FOREIGN PARTS

FOREIGN PARTS

A Singer's Journal

THOMAS ALLEN

SINCLAIR-STEVENSON

First published in Great Britain in 1993
by Sinclair-Stevenson
an imprint of Reed Consumer Books Ltd
Michelin House, 81 Fulham Road, London sw3 6rb
and Auckland, Melbourne, Singapore and Toronto

Copyright © 1993 by Thomas Allen

A CIP catalogue record for this book
is available at the British Library

ISBN 1 85619 252 0

Typeset by Deltatype Ltd, Ellesmere Port, Cheshire
Printed and bound in Great Britain
by Mackays of Chatham PLC

CONTENTS

Parkside
Allotments
Seaham . Sep. '90.

Parkside allotments, Seaham (p. 120)

LIST OF ILLUSTRATIONS

Cartoon depicting struggle for vocal supremacy: the magical "spot" on the stage of La Scala, Milan (p. 196)

The railway bridge over the Zambesi river, which separates
Zimbabwe from Zambia (p. 92)

For my father and mother who saw so much of me but missed so much more, I dedicate this book with all my love

A PARISIAN HORS D'OEUVRE

THE car battery that powers the seventeenth-century chariot in which the Grand Inquisitor sits has gone flat.

At the end of his interview with King Philip of Spain, the Inquisitor finds himself unable to scoot off stage. The King remains unaware of this as the scene in which he accuses his wife of adultery with her own stepson continues. The argument between King and Queen becomes long and convoluted, full of family tragedy, as one can appreciate in such a situation.

The ninety-two-year-old Grand Inquisitor is still having starting problems upstage – and this has not escaped the notice of the astute audience at the Palais Garnier in Paris. Loud murmurings are now heard from the auditorium. So much so that the King and Queen are also aware of the growing restlessness. The first thought of the singers, arrogant in their self-belief, is that the drama of their situation has stirred the audience from its normal passivity. They're less thrilled, however, by the laughter that seems also to be rising in increasing waves.

Meanwhile, the old man jerks and grunts in his arthritic efforts to become mobile once more. The royal couple are as yet oblivious of the third person who has shared the stage with them during their big scene.

Down in the pit, the Maestro has not been unaware of the disaster unfolding before his eyes. He bows his head, presumably in the belief that if he can't see them then he cannot be seen and has therefore absented himself from this scandal.

1

Several minutes into these heady dramas, and with an audience of a kind befitting a boxing match, the Grand Inquisitor has his brainwave. Still in character, he turns his old grey head towards the wings, where he sees two liveried flunkies. Slowly, he beckons them to come to him. Apprehensively, they do so. King and Queen continue their sterling work – unabashed, still, by events.

The three would-be churchmen go into congress. There follows a nod to the right, a hand signal left. Moments later, the purple-clad pair ceremonially turn the wheelchair, with all the pomp due a Pope's throne. Further nods and hand signals from the old man. The flunkies' work is completed only when the carriage, still with its ancient occupant, points downstage and towards the prompt corner.

Have I omitted to mention that the stage is steeply inclined?

The audience now holds its combined breath in anticipation.

A few seconds later, the G.I. gives an almost imperceptible signal, the two young men step away – and abandon their elderly charge to the inescapable effects of Newton's Laws.

Philip and Elisabeth have reached the climax of their duet at this most appropriate moment. Through the crescendo of the music, the mad monk gathers speed towards the corner.

With timing worthy of an international goalkeeper, the ninety-two-year-old leaps from his racing seat, hurtles through the air and lands in the wings in a blaze of Roman purple, milliseconds ahead of the moment when the offending carriage crashes into the proscenium arch.

The finale is accompanied by a deafening roar of approval from the bull-ring, and the King and Queen breathe the air of their success.

The baritone in the opposite wing watches throughout.

Chapter One

PRIMA LE PAROLE –
DOPO LA MUSICA

AND so the great year of Mozart has begun.

I'm looking out of the window of a house in Parsch – one of the posh parts of Salzburg – towards the fairy-tale castle and town, where Mozart was born in 1756. It's Easter Festival time. Mozart's chocolate balls – his *Kugeln* – are more evident than ever. Cheap violins decorate the windows of greengrocers, and Mozart's white-bewigged head peeps from behind rows of ladies' frilly undergarments and butchers' joints alike. What would Wolfgang Amadeus have made of it all? I hope lots of money – richly deserved, poor man.

It was in the stars, I suppose, that this year, 1991 – two hundred years after the death of Mozart – would be especially busy for a Mozart singer. So I shall describe the year, and a little more – after all, I shan't be around for the quarter-millenium in 2041 nor the three-hundredth in 2091.

For me, 1991 began with a production of Richard Strauss' *Capriccio*, in which I sang the role of the Count – rather different from Mozart's with which I'm more closely associated. On reflection, however, Strauss' Count is not wholly uncharacteristic for me – as the opera's theme concerns the argument over which should take priority, words or music. There's no denying the stunning genius of Mozart's music, but in collaboration with the brilliant da Ponte he achieved a harmony in music and words that is all too seldom heard.

3

With the intellectual exercise of the Strauss behind me, I set off for a two-week visit to North America for recitals, recording and orchestral concerts, before scampering home to defeat jet-lag, four days away from a single performance of *Figaro* in Munich on 21 February.

Since I arrived in England from California only on Monday, 18 February, I break with my normal comfy-but-cheap hotel routine and decide on the nineteenth-century comfort of the Vier Jahreszeiten, Munich, close to the opera. The psychological boost I'll receive from this hotel de luxe will help me cope more easily with any tiredness and the winter cold.

This proves to be a good choice. I arrive on the afternoon, a day before the performance, with forty-five minutes to spare before my one and only rehearsal. Having performed in this production in the past, I'm expected to remember pertinent details, but Susanna and the Countess are debutantes who've been given a couple of extra days' grace before having to present their wares.

Now, I know we can't all be Mr and Mrs Hollywood's favourite screen star in the crazy mixed salad that calls itself opera, but one problem becomes immediately apparent. My Susanna is a tiny Italian lady who, no matter how high a heel she wears – and what would Joan Crawford call these 'five-inchers'? – will find it hard to disguise the fact that she is something under five feet in height. That in itself must be a disadvantage for her – but those who know *Figaro* will be able to forecast a potential problem in Act Four, when Countess and Susanna exchange costumes and are mistaken for one another. Admittedly, this happens in the dark, but on this occasion the role of the Countess is to be sung by none other than Felicity Lott ('Flott'), one of the tallest ladies in the business at five feet ten inches. This stretches the boundaries of artistic licence beyond their elastic limits.

In some circumstances, and with more rehearsal time than we are allotted, it is often possible to disguise problems such as this by, for example, never having the two ladies too close together, by having the Countess seated for great chunks of time, or even by making Susanna work at a raised level on the stage while the

Countess operates below her. All three tricks have been employed in the past.

But at tonight's performance there is no way that even the most stupid of Counts could confuse the long, elegant hands of the Susanna who towers over him in the garden scene with those of the tiny figurine who had fitted comfortably into the crook of his arm with much room to spare during the first three acts. Someone should invent, for just such circumstances, an eighteenth-century shoe, built up seven or eight inches, that would go some way to disguising similar difficulties. Flott finds the whole thing amusing. I can't imagine what the audience is feeling. We singers forge ever onward. The conclusion is reasonably satisfactory. (Music before words, or dramatic truth in this case.) During the curtain calls there's a hint of interplay over the height discrepancy between Count and Countess in their regard for the '*Susannettchen*', but only the most observant onlooker would detect anything other than the best mannered British behaviour from us. In my experience, operatic disasters – or the potential for them – are often overlooked by enthusiastic audiences.

I return to my hotel to recover from both the performance and the remains of my California jet-lag.

The following morning I breakfast with my new English manager, Robert Rattray, and talk over the things he's to say on my behalf in his forthcoming meeting with the Munich administration.

He's taking over the management of my career from the lady who has done it, wonderfully well, for the past twenty years. Caroline Woodfield, a partner in the firm of John Coast, has been my wet-nurse, teacher, bully, buffer, bouncer and of course agent. On top of all of that, we've been the closest friends for all that time, and her announcement at the end of 1990 that she would be leaving our home shores, to be married and to live in New York, came as a tremendous blow from which I am still reeling.

Since I left music college in 1968, I've not had a singing lesson as such. That's quite unusual but I've found ways of dealing with singing and its techniques that have worked for me. I studied during four years at the Royal College with a bass-baritone called

Hervey Alan; he helped to refine what raw talent I had and did the sensible thing of allowing what was a very 'natural' voice to develop along very 'natural' lines. For me, singing began in a church choir, as a boy and a young man. This gave me discipline. Otherwise, a mysterious combination of sinuses, cavities in the face, vocal cords and physical set-up causes the voice which happens to be the one I have.

Other singers arrive at their 'instrument' by more technical means and from day one are aware of the position of the voice as it moves up and down scales.

After years of daily singing one becomes very aware of the sensations associated with a certain pitch, a certain volume. The Middle C, for example, may cause a buzz in the nose on a certain vowel. That's very much a simplification, but an indication nevertheless of how, after long use, a singer is able to self-diagnose, and correct, the path of his or her voice.

But teachers serve many purposes for singers other than simply voice mechanics. Many travel with their charges to important engagements and in so doing are there not only to fine-tune the voice but often to act as a support and confidence-booster. It can be a very important role and a considerable weapon in a singer's armoury.

What helped me was to have Caroline as a nurturer and believer. So much of what one does as an artist is dependent upon the state of one's mental and physical health. Added to that, the often underestimated quality of self-belief plays perhaps the most vital part. Time and again, I have observed artists delving deep inside themselves for something that might not previously have existed for them. Certain qualities and strengths, when found, can reveal to their audiences a little more of their true selves. I firmly believe that our bodies and minds are working at perhaps ten per cent of their potential. If we could just retain the learning curve we encountered first as babies and toddlers, when in those early precious months of life humans are able to assimilate skills only a computer can match, what giants we would be.

Caroline has played a huge part in my twenty-year learning curve. She was aided by my own temperament and work ethic – I try to be keenly aware and I've never been content to stand still. I've always sought to explore new artistic disciplines.

Hence the urgent need to meet with my new manager, since Caroline leaves for the USA in March, after which time Robert Rattray takes over the reins entirely. At that moment, I shall be transferring from the high culture of Salzburg and its Easter Festival to the easy-going climate of Houston, Texas, next stop on the Mozart Magic Carpet.

The term 'on the road' is so awful and yet it's one I am using constantly at the moment, for that's the position in which I find myself. I flew to America on 31 January (my son's twenty-first birthday) and, apart from approximately six days, I shall be in Europe or America until early November.

Some months earlier, I'd ordered a rental car that I could use during the five weeks I would be in Salzburg for the Easter Festival and the new production of *Figaro*.

22 *February*. The car duly delivered to the hotel, I pack my belongings into it, and set off, the twentieth-century troubadour on the early stages of his wanderings. Munich to Salzburg is a route I know well. I've rented a house, the same for Easter and Summer Festivals, and am due to meet the owner there around four o'clock.

Rehearsals are to begin the following day. It's a cold day and the remains of the heavy snowfall of the first *real* European winter in several years lie thickly over the landscape. The house is easy to find and sits on the low tree-clad slopes of the Gaisberg, with a view to the Muttsberg and Lattenberg Alps stretching towards Germany. To my right, above the trees, I can see the castle and cathedral.

The Gaisberg is one of my favourite spots in Salzburg. Here it was in 1985 that I would sit in a bathing costume, trying to acquire ✓ the tan I felt would make me look healthier as 'Human Frailty' in a production of *The Return of Ulysses*. The title role of Ulysses, which I also sang, could take care of itself, but 'Human Frailty' had been designed as a creature in a pair of sandals and nothing else, and I thought the extra skin of a suntan would help me over my initial nervousness. (I needn't have worried too much, as I managed to persuade the powers-that-be to let me wear a chamois leather loin cloth which, when finished, looked as though it had seen good service in the local car wash. There was, however, not much of it!)

The Gaisberg is also a place for watching madmen launch themselves into the abyss, tied precariously to their rainbow-coloured hang gliders. It must be the most exhilarating feeling to become a bird in that way – perhaps one of these summers I shall be tempted to try. Home, too, this Gaisberg, to the Swallowtail butterfly. In England it is only found in East Anglia, but here in Austria it becomes as common a sight as the Cabbage White but a thousand times more beautiful.

This weekend, with a clear blue sky stretching forever, the hang gliders are out in force, weaving slow, lazy patterns high above me, like so many multi-coloured butterflies. Nature can be so wonderful if one is only patient. I remember, when acquiring that all-important suntan, sitting in a multitude of clovers and vetches, all bright in the afternoon sun. The only noises came from bees and crickets, and the occasional distant cow bell. In the midst of all this quiet, myself being very still, a tortoiseshell butterfly landed on the drawing paper I was using, and over my foot slithered un-threateningly a slow-worm. Seldom have I felt so at peace with the world and nature.

23 *February*. The first day of rehearsal and, as usual, there's a hullabaloo at the cheering sight of old friends. New introductions are made. After so many years, almost all of us know one another, but there's usually one new face hiding somewhere in the middle.

The purpose of this rehearsal is to deal with our approach to the musical aspects of *Figaro*. Tomorrow we'll see the set and begin the 'geography' lesson once again. Bernard Haitink is to conduct. We know one another well, having first worked together on *Zauberflöte* at Glyndebourne in 1973, and since then on many other occasions.

With the forward planning that is so much an essential part of music, and particularly opera, the contracts for this production were issued three years ago. At that time, it was planned that √ Herbert von Karajan would be conducting, but first he suffered a setback which meant he had to withdraw from many activities, and then of course came the ultimate setback with his death during the Summer Festival in 1989.

Odd that, having auditioned for him in 1977, I should have had the opportunity to work with him after so many years only to be denied that dubious honour. I say dubious because he was of all things a stubborn man, very much used to getting his own way. Some have called him a tyrant – not without reason. His influence and effect were such that it was easy to be steam-rollered by his invitations. A 'yes' from von Karajan was for many a passport to success for life; for others, it was a professional death warrant. One could be so easily seduced by him into thinking oneself capable of certain roles. Had I accepted his initial proposition in 1977, I might well have been working with him regularly for the past thirteen or fourteen years. But the roles he offered me at the time, my instincts told me, were inappropriate and I continued to say so, in spite of his pressure.

I had flown to Salzburg in August 1977, having just completed my first performances as Don Giovanni at Glyndebourne. Outside the office of the secretary to von Karajan sat two American girls, wide-eyed with anticipation. They'd come there, it seemed, every day for the past four days in the hope of securing an audition. My audition had been long-arranged. A middle-aged gentleman gave me a cursory glance and indicated a practice room in which I could warm up. He was very off-hand when he returned to take me to the stage of the Grosses Festspielhaus fifteen minutes later.

I was shown to the centre of the platform and I shook hands with an unknown pianist. A voice with an edge on it like a chainsaw said: 'Good afternoon. What will you sing?'

'Valentine's aria,' I replied and launched into *'Avant de quitter ces lieux'* from Gounod's *Faust*.

'Very good. What else have you?'

Several of my offers were rejected and finally an aria from *Ballo in Maschera* was agreed upon.

At the end of that the voice was warmer. It was also getting closer. H.v.K. had left the darkness of the rear stalls and had come to see me.

9

'Tell me about yourself,' he said.

I resisted the temptation to offer him a catalogue of events since I was born. By now two other people were at his side. I recognised them immediately: Elisabeth Schwarzkopf and Walter Legge. Regaining my senses slightly, I told him of the recent performances of *Don Giovanni* and that I would shortly perform Count Almaviva at Covent Garden with Karl Böhm. He brushed these aside. I went on to say after that I'd be singing in *Pelléas et Mélisande*.

'Good,' he said. 'Golaud is a role for you.'

'I'm Pelléas,' I protested timidly.

'But you're a man when you walk on to the stage and Pelléas is a boy, a weakling, a milksop.'

I wondered for a moment how I'd play the role. Then I countered: 'I hope to play him as a strange poetic figure.'

'This can't be,' said he. 'But never mind. One day I shall record *Pelléas* and you shall be my Golaud.'

Goodness, I thought, my life has just changed before my very eyes.

He turned and left. I did the same. Somewhere in the wings a now much more deferential middle-aged man helped me on with my coat and ushered me back to H.v.K. for further discussions.

'Do you sing *Matthew Passion*?' he asked.

Walter Legge intervened – 'Oh, Herbert, I can help him with that' – before I'd had time to answer yes.

'And *Trovatore*?' The interrogation continued.

'No, I don't sing that,' said I.

'But with me, it's something you could sing. No problem.'

'No, I don't think so. It's not what I'm planning.'

He continued to insist.

When finally I agreed to his further suggestion that Posa in *Don Carlos* would be right, he turned and left – before Walter Legge could get out his next sentence.

It was like being caught up in the vacuum of a tornado. One moment he was there, and the next gone, as if by magic. It was very impressive, especially as he'd heard me for the first time that day.

The pressure began in the following two weeks. I stuck to my guns, and gradually we drifted apart.

*

Choosing suitable roles is not simply a case of assuming that all sopranos sing everything written for soprano, all tenors sing all tenor roles and so on. The art is in identifying those cases that are borderline – the roles that one can sing and 'get away with' as opposed to a whole host of others that fit like gloves and are central keystones in the maturing of an individual artist.

Such was the case with the two roles that von Karajan was bullying me to undertake. Certainly he heard something in my voice and in my personality that could be used in those parts. I could have sung them, but at that stage in my development they weren't exactly right for me.

The long lines of *legato* singing that are required for di Luna, the baritone role in *Il Trovatore*, are qualities for which I am known, but other aspects of the opera went against me. I was likely to find myself among a cast of leather-lunged heavies, all belting away at the top of their voices with a very loud orchestra under H.v.K.'s direction to accompany them. In 1977 these conditions were not ideal for me.

Pelléas et Mélisande, on the other hand, is an opera of subtlety and intimacy and the issues in the case of the role of Golaud are different. Apart from the fact that I've always found a thrill and excitement from singing the high-lying role of Pelléas, which converts into some incredibly sensual moments on the stage, my voice is not of the rough-hewn nature and earthbound quality for such a character as Golaud. He is the man of the forest, the hunter, the provider of food in this kingdom. Pelléas is poetical, aware of the feminine elements within him as much as the masculine. From that source and that knowledge is derived the nature of *his* passion. In vocal terms, Golaud needs a darker voice than mine was at that time, to contrast with the high, desperately fervent outbursts of Pelléas.

The *Figaro* with Karl Böhm was a wonderful success, and *Pelléas*, the opera despised by many and worshipped by at least as many, became enormously important in my development.

I prefer to think that as a singer I'm now enjoying a career which might well have been curtailed had I succumbed to H.v.K.'s overtures, as did so many others. That was the power of the man. I well remember sitting in Salzburg Airport following the audition with him, and writing in my diary the conversation we'd had, the promises made. He wielded magic.

The 1991 Easter Festival is the first without him. The dark empty foyers are gloomy and dead. The dampness from the underground car park seems to have permeated the passageways and the quietness of the place is strangely heavy even during the rehearsal period. Is my imagination working overtime, or is Herbert von Karajan's spirit badly missed? It will be some years, I suspect, before the Festival finds a new identity. For many people, von Karajan *was* Salzburg. But the truth of it is that Salzburg, and some of its public at least, have to learn that such a Festival is bigger than one man.

There has always been in-house fighting over the relative merits of this conductor over that one, that soprano over this. Take as one example the issue of Berlin versus Vienna in the Philharmonic stakes. New brooms are usually determined to sweep away the old order. They're right, of course. Time cannot stand still – though if it were to, it would surely do so here in Salzburg. Just look around in the streets. The predilection for regional costume is extraordinary. Anyone would think that film crews were still employed on *The Sound of Music*. But the *Trachten* pre-dates Julie Andrews and will surely outlive Hollywood. This Austrian obsession with Folk tradition is a curious phenomenon. The number of ladies in Austrian hats I saw this morning, for instance, all outdoing the others in sporting the longest pheasant-tail feathers. I have the feeling they're recently returned from a field-trip with Emperor Franz Josef, who, I am convinced, still pulls the strings from a lofty seat somewhere above Vienna.

Cake shops and clothes shops are filled with confectionery. *Torten* piled high with cardiac-arrest cream and, in the same kitschy colours, linen skirts in peach and orange and forget-me-not blue – the perfect ensemble for carrying home one's fresh-picked mushrooms in chintz-lined trugs. And always sensible shoes at the end of pit-prop legs and home-knit stockings. In the summer the protective winter bodice is discarded from the dirndl and fresh, creamy bosoms burgeon over the tops of taut chest-confiners. These have terrific erotic potential.

The commercialisation of the erotic in the twentieth century has blunted our sensitivity to what it is that fires the feelings between Man and Woman. In *Figaro* we've arrived at the opening of Act Three, when the Count puzzles over the events of Act Two. At the arrival of Susanna, he tries hard to maintain his coldness and detachment towards her. He no longer trusts anyone. But, with a few words expressed in the most delicate manner, she re-ignites all his former passion. And then begins their game of cat and mouse.

Time and again, Mozart gets it right. The way to success in seduction is understatement. We've lost so much, living as overtly as we do in the late twentieth century. How very sensual is the glimpse of the neck flowing into the shoulder, the promise of things to come when the moment is right, the suggestiveness of the unspoken. . . .

Rehearsals are not easy. A sixth sense tells us that in a few weeks' time what we will present here will be a clean new production, a good ensemble, well-rehearsed and beautifully musical, making little attempt to reveal new psychological insights. There is a lot to be said for this. It seldom happens these days that one can witness *Figaro* as a true representation of eighteenth-century life. But Salzburg is filled with ghosts. We fall easily into nostalgia and reminiscence. Many of us have been involved in memorable and remarkable productions and our musical lives have been filled with a rich kaleidoscope of characters from all parts of the world. We talk about past productions, and invoke the name of Jean-Pierre Ponnelle, a genius in his own field, a man so rich in ideas he was in danger, at times, of producing work almost too intricate to be taken in, even at third glance.

It could be, in the tense atmosphere – for Salzburg is certainly tense – that one's patience wears very thin. For the time being, however, I am relaxed, looking for new ideas to explore myself, returning in the afternoons to my house where I can put the rehearsals out of mind. After all, we've just come through a war in the Middle East. Norman Schwarzkopf may be an opera enthusiast, but he'd doubtless see our theatrical skirmishes in proper proportion.

Part of my time is taken up with painting and reading, and the rest in learning new recital programmes. The book I'm reading most avidly at the moment is Peter Matthiesson's *The Tree Where Man Was Born*. My interest in Africa began nearly ten years ago when I met my wife Jeannie. She was born in Johannesburg, though she'd lived in London for many years, married there, and had a family. Her parents and brothers were still in South Africa. When it was clear to us both that we were more than 'just good friends', a trip was arranged for me to meet family and country alike. It would be incredibly naive not to acknowledge the enormity of the problems of South Africa, the stupidity and cruelty that was apartheid, and the desperate need for solutions to difficulties which are a lot more complex than many people (usually those with little if any first-hand knowledge of that country) think. But, having fallen in love with the woman, I then fell in love with the place of her birth.

We've made several trips there in subsequent years. Sometimes I allow myself to think back to Junior School and to Mr Bowman with his roll-out maps. I never imagined then that I would one day visit so many parts of the world and hear for myself the 'smoke that thunders' that is Victoria Falls. When I count the hours spent in windowless rehearsal rooms and darkened theatres, when I need to find a balance for myself, I pack a simple bag with shorts, shirts and binoculars and make a life-enhancing visit to see the animals and birds of the huge continent of Africa.

The flags still flutter on the castle ramparts two miles away and below me the yellow house with the green roof falls under the shadows of the trees. It's the end of another busy day in snow-covered Disneyland.

At the evening rehearsal there is a pronounced change in atmosphere. A lethargy that one associates with routine is discernible. There is no malice, no violent row. Small murmurings in corners give the clue: this talented group of singers have recognised that nothing revelatory is being revealed. Will this be another in the long chain of 'chocolate box' *Figaros*?

*

It's some days later now. There are various forms of tiredness. I like the kind that comes of having worked hard and earned a good meal, an enjoyable drink and a sound night's sleep. I'm very much less fond of the kind that derives from having to stand around a rehearsal stage for long hours with minimum chance to perform and maximum time spent listening to a director voicing ideas loudly over a microphone. At least at that distance he's out of range of a frustrated artist's long reach. That makes me sound like an unpredictable hot-head. Nothing could be further from the truth. At times such as this I retreat further into myself, resort to a certain amount of sarcasm – usually out of earshot – and enjoy the banter of colleagues on and off stage.

Back at the Parsch house my painting is coming on. You might imagine I'd be producing Bosch-like nightmares in the frustrating circumstances of rehearsal. Not a bit of it. The recent picture is one of a sunlit snow-covered Untersberg, which is my guardian-mountain each day and the one to which I look for all weather changes.

Then there are the birds. My first food-shopping visit here included the purchase of a bag of wild-bird seeds. With the contents liberally strewn over my terrace and on the feeding table each morning, to the accompaniment of my less-than-authentic bird whistles, I now receive, on a regular basis, Great Tit, Blue Tit, Marsh Tit, Bullfinch, Chaffinch, Greenfinch, Robin and, once only so far, Nuthatch. It was the beauty of the Bullfinch that gave me the idea of attempting a painting of it. From my bird book I've now added to the same piece of paper a Bewick Swan and Caspian Tern, though they have yet to grace my terrace with their presence.

In the short breaks from rehearsal, we often retire to a nearby coffee house. Being Austria, the place is *sahned* out with cakes of all shapes, sizes and colours, *Schlag ober und unter* and for some reason – could it be Mozart, I wonder? – this particular establishment has as the centrepiece of its interior decoration the pipes of an organ. Kitsch was invented in this pink grotto!

The most recent professional problem has been my costume

shoes which were made, I believe, three centimetres too small for me. Small wonder then that the knuckles of my toes are now sporting red calluses. A new pair of shoes has been found and the extra two centimetres these enjoy make a world of difference. Now my shoes are only one centimetre too small. . . . .

The cast's overall feeling has remained the same – we are involved in a pretty conventional reading of *Figaro*. Experience teaches, however, that one should beware of making a snap judgement. What is extraordinary, and is seldom understood, is the basic goodness of people. I'm not aware of a wrong word or real argument. Everyone is very professional and gets on with the job.

There are producers who are completely inflexible and pedantic. There are artists who have strong ideas, built from long experience and acquaintance with a piece. Such artists know what will and what won't work. Rather than become embroiled in energy-wasting arguments, singers worth their salt will have discovered their own ways of making the points they wish to make. We don't want to appear confrontational or arrogant; but we have learnt to understand what operates best for us. With a little manipulation by the singers during the working hours of a rehearsal, the required result can usually be achieved.

I'm tired of reading in reviews and hearing in conversations all about the wonderful insights of producers. What about the ideas the performer brought with him to the piece, after many years of thought, performance and study? Perhaps the process has never been fully explained. Does anyone really think, for example, that the Canadian tenor Jon Vickers had to be coached finger by finger movement how to play Peter Grimes or Otello? Or that Teresa Stratas or Mirella Freni couldn't move a foot as Susanna until 'Sir' put in his first golden words?

Some singers require molly-coddling and nurse-maiding at times (not Mr Vickers, I must say). But most are well-rounded, mature human beings who arrive very well prepared to begin the task in hand. The mistake is made, I often think, in attempting to compare singers with actors of the straight theatre. Singers come in many different packagings, such as:

THE VOICE. In most people's belief it originates from Southern

Europe, but not always. So blessed with beauty of tone that nothing more need be done than open the larynx and pour forth. This, it need hardly be said, is a rare breed. Examples: Carlo Bergonzi, Joan Sutherland.

THE ACTOR. Originates from Northern Europe. The bearer of the torch that says everything must work at a theatrical level – and to hell with the singing. Very exciting on stage, this creature, who makes no records and many newspaper interviews.

THE MUSICIAN. Puzzling one, this. Wonderfully well-prepared in a musical institution. Phrases pour out of the larynx in a flow of base-metal tones. Often associated with operas in which the principal role is played by a trumpeter who can stand on his head and swim twenty-five yards backstroke under water. May make records for very obscure labels of the works of even more obscure composers. (No names and no law suits!)

THE SINGER-ACTOR. The Genuine Article. Someone in whom God has chosen to join together a voice and a knowledge of his/her body language such that one can be forgiven for asking the question: 'Is this an actor singing or a singer acting?' The singer-actor works hard at 'acting' because for this artist it's not just music and words. The 'whole' lies in the coming together of all theatre disciplines. He/she is often from Europe or North America. There are many examples: Gabriel Baquier, Elisabeth Söderström, Tito Gobbi, Sesto Bruscantini, Teresa Stratas.

Singers in each of these categories attract their own kind of public, too. The Italians who barrack the opponents of Panatta at Wimbledon will be there at Covent Garden to cheer and applaud the aces delivered by a Bergonzi. That's the nature of opera in Italy. Foreign to us, their behaviour, but then it's an art form we've taken over secondhand and try each season to come to terms with in our cooler northern climes.

In Salzburg, costumes were tried from the first week. At that stage they were merely being fitted to us. Two weeks on, the finishing brocades have been added and all is ready.

For Act One I have something that passes for an around-the-house eighteenth-century track-suit, in a kind of shot silk. This, together with a flowing housecoat, cuts quite a dash. Act Two sees me in a hunting outfit, made of softest leather and suede – I don't like to think which backs they came from. In Act Three I sport, as usual, something befitting court ceremony, namely a black silk suit with silver brocade refinements.

The wigs always look very different in this part of the world. In Britain we have an almost xenophobic idea about the design of such things. After all, we're dealing with a Spanish aristocrat in a French play set to music by an Austrian and sung in Italian. Too often, it seems to me, we take for our inspiration the pictures of Gainsborough, Hogarth, Reynolds, when, in fact, we should have been looking at the French-German-Spanish-Italian equivalent, which is different. There's no mistaking the fact that this wig is the product of a Continental house. It has two sausage rolls adorning the sides. The British wig of the same period will often have one roll; only in Europe am I presented with two.

The cast is given Saturday off. My wife and I, with Susanne Mentzer (Cherubino) and John Tomlinson (Dr Bartolo), decide to see some of the surrounding countryside. We take the well-trodden road to St Wolfgang for coffee on the terrace of the White Horse Inn, made famous in the operetta. In the summer it's crowded. Today the beauty of snow on the mountains makes the spectacle unforgettable. That and the clear light of a lovely day. We spend some time looking at the historic church, and then from the map choose a road that takes us away from St Wolfgang by a circuitous mountain route back to Salzburg. What a happy accident it proves to be. The lower section is heavily wooded and follows the course of rivers and frozen waterfalls. But as we climb, peaks begin to appear between trees on the slopes around us. Finally we arrive at the Alm, one of the venues of the Austrian Ski Club. Too little snow here now for proper skiing, though hardy *Langlaufers* can be seen making their inelegent way to this oasis in the mountains. Here, the beer and the bird-life are good. John and I enjoy one of the local dark beers and I spot my first Crested Tit. (Never had eyes for one on Loch Garten – only ospreys!)

This is the kind of relaxation for which we've all been craving. A day spent in good air, a walk in the mountains, a pleasant lunch – and home, not too late, by car.

It's Sunday, 17 March. Six days before the première. The Berlin Philharmonic, who are to be our 'band', arrived yesterday for their first rehearsals with Bernard Haitink. How strange to think of *the* Berlin Phil as our opera-pit orchestra. What a privilege.

Costumes are eagerly tried, on stage for the first time. Make-up too.

One of the great features of the Vienna Staatsoper is the care given to singers by Wardrobe staff and make-up personnel. They show an instinct for the welfare of artists, born of a long Viennese tradition of service. The same men and women are here to help us in Salzburg, and more than one member of the cast talks of them in terms of endearment. They share with us the ups and downs of performances, providing coffee or water when needed and a cool beer at the end of a long evening.

These days it's only at Covent Garden that I do my own make-up, just to keep my hand in, so to speak. Here, Gerhard, whom I've known in Vienna and Salzburg for many years, does his usual conscientious, professional job. I'm happy to leave the task to him while I get on with the *Independent* crossword. Otherwise, it's a fairly empty time, this. Not quite as boring as holding a petrol hose until the car fills up, but almost. (How long will it be before someone invents some absorbing game to help fill this awful time of waiting?)

Eventually, I'm declared ready, and decide to sit in the stalls to gain some idea of the balance of sound between orchestra and singers. The first shock is hearing John Tomlinson as though through the wall of a different room. John's voice is so big that most people would say it creates so much sound that it's as if he need be in another room. But this balance is not right. Nor is it difficult to see why. The orchestra is sitting high in the pit, and there are many of them. The Grosses Festspielhaus has a stage opening that is extraordinary in its width. Wonderful for *Fidelio* last season; but John Gunter's designs this year have been arranged to reduce that opening and create a much more intimate atmosphere. It's a new idea, and a very good one in my opinion, although it met with some initial opposition from the Festival powers.

It's good to be working with John Gunter again. I haven't seen him since the Buxton Festival production of *Hamlet* in 1980, which he designed incredibly successfully on a very tight budget. Tight budgets do not play a part in the Salzburg dictionary. How times have changed for us!

The balance of sound between voice and orchestra is the most common problem we encounter. A lot of time is spent by Bernard in trying to resist the temptation to allow the Berliners to take over entirely. His task is not easy. Each individual in this luxury orchestra is a star in his own right; many of them, I suspect, take none too kindly to being told to 'keep it down'. Their reputation is justly earned and Bernard has to tread carefully in asking them to adjust their 'thickness' of sound, now that they play the part of accompanists in the pit. I listen to them closely, and the unity of √ sound produced by the first violins alone is something I've never experienced before. It is as though I am hearing one huge sweet instrument, such is the ensemble with which they play.

My turn comes to make my entrance. Even the Berliners, like all orchestral musicians, used and unused to playing in the pit, cannot resist the urge to turn and see what new character has arrived and what fun is being had.

An amusing moment arrives when Bernard himself becomes so engrossed in the stage action during one of the recitatives that he forgets to give the orchestra the cue to come in. (Naturally, we take it as a compliment to our skills as actors/singers of the most accomplished category I've listed.) He's even more engrossed at the evening rehearsal when the goings-on are that much busier. By now the orchestra is feeling more at home and we're well on the way to finding a harmonious balance between us.

Act Two is the crux of the opera for me. From the first entrance into the boudoir of the Countess with a puzzling letter written by Figaro requiring a lot of explanation, the Count goes through enough emotions to fill a bucket. The band is still very amused and intrigued by the goings-on – a happy change from the blasé approach of so many regular opera orchestras.

The same procedure applies to Monday's rehearsal, this time concerning Acts Three and Four. Act Three is the high point for me. Dramatically, Act Two has me drained at the end. I have to recover strength for Act Three, as it begins with the erotic duet with Susanna, followed immediately by the Count's 'Vengeance Aria'. We try this two or three times, which leaves me more optimistic about the shape of things to come. Duet and aria sound and feel well in this acoustic. Act Four, despite the usual collision with trees and bodies in the dark, goes equally well.

Tuesday is the day of the 'pre-general'. This is the dress rehearsal of the Dress Rehearsal. I still haven't worked out why we indulge in so many of these luxuries. I often think it's because it's always been like that. Why didn't we call yesterday's rehearsal a dress rehearsal, and save ourselves a lot of nervous energy?

Some years ago, when I made my debut in Munich as Don Giovanni, we'd rehearsed very carefully for three weeks and were prepared for our Dress Rehearsal on a Saturday morning. I was already in costume and make-up, and was sitting in the make-up man's chair being fitted with wig and beard. It was at this moment that our conductor, Wolfgang Sawallisch, entered the room. '*Guten Morgen, Herr Professor,*' we all said.

He stood behind my chair. I watched him through the mirror in front of me.

'Tom,' said he, 'Donna Anna is not feeling well, and Donna Elvira has cancelled without voice.'

'*Schade,*' said I. What a shame.

'How would you feel at this your debut if we cancel the Dress Rehearsal altogether?'

'*Kein Problem, Herr Professor, danke schön,*' said I. And with that I was out of costume and out of make-up in about two minutes flat, and a *schönes Wochenende* was had by all.

Professor Sawallisch knew that a full house was waiting for this Dress Rehearsal. With them, he was *not* popular. With me . . . I would have kissed him, except one doesn't kiss Herr Sawallisch. He had just employed the best bit of psychology I've ever witnessed in the theatre. The result? The following Monday night's performance was a huge success. And I'm still working in and enjoying Munich.

The producer Michael Hampe's note to us is that all the recitatives are too slow.

My mind immediately goes back to London, *Figaro*, and Johannes Schaaf, the producer, whose note about the recits was: 'Why are they all so fast?'

The naturalism which resulted from the delivery of this dialogue at a speed dictated by the dramatic moment led to a series of *Figaro* performances which were notable for their flow and lack of boredom. Never, in my experience, has *Figaro* seemed so short, nor so truthful.

Dress Rehearsal day and suddenly my colleagues, who have come to work in a range of clothes from anoraks to denims to winter boots, look the international artists that they truly are, the men in whatever fashion befits them best, the girls in suits and tailored coats. The sense of occasion is upon us and will not now leave.

Television cameras are in place, as this Dress Rehearsal is to be recorded as a back-up tape to the First Night on Saturday – talk about turning on the pressure!

The rehearsal, despite one or two small hitches, runs smoothly and, though we reveal no new psychological insights, the production is 'clean', orthodox and looks good, much as we predicted. Balance of singers with orchestra now seems much better and all the 'business', so long worked out, seems to come together.

I have observed that all Countesses call Act Two of *Figaro* Act One, as it's the act in which they first appear. This is a fact of operatic life.

At the end of each act, indeed during too, there is no mistaking the warmth that the audience feels towards the show. I can see Jeannie smiling in the fourth row.

Lunch, which is around 4 p.m., we spend with Austrian friends in a nearby restaurant. They are full of curiosity about the rehearsals, and share with us various local scandals. It seems a certain Princess of these parts went recently to dinner with her husband. A fortune-teller was present and, after dinner, the entertainment took the form of palm-reading. The fortune-teller recoiled from the Prince's hand. After several minutes of persuasion, she agreed, perhaps unwisely, to reveal what she had seen. 'Turmoil ahead,' she explained. Sure enough, the Prince suffered a heart attack which, following his recovery, left him with an acute personality change. The sad Princess, we were informed, was slowly coming to terms with the fact that her husband had run off with his chauffeur and was blissfully happy. Such is Austrian Society.

There are now two potentially awful days to fill before the First Night. My requirements are: a good location for a walk, my bird book, a novel – I'm now on to *The Heart Is A Lonely Hunter* (I loved the film with Alan Arkin) – a supply of batteries so as always to be able to get the BBC World Service, and my paintbox. By these means, I arrive at Saturday in a relatively calm and sane state of mind.

During the 1988 Salzburg Summer Festival, having finished rehearsing with my accompanist, Roger Vignoles, for a recital we were to give at the Mozarteum, we filled in the yawning vacuum of time of waiting for the show by going with a family friend in the cable car from St Gilgen to the peaks high above. There – instead of the craggy mountain tops and boulder-strewn landscapes we might have expected – were meadows of endless summer flowers in all their glory and, to cap the experience, once again, the Swallowtail butterfly. My preoccupation with our natural surroundings stands above all else in helping me to maintain the balance I find so essential to my chosen way of life.

This year, though, I've discovered painting in a big way. Drawing was always there and reasonably straightforward, but I've previously felt intimidated by paint and brush. No longer. These new acrylics, and the system for keeping them soft and usable, keep me wholly occupied. I find no problem in whiling away the hours – indeed a performance will now seem a niggling intrusion into this other life!

Learning how to deal with the time between appointed high moments is a difficulty familiar to anyone whose life is governed by a diary prepared several years in advance. The singer knows almost to the minute when he has to be on peak form to deliver the sound everyone expects. The tournament golfer prepares each shot meticulously and lives on raw nerve endings while walking down fairways between shots. The answer for both artist and athlete probably lies in how well or otherwise he controls his breathing. Tony Jacklin in former years could be seen taking time at various moments to bring his diaphragm as much under control as he could manage. Likewise the singer, who, it has to be said, is probably much more conscious of his breath control than most others, must steady his mind, and in turn steady his breathing, before the required delivery.

I played golf up to county level and then found I was unable to play often enough to sustain that standard. A number of people told me that I was sufficiently talented to turn professional. I think I knew better, having observed the superior skills of those in County Durham, let alone on the national or international circuit.

I enjoy fewer ulcers as a singer than I might have done as a pro golfer.

23 *March*. Saturday finally arrives and I begin the day quietly. Jeannie is well aware of my special routine and sits calmly by, embroidering before putting together something for lunch. Why can't we do it now and get it over with? Why must I wait till six o'clock this evening in order to display myself before punters who are at this moment enjoying what for them is a lovely Spring holiday, with a leisurely lunch, a bottle of wine, a nap and *Figaro*? The condemned man must feel only slightly worse. As the day wears on I grow more fidgety, making countless little trips to the piano to try a note or two. Time ticks by slowly. At least with a six o'clock start I have to be there for make-up at five o'clock, so the afternoon is foreshortened. The added presence of television cameras and their attendant lights does nothing to lighten the pressure of a First Night of a new production in the Salzburg Easter Festival.

Is it too late to become a rival to Nick Faldo, Ian Woosnam and their like? I'm afraid the answer is probably yes. And the further truth is that singing is all I know how to do. It's what God seems to have put me here for, and an ethic learned in childhood tells me I have to do my best and get on with it.

I leave the car in the hollow mountain Salzburgers made their car park and wend my way to my dressing room. Already I feel better. Being in the theatre helps enormously. I'm early, so the place is quiet. Colleagues haven't yet arrived.

Franz, my dresser, welcomes me with a warm handshake and helps me off with my coat. He makes the immediate offer of coffee – always gratefully accepted. Gerhard, make-up man extraordinaire, is pleased to see me here in good time – I have kept him waiting in the past. I put on the basics of the First Act costume, Jeannie sits near the piano quietly reading, and Gerhard begins his work.

During the next half-hour the atmosphere changes. Bernard Haitink is the first to call on me. Always quiet, he too feels the weight of the occasion. He's taking over the mantle of Herbert von Karajan for these performances and, despite his own celebrity, that must be a strain, especially here in Salzburg.

A woman's voice now permeates from somewhere down below. Dawn Upshaw, the American Susanna, has arrived and goes through her own particular warming-up schedule. Another woman's voice is added: Susanne Mentzer – Cherubino. Her method of finding a voice is radically different from that of Dawn. To each her own. On other occasions I've heard the American tenor Neil Shicoff give a passable imitation of a budgerigar trilling away, and a dozen girls in warm-up sessions rival Florence Foster Jenkins. The end result, thank goodness, bears no relationship to this early preparation. Strangest of all, tonight, is Ferruccio Furlanetto, our Figaro – what operatic alliteration this is – who starts several feet below the keyhole of Middle C to launch upon a series of rising scales with his own syncopated piano accompaniment. Who says singers aren't musicians? This method I've not heard before.

I have a confession to make: after all these years I've not found a system. I give myself an A, as per orchestra, and set off on the bass aria *'Quia fecit'* from J. S. Bach's *Magnificat*. Don't ask me why. It's a good tune and serves the voice well. Not something I'd choose for *Il Barbiere di Siviglia* or *Billy Budd*, perhaps, but appropriate to the delivery of Mozart that lies ahead. To make an analogy with wine: the works of Rossini resemble Asti spumante, Benjamin Britten reminds me of a fine medium sherry, and the music of Mozart is champagne. . . .

Visitors knock, say hello, and leave me be. Some colleagues, though as far as I know none on this occasion, hang notices outside their doors, especially on first nights, requesting not to be disturbed. I well understand this as there can often be a stream of folk who, all with the best of intentions, nevertheless add to the confusion and tension of the occasion. Thus far I've not used this ploy, though this may be the year to begin.

A tannoy announcement warns us that the performance is soon to begin. Orchestra members are called to their places in the pit. Beginners hear their names for the first time. And so it starts. Little by little the well-rehearsed moments trip by, some better than others. The singers are in a fair state of nerves before a première audience, and also recorded and on radio and television. A tall order. But the notoriously cold and stiff first-night audience begins to belie its reputation, applauding enthusiastically despite the pain, in some cases, of bringing together the emeralds on one hand with the diamonds on the other.

From the well-lit stage I can pick out several familiar faces in the auditorium. On the backstage television screens that help to confirm that we still have a conductor up front, I can see in the second row two friends from Yorkshire. The place is a sea of bare shoulders – yet Easter is the less dressy of the two Festivals. Further back in the stalls, in the twilight zone of row R or S, sits a lady on a strategically chosen aisle seat. Her voluminous white gown spills from stage left to block the aisle at stage right. Cinderella in search of a ball? (I have it on good authority her companion was not dissimilarly attired and they both sported mother-of-pearl opera glasses!)

Much kissing and hugging after the final curtain. 'The men in black', as designers, producers and chorus trainers are known, appear on stage for their plaudits. The feeling is warm. It appears we have successfully entertained those who came.

And so the première is past. Producer leaves for pastures new, the cast say tired good-nights and Salzburg shuts up shop for the evening.

I look forward to the second performance in three days' time. By then, we will no longer be a cast of zombies, but real people enjoying themselves in one of the great comic masterpieces of all time.

In Austria we get our shopping done by Saturday lunchtime, because after that the country closes down. The observant onlooker can spot well-known musicians streaming from the Festspielhaus at noon or 12.30 to gather up what bread and vegetables remain on the colourful market stalls. The victuals have freshness and quality. No-one should be vitamin-deficient here, unless of course they miss the Saturday midday deadline.

Time to remark on another feature of Salzburg: what would pass elsewhere for an ordinary but well-ordered restaurant and, indeed, is so during daylight hours is by night and at Festival time transformed into one of the accepted black-tie spots where dinner can be had at Festival-related prices. Elegant dress in rustic farmhouse surroundings. I wonder how long it will be before pressure for more space makes the ubiquitous 'Chinese' into a haunt of the black-tie brigade. I can even foresee the burger bar in the Getreidegasse welcoming the jet-setting throng.

It's all about people-spotting. I hear that on our First Night a lady not unlike the subject of a Tretchikoff painting was to be seen in the foyer during the interval. Her costume was of such complexity that her designer had to be in constant attendance. A Royal-wedding-length train spilled from her shoulders and spread across many square yards of floor area in a carefully arranged series of folds and turns. She could not move, of course, for the entire interval. The designer must have been well pleased and everyone else a little taken aback.

*

The day of the second performance arrives. How different the feeling. I'm kind to my wife. Had we a dog I'd not be kicking it. Today I'm tolerant, unfidgety and much more in control. Now, as predicted, we can start to enjoy the production we've prepared over the past month.

I arrive at the theatre very shortly after having cleaned off the last of the paint that is becoming such a familiar sight on my shirt and fingers. It's soon apparent that everyone is much more relaxed. We have shed the fetters that were there for the première. There's a greater freedom of music and movement.

It's snowing. Jeannie has decided we should go home to London for the Easter weekend, leaving on Maundy Thursday (*Gründonnerstag*). We plan to dine with Caroline Woodfield, my agent for the past twenty years and for the next four hours, and on Friday to meet with Robert Rattray, my agent, I hope, for the next twenty years, by which time. . . .

This dinner is a special celebration. Jeannie and I marked our third wedding anniversary on 12 March in Salzburg and Caroline is about to leave for the States and a new married life. Years before, Caroline's partner John Coast, formerly my joint-manager until he retired, had persuaded the long-serving, redoubtable stage manager of Covent Garden, Stella Chitty, to allow a bottle of champagne to be presented to me on stage at curtain call following my first Don Giovanni in the house. She allowed this unprecedented act, remarking that, while it was customary for flowers to be presented to ladies, the Royal Opera House flunkies had not previously provided a similar service for gentlemen singers. This bottle I had uncharacteristically put away for a special day. Now is the time to dust it off. Over the champagne we reminisce a lot, but talk even more of the future and of Caroline's new life.

Friday, 29 March. Robert arrives for coffee, stays for lunch and in between talks much sense about our work together. Some instinct tells me my career will be safe in this man's hands. He's a nice person, bright and sharp. It will be interesting to see how things shape under his management.

There's time for a dental check-up, a visit to my son Stephen, and the sorting out of the clothes I'll need for Houston. Golf shoes and trousers take first priority. After that it's anything light that will reflect the sun. What a change from wintry Europe. Jeannie suggests I might like to go to the film of *Cyrano de Bergerac*. She sees me in the role for some reason – is my nose really so good in profile? I have a preconceived idea of what to expect from Gerard Depardieu, and go with a slight doubt at the back of my mind. I needn't have worried. The movie is wonderful. I cry and cry. The final twenty minutes, when Cyrano visits Roxanne in the convent, are unbelievably touching.

With the emotion of all that still in my mind, I return to Salzburg on Easter Sunday.

The following day, the day of the third and last performance of the Easter Festival, I spend quietly at the rented house, having a latish breakfast, feeding my birds and making a leisurely lunch of pasta with a tuna and tomato sauce. Preparing food is something else I find relaxing. Nowhere near as good a cook as some of my colleagues, I do enjoying cooking for others on occasion. But I follow recipes more or less implicitly, only rarely reaching for extra spices or *herbes de Provence*. Jeannie, on the other hand, professes to hate cooking but at certain times has a flair that would seem to suggest she missed her vocation.

This third performance produces yet another emotion, different from that of the first and second nights. Now we're at the end of this all-too-short run and are aware that we'll separate and go our own ways as of tomorrow.

Our Basilio, Ugo Benelli, tells us that he became a grandfather during Easter. This is somewhat frightening. It's not so long ago that colleagues were announcing marriages and babies. Well, just as policemen look younger, so. . . .

Susanne Mentzer isn't sure whether she can finish Cherubino this evening because of a cold. An understudy sits eagerly in the wings, while trained ears listen for signs of any problem. As is often the case on these occasions, she sings as beautifully as ever, and – dare I say it? – no-one would know. *She* knows of course.

We've all been in the situation of trying to decide during the course of the day whether the voice will last out or not.

Performance safely negotiated, we say our fond farewells until the Summer Festival. Some pressure is being applied to return for repeat performances in the 1992 Season. I shall be in Japan with Covent Garden and going immediately afterwards for rehearsals in Los Angeles. There's no way I can take in Salzburg as well.

I've always thought that what we should do after final evenings is pool the resources of our fridges and larders and have one huge international fry-up that would reflect the tastes of the many nationalities involved in such a production. Imagine the scene. Ferruccio, our Figaro, could provide good pasta and a lesson in how to cook liver the Italian way. John Tomlinson, our Bartolo, who comes from Oswaldtwistle, could bring along a favourite black pudding. Our two American colleagues could contribute a mixture of potato chips and vitamin-enriched space technology. And so on.

I'm still waiting for it to happen.

Generally, we're all in a rush to be away on the first available flight. Sandy Oliver, who sang Don Curzio, has to get to Brussels to start rehearsals the very next day. He can't drive. Instead he has to take a 5 a.m. bus to Munich where he can catch a plane.

Occasionally, after a month or more together, it feels like time to move on and see some new faces. There is a symptom known as colleague fatigue, even with the loveliest of friends.

I take my rental car out of the mountain parking place for the last time and wend my way 'home' to Parsch bei Salzburg and a simple meal of left-overs from fridge and freezer. Before going to bed I prepare the coffee machine. The most stimulating early morning smell is that of fresh-brewed coffee and good bread. My flight home is at 7 a.m. via Zurich. I'll be lucky to get four hours' sleep. My alarm rings at 5.30. The coffee helps me wake and I leave the house in darkness. I switch off the lights, lock the door and post the key back through the letterbox for the owners. I know the place so well now it will feel like coming home when I return in the summer. More keys dropped through boxes. This time, those of the rental car. I meet up with Susanne and her family. They are with me on the flight to Zurich, after which they travel to Chicago.

Now I have a day to look forward to some family life of my own before changing the mountain landscape of Austria for the flatlands of Texas.

Chapter Two

MOZART IN TEXAS

THE two Mozart operas in which I'm to perform in Houston are *Don Giovanni* and *Le Nozze di Figaro*. The productions are not new. They originated in Sweden's Royal Drottningholm Theatre, the work of the young Swedish producer Göran Jarvefelt, √ and designed by the German Carl Friedrich Oberle. Sadly, Göran died in November 1989. He was a young man of great talent with much still to offer, having already established a considerable reputation. The performances are to be dedicated to his memory.

I sang in his production of *Don Giovanni* in Houston in 1986. My memory of this is of the way in which the disastrous decline of Giovanni was demonstrated.

I keep a reasonable, though not fully comprehensive, record of photographs of past productions in which I've been involved. A year or two after playing this Don, I flicked through my files and was repelled by some of the images I saw. I found it hard to come to terms with the fact I was looking at myself in these pictures. Murnau's Nosferatu figure is the obvious comparison.

The sets are constructed to suit the requirements and ambience of the Court Theatre of Drottningholm and are an acoustical joy, being made entirely of wood. They are further enhanced by the sound of the new Wortham Theatre here in Houston. The same firm of architects who put together that extraordinary arena known as the Astrodome also designed this theatre. I can only say I wish all theatres were as easy on the singers. The merest whisper of recitative is audible in the farthest reaches of the auditorium. That means, of course, that all asides are likely to be heard – those of da Ponte as well as our own ad libs, which creep occasionally into our play.

The conductor for both operas is Christoph Eschenbach, the German pianist/maestro who took charge of the *Figaro* when I was last with Houston Opera. He is now Musical Director of the Houston Symphony and as such is the big music cheese in the city.

Houston, while not at the forefront of music-making nor in the full glare of the operatic spotlight, is nevertheless very attractive to many artists. This is for two reasons. First, the care that goes into the preparation and presentation of a work for the stage under the watchful eye of the intendant, David Gockley, now twenty years at this post, and secondly, the consideration that is shown to each individual artist, from the moment of his or her arrival.

I arrive in Houston on Wednesday afternoon, 3 April, to be met by my assigned hosts, Donald and Rhonda Sweeney, who have 'looked after' me on two or three previous occasions. Their brief is to see that I don't starve in downtown Houston, that my special requirements are catered for, and that I know that they are there if I have any troubles. It's simple courtesy, but enomously important in a life spent largely away from home and on one's own. There's always the chance that a designated host may be too intrusive or absent when the need arises. In my experience that has never been the case and I'm full of admiration for the way in which the system works. I struck up an immediate friendship with the Sweeneys from our first meeting.

Things to do in Houston. Well, we're an hour's flight away from New Orleans. Jeannie and I flew there for a couple of nights on our first visit. We listened to good jazz and drank mint juleps in the French Quarter, and later a street musician in Jackson Square beguiled us with his playing of Mozart and Rifkin, among other things, on the glass harmonica. The Lyndon B. Johnson Space Centre is in Houston and here, on our last visit, we sat in that well known control room behind the glass screens of the visitors' gallery, watching the progress of a Shuttle across a giant screen. It was much smaller than we'd imagined from television pictures and the tension of each passing moment of a mission consequently that much greater.

Somebody heard I liked sailing. Six or seven of us set off in a chartered boat, thirty-six-foot, loaded with the contents of three boot-loads – rather, trunk-loads – of food and drink. Once away from the tangled maze of pilons and overhead tension lines that are so much a part of the landscape, we were out into the Gulf for a restful day of sailing.

Golf, needless to say, has occupied my time on occasions but when asked what I would like to do with a spare day I expressed a desire to see some birds. My host reached for his gun and prepared for a day's huntin'. Calming the fever of this typically Texan reaction, I explained that a set of binoculars was all that would be necessary. The blood-lust drained from his face as he contemplated the wimpish creature before him.

'Well, that's a new one on me,' he ventured, clearly unacquainted with Audubon and his followers.

We left in his car the following day for a rice-growing area outside Houston. The previous week he'd been here, he explained, and blasted heaven knows how many geese out of the skies. The silly birds were back though, in vast numbers, offering me wonderful viewing and my host an experience he's probably still trying to fathom.

If memory serves me right I swore never to breathe a word to his macho Texan pals, but I expect that Houston dinner parties echoed to his banter as he recounted the tale of the strange Englishman who turned down an offer to go huntin'!

We open on Wednesday, 10 April. It is now Thursday, 4 April. I've arrived several days after the others, having been involved in the Salzburg work. I'm trying to ignore the tugging fingers of jet-lag.

By now, the rest of the cast have been in rehearsal for several days. As they are new to the production, I hope I'll quickly be able to catch up, knowing it from previous seasons. The assistant producer reminds me of the geography of the set and one or two salient points.

*

When I first embarked upon the role of Don Giovanni, I laid down what I thought would be certain permanent stipulations. Principally, they involved my desire to work with a Leporello with whom I was already well acquainted. The reason for my concern must be obvious. Don Giovanni and Leporello enjoy a very close working relationship on stage. I believe the greater the understanding and knowledge the singers have of one another the better. For a time most of my performances were with a long-time friend and associate, Richard van Allan.

That first production at Glyndebourne in which I played Don Giovanni was memorable. It was 1977. Benjamin Luxon had opened the performances and I came along some time later with the next cast to see the season to its close. The setting in the small theatre was sombre. John Bury had designed a gloomy set, largely black, and Peter Hall added to that gloom by having Elvira and several others shelter under umbrellas, fending off the oncoming storm.

Giovanni himself was dressed as a Regency fop, though there was nothing foppish about his behaviour. Well-mannered, superficially at least, his true nature came to the fore and was most forcibly expressed by his use of his sword-stick. There were many features in Peter's production that have served me in almost every production since.

In 1969 I'd been a member of the renowned Glyndebourne Chorus for one season, taking among others the part of a servant in the *Don Giovanni* production then playing. Richard van Allan was one of the Leporellos that year. Here, eight years later, he was my companion. Always the thorough professional, this experienced Leporello offered his new Giovanni much good advice. We developed a very close – almost telepathic – understanding, which we can enjoy to this day.

When at La Scala, Milan, I began rehearsing Don Giovanni for Giorgio Strehler, he spent hour after hour worrying over the key relationship between Don Giovanni and Leporello. It was as though he couldn't proceed until he was convinced in his own mind that, whatever guise these two characters wore, however dark it was, and however large the amount of artistic licence taken, one could always be mistaken for the other.

The Leporello of one's dreams is not, alas, always available. There are those who take on this role as if it were any other part and sing a series of notes. There are others, my soul-mates, who *become* the manservant, who know how to behave when with the Don and who take pride in serving his dinner with utmost professionalism.

In Houston, I meet a new Leporello, the Swiss Gilles ✓ Cachemaille. Part of the success or otherwise of this show may depend on how well we 'get on' and how thoroughly we come to know each other over the next few days. He's quiet, perhaps because of his poor English, but seems to have a natural clown's way of playing the role. It's odd how national characteristics become apparent at such times. Gilles could not be mistaken for an Italian or Englishman. His Gallic way with the role is instantly identifiable and comes from his musical background and the French theatrical tradition with which he's most familiar. We should have fun.

Karita Mattila, looking beautiful and extremely slim, the result of a recent diet, is the Donna Anna. Donna Elvira is the young American Renée Fleming, who will also sing the Countess in *Figaro*. Don Ottavio is a friend from *Barber* in London, the South African tenor Deon van der Walt. John Macurdy, another American, sings the Commendatore, and two local singers, Stella Zambalis and Grant Young, Zerlina and Masetto.

Maestro Eschenbach is with us for this, my first rehearsal, and it is soon apparent that he has some very definite statements to make about the piece. Never before have I had to sing a tempo as fast as the Act One finale or the 'Champagne Aria'. But, as he explains, when I ask him, the work is about life, and a life that hurtles ✓ cataclysmically forward. 'Go for it,' I tell myself (falling immediately into local slang), hoping I've got the energy to see this through. But maturity has taught me that things which may not appear to be right at first often fall into place once the orchestra arrives – after all, string players in particular have to play at these speeds, too, and have many more notes.

Perhaps only once, with Karl Böhm during *The Marriage of Figaro*, did the thought cross my mind: No-one ever taught me how to sing so slowly! Now I find that Eschenbach also requires some of the slowest tempi I've experienced. He goes to extremes.

After the morning rehearsal I am required at Wardrobe to try on costumes for the production. This being Texas, today no-one is allowed into Wardrobe without a hat. I can give no reason for this except that it relieves the potential tedium of the day in this windowless, air-conditioned basement. That's good enough for me. Most of the personnel of the Wardrobe department are ladies. They work away diligently in the undercroft of the new theatre building. The fact that serious questions about costume detailing are being asked by the Wardrobe mistress nonchalantly sporting a ten-gallon stetson, whilst others wear a range of hats from Minnie Mouse ears to an Eliza Doolittle bonnet, causes no problem for anyone. It's all in a day's work.

There are many signs that point to the youthfulness of America. Its native Indian roots, it seems, are too little known, while its inherited European culture combines with Eastern and Caribbean influences to make the strange salad that gives the United States its uniqueness. The hi-tech brilliance of the various Disney enter-prises are what artistic America is about. And why not? To make my point I'm deliberately omitting the vast contribution of great painters such as Hopper, Pollock and Rothko.

I've noticed before that in North America one of the problems of period costume is in providing the correct footwear. Giovanni, for instance, wears at different times long leather boots and white tongue-and-buckle dress shoes. In London, a Wardrobe master or mistress can pop round the corner to one of several workshops and find a range of such shoes. Here, though, it's usually a question of adapting a modern shoe to look like the eighteenth-century original. Once, in Ottawa, I had to go to a tuxedo hire shop with a Wardrobe master to find suitable footgear. We finished with two pairs of white-and-black patent leather shoes of a design more normally associated with Las Vegas wedding parlours inspired by the proximity of Mexico and its medallion-man influences. You can imagine the aesthetic pilgrimage the shoes made before they were considered suitable. All I missed was a luminous pair of bell-bottomed trousers and shades. That was a production of the Russian masterpiece *Eugene Onegin*.

Eventually we settle upon shoes and shirts for the Don that will convince and I snatch an afternoon nap before the long ordeal of this evening's rehearsal. We're scheduled to run from 7 p.m. to midnight. With an extra half-hour to show me one or two important points on stage that I may have forgotten, that makes a five-and-a-half-hour rehearsal. Having come only yesterday from Austria with an eight-hour time difference, I'll finish at eight o'clock in the morning according to my body-clock. I do this sum in my head and decide on the best course open to me – to ignore jet-lag and to work right through. At times like this I can only draw on reserves deep within myself and hope they will provide enough energy. I enjoy the challenge.

Apart from one or two hiccoughs, the rehearsal goes well. The costumes fit, the tempi work, I don't kill anybody and nobody kills me in this dangerous piece.

I return to my apartment ready to enjoy as much rest as possible. Rest, I believe, is the secret, whenever faced with a difficult timetable crammed with rehearsals and performances. Singing an opera means using the muscles of the throat for extended periods of time. Provided they're used correctly, as any other muscle, and allowed to rest when not required, theoretically there should be no harmful effect.

Saturday, 6 April. We gather in the afternoon to sort out details that need working on, following last night's rehearsal.

My principal concern is to try to get to know Gilles a little more. Were we straight actors, perhaps I would not hesitate to throw him about the stage and rough him up when necessary. With a singer I have more inhibitions. Fortunately Leporellos rarely fall into the wilting-violet category. Most of them have learnt how to tumble and roll, without too much harm to themselves other than the occasional bruise, and still be able to sing. I have to be sure Gilles is of this type and not a fragile creature who will not be able to cope with so much of what we do on stage.

There's little time for any of these theories to be put into practice.

Tomorrow is the day of our public Dress Rehearsal. I spend it quietly, with a mid-morning breakfast, and try to while away the remaining hours with occasional dips into playing the piano, reading and painting. It is the most frustrating time to be a prisoner within this apartment. This part of Houston is featureless. It's also considered an unsafe city in which to walk. The weather is warm and very humid. Staying in is clearly the best of the few options open to me. Time passes slowly but eventually the moment arrives and I take the car to the theatre.

I'm an hour ahead of curtain time. Too early. In an ideal world I'd prefer to arrive ten minutes before the overture of this production and go straight on. This version has Don Giovanni go into very extreme decline. In order to make the most of this extraordinary change, I create a figure who is initially, in appearance at least, as pure as the driven snow. A white-faced Japanese-like mask is the starting point. A white band passes across my forehead and a tightly-dressed wig of jet black completes the look. Did someone say *M. Butterfly*?

I have developed a habit of listening out for the first bars of the Giovanni overture. In this ominous music there always lies a clue to the kind of evening I may expect from conductor and orchestra below me in the pit. Tonight, it sounds suitably threatening. The sword-fight works well. I wouldn't like to enumerate the performances in which not a sound of crossed swords was heard, as both Don and Commendatore managed to miss one another in the dark, caught in the dilemma of trying to look realistic while at the same time exercising extreme caution. Arias follow recitatives and duets, quartets and finale speed by under Eschenbach's baton. The various vocal landmarks I single out along the way in the opera pass by, each successfully negotiated. Where necessary some of the singers 'mark' certain sections of the music, that is to say, they do not sing with full voice. The dress rehearsal audience may well feel cheated of a performance when an artist saves his or her voice in this way, but the very good reason in this case is that a number of us are also singing in other operas in this Festival. With a first night 'just around the corner', as well as a continuing rehearsal schedule, it is to be expected that something is kept in reserve.

I'm feeling very fit, and anxious to begin, aware of the 'buzz' that Giovanni gives me. No matter how many times I sing this role, it continues to intrigue me. The variety of possibilities in the recitatives is my principal driving force. I hope that no two nights are ever the same, though they may appear so to many. Tiny, subtle differences of inflection are enough to conjure up a new chemistry between artists that may lead to fresh revelations and the constant renewing of this extraordinary work.

The question of how to complete Act One of *Don Giovanni* is vexed. Seldom is the escape or otherwise of the Don made plausible, partly because of the threat under which he's held by Don Ottavio. (Some would say that this is Ottavio's only manly gesture of the evening.) Peter Hall had the Don walk brazenly to the front of the stage, and take a deep bow to the audience, with a demonic grin of confidence and daring growing on his face. I liked that – it appealed to me. Jarvefelt's solution is perhaps even better. Giovanni initially attempts an escape upstage, through the other principals, but is prevented from doing so by the chorus. He returns to the front of the stage just in time to be cut off from his pursuers by a descending wall. He turns, realises his narrow escape, laughs relievedly, beckons Leporello to follow, and flees, laughing all the way. The audience is shocked by this. No music accompanies the last moments, it all being acted out in silence as a mime, save for the Don's laugh. A wonderful moment.

Because of the complexities of Don Giovanni's decline, as called for by this production, I spend the entire interval going through a change of wigs and hair pieces. First, the white band and wig must be taken away. My suffering hair is then covered by a bald pate held in place by a glue I've not previously encountered (it's normally used in medical procedures). Wisps of greying hair are draped around the back of the pate. The black wig of Act One then goes over everything, though now it is looking a little distressed – a reflection of the hazardous life it and I are leading. All this takes considerable time, and David, the wig-man, has to work calmly and steadily through the intermission in order that I'm ready for beginners call.

An example of the different ways in which one can handle the recitative comes early in Act Two. This act begins with Giovanni and Leporello in flight from their most recent crazy escapade. Leporello makes to leave – yet again. Don Giovanni calls after him: 'Leporello!' It can be simply that. Full of his own madness and bravado, the Don calls for Leporello to come back and stop being so pathetic. An alternative is to inject a sense of loss and desperation – 'Leporello?' – with an unwritten 'Don't abandon me' after it. There's enormous relief, however brief, to be conveyed when the Don hears the reply of Leporello from the gloom: 'Signore.' He knows he still has him at the end of his line like a weakly struggling fish.

None of the dialogue can be taken for granted. Each time I come to any of the lines they can mean something fresh. Something more revealing about the character of Don Giovanni, something new in his relationship with Leporello. It becomes intriguing to ponder on the relationship between Mozart and da Ponte, and their understanding of human behaviour in their pre-Freudian world.

Giovanni has three contrasting arias during the course of the evening. The 'Champagne Aria' of Act One shows him at his manic worst, arranging the ideas for a party at which he'll demonstrate his considerable powers.

The other two are close on one another in Act Two. First, the lovely canzonetta *'Deh, vieni alla finestra'*, sung to a mandolin accompaniment as he woos the maid of Donna Elvira. Following this comes a buffo aria, in which, to save his skin from the anger of Masetto and the band of armed men he's gathered about him, Giovanni takes on the guise of Leporello and describes the man they should be looking for. Nothing of the real nature of Don Giovanni is deeply revealing from these arias. Where we see the inner man is in some of the other duets and quartets, and of course the recitatives.

The frightening coup of our production comes in Giovanni's last moments as he descends to the inferno. Only then do I tear away the now-dishevelled black wig to reveal the wisps of grey and white hair that lie on the bald pate beneath. This comes as a shock for the audience. It caps a number of wonderfully revealing moments in the production.

The finale draws to a close. With what energy I have left, I congratulate my colleagues and the design team, led by Carl Friedrich Oberle.

Monday, 8 April. A full day of rehearsal for *Figaro*. Don Giovanni has to be forgotten for the moment; he sits on the low back burner waiting for his First Night on Wednesday.

Almost all the details of the *Figaro* production seem new to me, though I sang in it here in November 1988. I suppose the brain needs to eliminate some details from its memory banks in order that new material can be absorbed. The cast is largely new since the previous time, with the exception of Judith Christin, who plays a virtuoso Marcellina. Watching her is like having a compilation film of all those matronly ladies we know from great comedy, opera and pantomime. She would be wonderful as Mrs Peachum in *The Beggar's Opera* or in a Restoration comedy, and that's before I've taken into account her fine singing. She's worth a trip to the theatre for her stage personality alone. She's a lovely person, whom everyone is happy to have around, as well as a fine actress-singer.

Renato Capecchi sings Doctor Bartolo. I well remember the first recording of *The Marriage of Figaro* I owned, on which Renato sang Figaro. He has a wealth of experience behind him and I look forward to watching his buffo playing for which he's justly renowned.

Christoph Eschenbach makes an appearance at the *Figaro* rehearsal. He's still excited by the events of last evening's *Giovanni* Dress Rehearsal. He can't stay with *Figaro* long as he must also attend an orchestral rehearsal of *Così*. He has the trio of da Ponte operas in his charge at this Festival.

Playing the lascivious Count to the Susanna of the pretty Italian, Nuccia Focile, is not difficult! She's taking on the role for the first time, and will I imagine enjoy many years of success with it.

Today I'm buoyant – though understandably tired. I take in as much as I can of detail for the four acts of *Figaro*, and look forward to tomorrow's rest day in anticipation of our *Don Giovanni* première.

10 April. I arrive at the theatre an hour before curtain in order to begin make-up and wigs. Everything fits, all goes smoothly and after what seems an interminable wait those ominous chords sound once again. First Nights are always busy. So many people want to call by the dressing room to pass on best wishes.

With the help of surtitles the audience is more responsive than most first-night audiences used to be. At first I thought the intrusion of surtitles into the theatre was a retrograde step. But now I find them enormously helpful in watching performances of operas whose texts are not familiar to me. Used properly, they are unobtrusive and detract not one bit from the enjoyment of an evening.

Act One ends with the planned shock to the audience as Giovanni survives all threats and goes his ruthless way on the slide to hell and damnation. In Act Two I'm a little out of breath, having attempted to put on Leporello's boots as part of my disguise – they are at least one size too small for me. Oh, the pains we suffer for art's sake!

At the conclusion there is a rapturous reception. I'm tired, still jet-lagged, but stimulated by the accomplishment. It is satisfying to play this role, to explore the dark corners of Giovanni's mind, and to feel at the end of it all a sense of having arrived at some goal.

A lot of my playing of Giovanni is purely instinctive; but doubts about my interpretation were abandoned some time ago in Milan. I have a friend there, a lady psychiatrist who specialises in the treatment of sexual problems and difficult relationships. Having seen my performance at La Scala, she told me that she recognised many of her patients in my stage character. We enjoyed a quiet drink at a nearby bar, where I endeavoured not to twitch too much in front of this expert of the mind!

Contrary to popular opinion, first nights are not always the occasion for glamorous post-performance parties. Tonight the cast and production team are invited to a private house for a quiet buffet dinner. I sit and rest my rather weary legs.

*

11 April. The euphoria of the *Giovanni* First Night now behind me, I haul my aching body into some sort of order and set off for my *Figaro* rehearsal. Last night the plush of the theatre, this morning the drawing board of the rehearsal room. There is a considerable strain attached to the playing of Don Giovanni. I've likened it to an ascent of Everest – without oxygen. At the start of the evening, having dealt the fatal blow to the Commendatore, the Don begins the enormous uphill climb that culminates in his invitation to a 'celestial supper'. At that early point of the evening the task seems very daunting indeed. No surprise, then, to be suffering somewhat on this, the day after.

But the magic of 'Doctor Theatre' is a wonderful cure. The *Figaro* schedule will no doubt be as intense as the *Giovanni*.

We begin the process of repetition. The day is a full one, going over some of the details that were only sketched in at my first rehearsal. I'm getting to know various members of the cast a little better.

13 April is the date set for our second performance of *Don Giovanni*. Gilles has returned to Europe to fulfil a long-standing engagement. He was, it seems, a late replacement as Leporello and never free to sing this second performance. His place is to be taken by George Hogan. This is where things start to become crazy. With opportunity only to run through the words of some recitatives before we begin, I work for the first time with Leporello-George. He does very well. Second performances can fall notoriously flat, but this one is not at all bad.

Life is like a roller-coaster. In the evening, the high of performance; the following afternoon, the basic essentials of a piano dress rehearsal for *Figaro*.

In the past two days, my costumes for the Count have been reassembled from the previous performances in Houston. Since that time, two years ago, they've been through other hands, or rather on other bodies. Inspection shows the journeys they have made among other companies in America. The cuffs of shirts are ragged, buttons have gone missing, hems hang unevenly. But the magic ladies of Wardrobe have an eye to all these things. By the time of the piano dress, most flaws have been covered up.

It is by no means a smooth run. Several times it is necessary to stop to check moves. It's difficult to get the Act Two finale right. Mozart was a composer of genius and the development of this particular passage of music is surely among his supreme achievements. Peter Shaffer recognised that in *Amadeus*.

Jeannie has arrived at the apartment by the time I finish. I couldn't get away to meet her at the airport, but the Houston system has moved into action and friends she made on a previous visit see that she is safely collected and delivered. She brings news of home, letters and bills that have piled up over the past two weeks, plus her welcome company.

The following two days are spent in correcting faults that arose in the piano dress. There's time, too, to work with Christoph in setting tempi and dynamics of arias, duets, trios, ensembles. How he compartmentalises each opera, day after day, astonishes anyone outside music. Anyone inside opera learns to be aware that the brain we humans have is capable of dealing with many things at once. 'Every man to his job' is an adage that applies in music, too.

17 April. Dress Rehearsal day and people flock to this as they do to a first night.

I'm beginning to have to make a conscious effort not to react on stage at the moment the audience reacts to the surtitles they're reading. Before the invention of the surtitle, a lot of what was regarded as 'operatic acting' (and rightly criticised) was a result of the lack of understanding among audiences. To compensate for this, singers developed a system of semaphore to show how passionate they felt, that they were writing a letter, or that 'no horses fell from the window' – important moments in *The Marriage of Figaro*. Surtitles should, theoretically, help us rid ourselves of such bad habits, and to play much more in the style of the Royal Shakespeare Company.

Our Susanna, Nuccia Focile, does the most erotic version of *'Deh vieni'* in the last act that I've ever seen in my life. This surely has to be the utmost torment for Figaro. Our Countess, Renée, sings beautifully with lots of vocal control, as befits her age and talent. She's clearly enjoying this early stage in her career when nothing is a problem and she can hang on to notes until the cows come home, making them swell or diminish as she wishes.

My only concern is that in the process we may finish up with Donizetti rather than Mozart. The difference of singing styles between those two composers is considerable. In Mozart it is forbidden to join up two notes that are, say, five or six notes apart ✓ by the use of a slow slide or *portamento* either going up or down. Conductors squeal at this just as we squeal when someone runs fingernails down a blackboard. To employ this same effect in Donizetti, however, is acceptable stylistically and indeed gives the special colour that one associates with the music of this slightly later period. The singer is also permitted to make long pauses on certain notes before tumbling away from them in cascades of sound – the sort of thing Dame Joan Sutherland excelled at in *Lucia di Lammermoor*, for example. The same technique is considered very wrong when singing Mozart.

The following day I have an interview with one of the two classical radio stations here. It means going to the fifty-first floor of a very new high-rise building. The interview is brief and concerned mainly with the interpretation of Don Giovanni. Equally interesting to me is to hear that a Peregrine falcon regularly perches on a ledge outside the studio windows. Alas, it doesn't turn up while I am there. I resolve to make a bird-watching trip along the Texas coast during my stay, and will get myself better organised than on my last attempt with gun-totin' Jim.

19 April. I spend the early part of the day painting. If I allowed it to, this could occupy my every waking hour and, who knows, may do so one day. I'm improving, I think, but am as yet reluctant to let anything be seen. The odd effect is that it makes me look at everyday life quite differently. I see compositions for paintings as I drive along the street here in Houston. At first sight there would appear to be few suitable subjects. But once the scales are taken away from my eyes, I begin to see shapes, forms, masterpieces leaping at me from the most unexpected corners. I can feel an engine inside me beginning to turn in my eagerness to try to capture so many of these things in paint. I can find the time – if only I had the skill to support it. But I'll keep trying!

Jeannie and I have lunch in a local restaurant. It has been highly recommended. She orders a simple pasta and salad dish and I choose macaroni with some fresh seafood. I can't tell you the number of times I've heard her say: 'Darling, don't eat seafood before you sing.'

I rest during the remainder of the afternoon, as the performance starts at 7.30 p.m. At the time when I should be awake and getting up, I'm feeling very drowsy. All I can think of doing is going back to bed. I feel extremely weak, my knees buckling under me. It's now 6 o'clock and I'm due at the theatre by seven. We begin to suspect something amiss – 'How many times have I asked you not to eat seafood before a show?' were the words my wife used.

Putting thoughts of illness aside, I make my way to the performance. David Gockley, the General Manager, must be told how I'm feeling and also Christoph, who is to conduct this weakling Count. Other than that, I try to put it out of my mind.

The performance proceeds. I feel a little weak but 'Doctor Theatre' is working his magic once again. What is that numbness or anaesthesia that assails us when we step on to the stage? It's an extraordinary phenomenon that some clever person should surely utilise. Or is it unharnessable, like wave energy? Perhaps it is to orthodox human response what acupuncture is to orthodox medicine. Whatever it is, it's on my side this evening. I breathe deeply to try to use whatever resources I have and it works, thank God.

A party is held in a private house following another happy success. Rather than spoil the evening, and feeling elated rather than drained, I go along. It's another opportunity to meet some old Houston friends and to enjoy their Texan warmth and hospitality. Sadly, we seem to find it so hard in our European society to smile and be pleasant with others. Encountering kindness at this level, the cynic has to ask: 'But what's the catch?'

47

The food poisoning, or whatever, went away during the evening.

21 April. Spoke too soon. I have a *Giovanni* matinée this afternoon. I have spent a fitful night unable to find any restful position in bed. I recognise these signs – clearly something is wrong. By 9 a.m. I'm finally sick.

I'm now familiar with the grouting round all the tiles in the bathroom, as well as several features of the floor. This is the real thing I was waiting for two days ago. It went into hiding somewhere inside me, just long enough to lull me into a false sense of security.

Jeannie calls the opera house. She explains. Within five minutes a doctor has telephoned with first-aid advice. He advises a sports drink that will replace the electrolytes in my body (which makes me sound like a car battery) and Coca-Cola – instant correction for the rolling-boil stomach.

I feel like death. The matinée begins at 2 p.m. – now only three hours away. Interestingly, I've not drunk coffee for a couple of days, since the last 'funny bout', and just at the moment I don't see myself ever drinking it again. You've no idea how amazing a statement that is for as dedicated a coffee-holic as myself.

I put on three articles of clothing – trousers, underpants, shirt – and a pair of espadrilles. I simply can't be bothered with any more.

When I arrive at my dressing room, all the people who need to know are alerted. Anne Owens, who does a marvellous job in artists' relations here, meets me with an assortment of bottles and cans. I start immediately replacing those missing electrolytes.

It seems hardly necessary to put on the stylised white clown make-up. Nothing can match this natural pallor. A young under-study is standing by – poor lad. I know this because every now and then someone from the Wardrobe department comes in and removes a pair of shoes or boots, in the hope they'll fit him, returning them five minutes later. They think I don't notice, but I do.

People call in and wish me well. I wonder what I'm doing here. Having previously described this opera as being rather like climbing Everest, what possible description will satisfy today's situation? I try to put thoughts of the whole out of my mind, and begin to think in terms of scene by scene: if I can kill the Commendatore without mishap, I can have a rest before my next entrance; the next scene is a trio and recitative, not very taxing. But the comedy needs precise detail. And I'm not in the mood for detail, precise or otherwise.

The witching hour arrives, the ominous chords of the overture especially portentous today. The audience has been made aware of my predicament via a front-of-tabs announcement.

In the first scene I go through a more restrained tussle with Donna Anna than normal. Karita Mattila is a strong Finnish girl, but on this occasion she's gentle with me. John Macurdy arrives as her father. I despatch him. It is then that I begin to feel unwell. I tell myself this cannot be.

Despite the assistance from the surtitles, the audience is quieter than normal. They're watching a man with food poisoning trying to play Don Giovanni and they've no idea where or how it will end. Nor have I. *Dallas* has become *Houston*.

I get safely into the wings and begin to recover. First scene successfully negotiated. That's one down and several thousand to go.

Our second scene goes smoothly, the audience still watching me, T.A., rather than me, D.G. It's almost tangible. There are various sorts of quiet in the theatre and this one is unmistakable.

At a time like this there is the chance to take out a part of oneself as though to observe from the outside what the body, the person, is doing. I'm conscious of this self-examination, curious as to just how far I can go and what the body and mind can tolerate. Once again I find that, when we push ourselves, there are available to us huge reserves which are seldom if ever called upon. I'm not, of course, comparing struggling on stage with food poisoning to what has to be endured by a long-term hostage, but listening to Brian Keenan on the radio during *Desert Island Discs* I felt very strongly that here was a man who had been pushed to the very extremes of self-examination. I make this analogy simply to use Keenan's courage as an example of what can be achieved in the struggle of mind over matter. I doff my humble cap to one who survived as he did.

There is a kind of sense and order to my first few scenes in this opera. The first hurdle is the so-called 'Champagne Aria'. So called because of its bubbling, vibrant nature – as far as I remember, I've never been involved in a production which required me to raise a glass in salute. The aria needs a lot of breath control and agility of voice. Rather than rush headlong at it like a bull at a gate, I opt for a quieter approach, trusting this will be interpreted as yet another facet of the Don's scheming and his dangerous psyche. It seems to meet with approval. I find I've learnt something. Perhaps in normal circumstances I cause too much genuine tension in myself, instead of relaxing and externalising the effect I wish to make. It sounds simple, written like that. Indeed, it's a lesson I thought I'd grasped a good many years ago. Clearly, we never stop learning.

Following this, I'm hopeful of being able to complete at least the first half. We'll see how I feel after the Act One finale.

Applying the same principles – and losing nothing dramatically, I suspect, into the bargain – the next ten scenes also go well. Gratifyingly, the audience is hushed at the final chord of the finale (still wondering when I'm going to drop, I imagine) which means I can turn and face them in the silence, laugh demoniacally, beckon Leporello to follow, and flee to the darkness and security of the wings.

Oh, what an old ham I am at this moment!

I long to lie down and sleep now. But the timetable requires me to go through the usual wig changes. I stock up on more electrolytes.

The next big hurdles lie directly ahead. A roustabout with Leporello. A trio involving the Don and Donna Elvira. The delicate Serenade to Elvira's maid. The buffo aria that results in Masetto lying bruised and battered on the ground, wounded by 'Leporello – or some such devil', as he later tells Zerlina. It's a long section that lasts twenty minutes or so. I'm always glad to see the back of it because of the contrasting moods and the amount of energy demanded in acting all this out. It precedes the only real rest I get in the opera. Now I really can go to sleep. I'm sorely tempted, but I'd never rouse myself to performance pitch in today's condition. I opt for more electrolytes.

The performance isn't over yet but I'm fairly confident now that I shall be able to complete my part. My colleagues are very considerate. They've spent the afternoon offering me encouragement and placing buckets strategically in the wings. The white make-up I wear hides my true colour. Occasionally I've leaned against a wall of the set. It's so good to be able to lean like this. I wander off in character and lean in character – it's surprising how many changes I could have made to help me this afternoon without undermining the show. It occurred to me to sit on the floor for part of the time but I didn't find this expedient necessary in the event. I revel in the cemetery scene, always bizarre, filled with fears and superstitions. I can make any changes I wish to help me today in the course of the recitative. This is the part I find most interesting. Giovanni works for me by way of these recitatives and in this production there's greater scope in the graveyard scene than in most others, because the Don by then has become so deranged.

The element of superstition and the part it plays in *Don Giovanni* is, I think, enormously important. Anyone who has visited a church or cemetery in Spain can hardly have failed to notice that there is an overpowering sense of power and gloom in the atmosphere. Certain areas within the Cathedral of Barcelona, for example, struck me on my first visit to be heavy and black with significance. Here was work in a religious context, most certainly, but derived more from the Inquisition, the *Auto da Fe* and all its evils, than from the gloriously golden aspects of Christian faith. The devil himself seems an equal partner with Christ in portraying the course of human life. Superstition must surely be written into this kind of faith, too, and that is the primitive fear upon which Giovanni plays when he terrifies Leporello to such a degree in this graveyard scene. Beliefs as ancient as Christianity – and far older, too – are present.

We escape safely over the wall.

The supper scene arrives and today the worst aspect of this for me is the sight of food on the table – even these small pieces of chicken. I do my best to avoid confronting them. In this production

I look pretty 'far gone' by the time Donna Elvira arrives to make one last attempt to save me. Today, she can see immediately that I'm beyond redemption. I'm beginning to feel like a spent force. But the show is almost over. I'm in my normal vocal state, which must be some sort of miracle.

The ending I can play as crazily as the producer demands. The Commendatore freezes my hand. I vie with him for decibel counts. I feel around with my feet to locate the trapdoor safely without making it too obvious what I'm about. I rip off the black tousled wig and reveal the Don's true wispy baldness beneath, before disappearing on a scream rather weaker and less blood-curdling than I'm usually able to muster.

But who would know? I've finished. I've got through the show with an audience that changed from waiting for me to have an accident at any moment to one that gained in confidence that things were going to come to their conventional conclusion, much to their relief – and to my own.

Jeannie more or less carried me home and I spent the rest of the day lying down watching my favourite film channel on television.

Everyone else in the company went off to the big party of the Season. It was held in a downtown disused Victorian ballroom. Disused as a ballroom because it is in an area that has been caught in the poverty trap that one can see in so many of the Tex Mex areas of Houston. The theme of the party was 'Così fan rootin' tootin' Tutte'; the brief, needless to say, was wear anything Texan. I was sorry to have missed Karita in her denims and pink leather cowboy boots. Quite a sight on this blonde Finnish bombshell.

Monday is a rest day and I make the most of a short session in the pool. I manage six lengths of breast stroke before getting thoroughly bored, while Jeannie is doing about twelve. For the moment at least I can still beat her at golf, but I have the feeling it might not last long.

People here are very fitness-conscious. Some American youths buy a new pair of trainer shoes from a specialist shop every three weeks or so. Trainers are one of the status symbols of the 1980s and

1990s, and the promotion of a shoe that self-inflates for tennis, aerobics, basketball, or whatever your particular torture is, means that these same folk are reaching into their pockets for something like $170 every three or four weeks to stay in fashion. The business community who stay fit are a different sort. It's common in American cities now to see smartly dressed women leaving their offices at midday and in the evening in grey and blue pin-stripe suits, elegantly tailored for the modern executive lady, but on their feet are white socks and trainers. Walking is an important part of the fitness regime.

The Mozart Festival continues on the following day, Tuesday 23 April, with the second performance of *Figaro*. I feel rather weakened still from the events of two days ago and do my best in this performance to give myself a slightly easier time.

The Houston public is being satiated with Mozart night after night. Normally used to hearing two operas in any one period of the company's work, they now have before them five big Mozart blockbusters. Sadly, it appears to be reflected in the ticket sales. Those who attend are very enthusiastic, but each evening I can't help but see from the stage that there are several large gaps in the Stalls. This must surely be disappointing for the management, but it was a brave undertaking.

Wednesday is a single rest day before the final *Giovanni* on Thursday.

The longest run of any one opera I've been involved in was the *Don Giovanni* at Glyndebourne in 1982. I had an opportunity of seeing a little of what it must be like to watch a show develop and change as in a West End success. Although we did fourteen performances only, things most certainly did change and I learnt a great deal from that experience, especially from a greater familiarity with and understanding of the artists with whom I was working. As usual at Glyndebourne, the production had been very carefully prepared over several weeks. First, the cast would be called together for music rehearsals, when the head of music, Martin Isepp, would drill everyone into a particular blend that would be that year's hallmark for Mozart. On stage, the same process went on, as the production was regenerated from its original concept.

At the end of those long working days we would all drive off to our own houses. Cottages, bungalows and seaside flats were taken over by visiting artists of the Glyndebourne season. Close friends were made during those festivals in the Sussex countryside and there started a nostalgia for a very special place that has lasted throughout my career. Here in Houston, we have had a very short time with only four performances. Nevertheless, with my greater experience it seems to have become possible to find something new for each new production. I have learned to allow instinct to dictate minor changes at odd moments. I won't forget the Houston *Giovanni*. There's a wildness that stays on the thin border between utmost sanity and utter madness.

I'm so happy with the end of Act One. The audience is in our grip at the close of the music. It waits in perfect silence while Giovanni makes his escape. It gives me great pleasure to have participated in so theatrical a drama. New ideas have been stored away.

This role becomes more and more fascinating. Several key points spring to mind. Stillness – I now lay great store on the power of stillness. An almost hypnotic concentration – such as those moments when Giovanni, at his own party, sizes up Zerlina as his next prey. In this scene I try to make Zerlina feel as uncomfortable as possible on the stage, as though Giovanni had stripped her naked in front of everyone. Giovanni is, I think, like a cheetah. It's fascinating to watch a slow-motion film of this animal as it first selects its target, then stalks it, and finally begins the run that will demonstrate how it moves in complete harmony with all its constituent forces. And, all this time, and with all that energy to unleash to its service, the head of the cheetah remains in one position at one level. Its concentration is of white-hot intensity. Stalking Zerlina, I try to emulate the cheetah.

I say farewell to some of the cast. Others will remain to fulfil duties in the other operas. During all this time I've seen very little of my colleagues. The schedule is fairly tiring for everyone. Like most artists, each singer has a personal ritual of discipline that will get him or her safely through. No big parties, no balls, no all-night gambling and drinking sessions – we're all very good. It sounds terribly boring, don't you think?

*

Overnight, an immense cyclone hits Kansas in the mid-West and many people lose their lives. I've seen photographs of these effects but nothing like the tragic news footage that appears on television the following day. I remind myself that Texas is almost the size of Europe. The area of Houston is spared and our weather oddly changes for the better. On what turns out to be a hot sparkling day I manage my only game of golf during the entire visit. Surprisingly, I play quite well knowing that had I a second opportunity tomorrow I'd probably play like the proverbial rabbit. The remaining performances of *Figaro* pass without incident. Jeannie leaves for London a few days ahead of me to see to one or two domestic matters that inevitably arise with these long stays away from home. I'll find it hard to leave the comfort of the apartment which I've come to regard as home. America has a way of spoiling you for life anywhere else.

Stephen, my son, meets me at Gatwick and we have lunch *en famille* at home, having got over the awful business of unpacking. It hardly seems worth it, since I'll be leaving for Cologne on Sunday afternoon.

Saturday morning is spent with Angela Halliday, my secretary-cum-bookkeeper. It is essential to ensure that certain bills and letters are dealt with during my absences. Angela stands between me and the bailiffs.

Saturday afternoon I spend at Stamford Bridge with a doctor friend who has tickets for Chelsea's match against Liverpool. Why not! I'm full of energy and we decide the change will do me good. I'd rather see Sunderland at Roker Park, but I'd not have had time for the trip there and back in any case. I enjoy the match very much – Chelsea win 4–2. I'm ashamed to say the last and only time I was at Stamford Bridge was as a student in the 1960s to see the famous Leeds team play – Bremner, Giles, etc.

We've invited half a dozen friends for dinner, knowing that if I don't see them during this short period at home the chances are I won't see them for the rest of the year. It's a lovely evening of reminiscing and story-telling.

On Sunday I get up early to repack with a new wardrobe of slightly warmer clothes for northern Europe.

Before I leave, I have a morning rehearsal of *Die Zauberflöte* with Sir Charles Mackerras. I'm recording Papageno with him later in the summer, and this is our one chance to rehearse. It's seven years since I sang the role of Papageno and, though it's Mozart, it's a million miles away from Don Giovanni. Against the challenges of the Don, Papageno's part seems short and simple.

This hectic weekend almost over, I now race home to have lunch with Jeannie before leaving for the airport.

Chapter Three

A COSY NEST
IN COLOGNE

I'M flying to Cologne – my debut in this Opera House – for a new production of *Don Giovanni*. Carol Vaness, who's to be the √ Donna Anna, is in London and hopes to be on the same flight. We're old friends from Covent Garden, Glyndebourne and the Metropolitan. We meet up in the departure lounge and spend the short journey catching up on news and gossip. Carol is a very powerful personality and always to be relied upon for strong opinions on all matters musical – and on most other matters under the sun.

Despite all my travels and experiences, I'm still nervous about arriving at a new location. I was in Cologne only once before for a recital at the Opera House. Carol and I are staying at the same apartment house, ten minutes' walk from the theatre. It's wonderful to have friends close by. So much of a singer's time is spent alone. Eating by myself in a restaurant I find a miserable experience. A book helps but is nothing like the company of a friend.

Karita is in Cologne too. This time she is singing the role of Donna Elvira – a quick change-around from Houston. She informs me that her departure from Houston was delayed because the Kansas cyclone finally got there.

Monday, 6 May. Our first rehearsal is in the fourth floor rehearsal room of the theatre, amidst the bits and pieces of scenery of a dozen other productions. This time the Leporello is someone I know quite well. Ferruccio Furlanetto – Figaro from Salzburg.

57

The production is that of Michael Hampe. There's something about German producers and their work method that is different from many others. They operate with a huge back-up team of assistants, all scribbling furiously in their books as soon as anything from the rehearsal stage needs to be registered. Production scores of operas are twice as thick as the normal vocal score that we use. Between each two sheets of music is interleaved a plain sheet of paper. On this the assistants can draw their plan of the stage set and furniture and plot the moves of the singers as the production proceeds. In this way, at the end of the rehearsal period there will exist in the theatre a copy of the production of this opera, which can be taken down from the shelf at any time in √ order that it can be re-produced by a house assistant.

What surprises us on this first day of rehearsal is that the blank pages aren't blank. In the master copy they're filled with the lines and details of the production that Dr Hampe invented in Salzburg, five years ago. For two of the cast this means going over a lot of old ground. Ferruccio has sung in every performance since that original and Carol Vaness in subsequent revivals.

During the course of the day we meet our conductor. James Conlon is now General Music Director (GMD) of the Cologne Theatre. He reminds me that it's about ten years since we last √ worked together on *Zauberflöte* and *I Pagliacci* at Covent Garden. As GMD he has a difficult task here. There are many commitments, not only to opera but also to ballet and concerts. Establishing a work schedule is not going to be easy.

The theatre enjoyed a tremendous reputation for its Mozart operas several years ago, under the joint leadership of John Pritchard and Jean-Pierre Ponnelle, when such singers as Margaret Price and Lucia Popp were regular visitors. Now there's a conscious effort on James's part to try to re-establish that international reputation. The emphasis has swung in the intervening years from a theatre of great music to one of good music theatre. (*Prima le parole, dopo la musica.*) The theatre itself is relatively small – just over two thousand seats – and looks every bit as faceless and unaesthetic as anything that ever sprang up on London's South Bank. But appearances can be deceptive, and the damage done to

Cologne by Allied bombing in the Second World War is the reason this building and many others look the way they do.

Inevitably, when one performs a role many times, there are certain favourite moves, dodges, tricks and accents that are a part of the trademark by which a public recognises a particular artist in a particular part.

In just the same way as one develops habits in life, so a character acquires habits as he grows within an artist. The logical development of this is that certain behaviour patterns become those of the character being played and not of the artist playing him. This applied to the art of Laurence Olivier, Ralph Richardson, Edith Evans, Tito Gobbi, Maria Callas and many others.

I am familiar with the role of Don Giovanni, and I am now an experienced singer-actor, so I begin to reveal some, though not all, of my trademarks. Dr Hampe has other ideas. He's entitled; it's his production. But without a sense of sharing, of give-and-take between us, I'm anxious that I will feel too strait-jacketed to give of my best.

I believe that the fruitfulness of any working relationship, and the ultimate success of any production, lies in acknowledging the various wisdoms brought by everyone to the scene. It should not be a one-sided process of dictation from behind the well-staffed producer's table. I know the state of play when I'm told not to wipe the sword cynically over the body of the Commendatore. He's died a moment before as a result of a blow delivered by me. Could we perhaps discuss whether there's an argument for my interpretation? It seems not. I'm simply told not to do it. Let us hope there'll be a sense of glasnost as time goes by. If we both dig in our heels, it could be a long process.

It's very difficult to let go of favourite moments. One has to adapt, of course. I give myself a gentle reminder to remain open to any ideas that come along. In this way I'm a little less stubborn than I used to be. I used to argue for hours over the whys and wherefores of Billy Budd. Now, I'm rather more inclined to let nature take its course.

But Giovanni is a person I understand. It would be very difficult to say why. I have no medical qualifications and can't therefore explain his state of mind psychologically. An historian might produce a very sound argument for some other interpretation. But instinct tells me that Don Giovanni is a very rare creature in the entire panoply of mankind. He has opened his whole being to all worldly experiences several times over. He is capable of anything, like a modern-day supernatural creation of Hollywood. His horizons know no bounds – he would appear to be indestructible. He is a man unfettered by the morals and restraints that affect other people's lives. He can at one moment appear a saint, and the next, the very devil incarnate. Now, he is the most attractive personality on earth; now, a repulsive creation from the depths of Hell. He was brought out of me when I first performed the role in Glyndebourne in 1977, and I've been trying to reveal more and more of him ever since.

Some years ago, at La Scala, Milan, I went through the most taxing rehearsal process of my life. Long hours in the theatre, beginning at 10 a.m. and finishing sometimes at midnight, seemed to me to represent a Giorgio Strehler System.

What interested me most was the time we spent exploring the relationship between the Don and Leporello. Acknowledging the long-held theory that neither one could exist without the other, we now went some way beyond, into the role-sharing and occasional reversal of the master–servant relationship. There is never any doubt as to who is the real master. Giovanni is always too dangerous and unpredictable to allow Leporello too much liberty. The occasional loss of aristocratic dignity makes Don Giovanni an even more rounded character.

There are so many theories about their relationship. On at least half a dozen occasions during the course of the opera, Giovanni puts Leporello into life-threatening situations without a second thought. From the outset, Leporello is forever threatening to leave his master. But Giovanni knows that the scrapes they get up to are food and drink to him and a heady source of enjoyment for his servant who would never otherwise have such experiences.

They are like parasites feeding on one another. Don Giovanni cannot operate without his straight-man and is incomplete as a person otherwise, and Leporello cannot resist the life-enhancing effect of being in the operating sphere of the dangerous, many-faceted figure of Giovanni.

The pair become a knockabout comedy duo with well-practised routines into which they can launch at a nod or a wink.

The set is in place for us to work on stage by the second or third day. At the moment the colour is bright copper, like a newly minted penny. This will change when it is mottled by the painters. Then it will resemble more closely a rose-black marble.

This first sight is always interesting. For some technical reason, which I never fully grasped, the balcony is connected to a staircase in a way that prevents the audience from seeing Giovanni and Donna Anna during several bars of singing at their first appearance. James Conlon is not with us for these early days of rehearsal and I doubt he'll like it. Try as we might to find one, there is no obvious solution. I bet I'll end up coming over the balustrade and climbing down the wall into Donna Anna's hungry clutches. We shall see.

Karita professes to be much happier with her role as Elvira. Carol is philosophical about the technically more demanding task that Donna Anna presents – while singing it sensationally. I know hardly anyone who'd opt for Anna if Elvira were offered. Anna spends the entire opera being miserable and in torment – not surprising, after the violent death of her father. She's not helped by having that milksop of a man, Ottavio, by her side. I've seen no singer who can make much of Ottavio's character. It's the role – he's a terrible bore, a bank manager with the instincts of a school prefect and the voice of an angel.

It's fun watching Ferruccio. He has that clown facility that is the descendant of the *commedia dell'arte* tradition. Since Don Giovanni is also in his repertoire, he really has a special insight into the relationship between the two men.

Once again I'm conscious that Giovanni and Leporello are sizing one another up. How do we want to present certain lines of recitative? How physical or otherwise will be the various fights between us? I hope he'll play along with my preferred course: moments of uncontrolled anger and violence tempered with subsequent unsettling softening of character. This quicksilver ✓ schizophrenic nature is Giovanni for me. The opportunity to play these extremes on stage is one of the most satisfying experiences I have in the opera house. It generates an awesome power in me – for the time I'm on stage only, I promise you. This is another aspect of 'Doctor Theatre' at his magic work. It would not be advisable to be in my way at these moments. I feel omnipotent, capable of superhuman feats. In the straight theatre, the player of Kean, Lear or Othello must have similar feelings.

Dr Hampe is sticking rigidly to the production book of Salzburg five years ago. Robert Minder, his Austrian assistant, knows the production from the book and from their work together with Herbert von Karajan. He keeps the good doctor informed of who went where and when. I find myself raising the question: 'Are we going to follow action for action as written in the book or would it not be better to use the weeks of rehearsal to try to come up with some new ideas?' This elicits no immediate response and I sense that it could be the germ of trouble for me over the next few weeks.

The length of time allotted for rehearsals is becoming more and more of a talking point wherever we go. A growing number of producers these days insist on a minimum of six weeks' rehearsal, and as I write this it has probably gone up to eight. Some producers certainly have the talent to hold one's interest for that length of time with their ideas, their anecdotes, their intellect or their personality. Others don't. In any case I believe it's too long. Frankly, I'm not prepared to give up six or eight weeks of my time to do something I've done more than a hundred times before. Sometimes a producer is not sufficiently familiar with either text or music, and requires human chess pieces he can play with on his board. Singers arrive at a first rehearsal with the work already memorised and well-prepared. That makes an over-lengthy process unnecessary.

I stood in the wings of the Royal Opera House Covent Garden at the final performance of *Figaro* several years ago, talking to Johannes Schaaf who had directed a very successful production.

'You must be pleased, Johannes,' I said, 'and sad that it's over.'

'Only sad, Tom,' he said.

And then he explained. 'If I'd had three months, I could have made it perfect.'

'You're wrong, Johannes,' said I. 'How would you have known when you'd achieved perfection, when it doesn't exist? And having been satisfied on one occasion, you'd then watch a subsequent performance disintegrate, because we're involved in a constantly changing tapestry. You simply can't have perfection.'

I would argue strongly not for interminable rehearsals but for longer runs of performances, so that we can find more time to discover further possibilities in our own roles and our relationships to other roles.

But perfection – forget it!

Free from other commitments, James Conlon arrives in the Opera House. We spend two afternoons with him working on the musical details of the piece. The subtleties of dynamics for the various ensembles are discussed, tempi for arias are agreed upon. We work out where and when to breathe during arias, so as not to lose time against the relentless pattern of the orchestra. All the usual things that are now such a part of our everyday lives.

This mixture of stage work and music studio work is often a welcome respite against the business of being forever on the rehearsal stage trying to find new insights. Fresh thinking is as likely to be found in the music studio as anywhere.

What is quite amusing about these music sessions is that one often finds oneself eliciting the sympathy of the conductor as a confessor figure.

An imagined dialogue:

'Oh Maestro, I'm not sure if I can make that *rit* at that moment because he wants me to do three somersaults and a back flip finishing on the High C – whilst doing the splits.'

Maestro: 'Oh no no no no no. He has to do some something

different. You'll have to come straight to the front of the stage – ignore the people you're talking to, maybe they could come too – and watch me like a hawk so that we make music together.'

'Oh Maestro, do you think so? He'll not agree to it. He doesn't understand my difficulty here.'

Maestro: 'Leave it with me. I know how to handle him. This is *my* music – *he* can't do this.'

And so on. Variations on this theme have been played out in almost every production in which I've been involved.

The exceptions are those delightful gentlemen Maestri who see it as part of their task to share with us the whole experience from day one. Naturally they may have to disappear to rehearse the orchestra at some point. But what I can't understand is the arrogance of a conductor who arrives three or four weeks into rehearsal, doesn't like what he sees and then proceeds to destroy the fruits of weeks of work by asking everyone to forget about acting, face the front and sing. Ugh! It's death to opera.

Jeannie has arrived and begins nest-building immediately she settles into the flat. I introduce her to those members of the cast she hasn't met before. We're living in a fairly Bohemian area, full of little boutiques and cafés, sex shops and gay saunas – something for everyone you might say. We wander round the city. She's always surprised at how quickly I get to know a place. I have a much better sense of direction than she – or, more correctly, I have one and she hasn't. I guarantee that if she chooses to go left, we should have gone to the right. She blames it on having been born in the Southern hemisphere.

In the middle of the second week, Kjell Magnusson, our tenor, announces that he has a serious family problem. His father is near to dying. From the description he gives it's clear he's had some form of severe stroke and Kjell thinks he will not last long. We work on but for Kjell it's not an easy matter, though he covers it with a brave face.

It's an awful dilemma to be far away from parents at such a time. It happened to me with my own father in 1987, and the psycho- logical blow of somehow having neglected him to go about my business thousands of miles away was very difficult to deal with. Somehow one never seems to be conveniently placed when the dread moment arrives. Flying back from South Africa for my father's funeral was among the lowest points of my life. One of the great sadnesses is that no longer can I pick up a telephone after a performance and give him a report on how things have gone.

From my early childhood my father was all-important in my life and thinking. My mother kept us fed and made sure the house was clean. But Dad was my influence.

There'd been very little money when he was young but something special in him niggled at his insides. He would save up what little money he made as a butcher's lad to buy an old clarinet; on another occasion, a violin, and on yet another, a banjo. At the age of three I was as familiar with the arias of *The Messiah* as I was with the playing of Charlie Kunz whose style Dad would try to emulate on the piano.

It's odd, late in the twentieth century, to be writing about the people of a generation who seemed to be more in touch with the bad times of the Depression than the brighter post-War years. But it's like that in a north-eastern mining community.

While all of my mother's family (she was one of thirteen children) were miners, the influence of my paternal grandfather and his canny wife saw my father, on leaving school at fourteen, taking on the butcher's lad job rather than go down the pit. A few years later he was collector for a hire-purchase firm based in Sunderland. His task it was to go with his book from house to house, collecting the dues for the three-piece suite and the curtains, and all for a very small wage.

By the age of twenty-one he'd saved up a little money to buy a motor bike, and shortly afterwards was involved in an accident with a lorry which caused the loss of his left leg. His fiancée, my mother, stood by him through the difficult months of depression that followed. The bosses of the firm for which he worked could see no way that he could continue. My dad had different ideas. Not yet ready for the artificial limb, he took to crutches and, with the encouragement of my mother, set about his job as he'd left it before the accident. There were times when he must have been exhausted and deeply frustrated. But he kept going, and worked for that same company until his retirement.

When I was about twelve or thirteen, I expressed the desire to play golf, but only if Dad would join the club with me. He was then forty-seven. For a couple of years we shared one bag of clubs: I would play my shot and then run over to him at his ball with whatever club he needed. Golf became his passion and he played until told to give up for medical reasons. The course at Seaham is quite hilly and several holes lie across fairly severe slopes. He insisted on carrying his bag across his back, determined to enjoy the exercise and fun he'd been denied earlier in his life. On three occasions at least that I can remember he swung at the ball, only to have the hip pivot of his leg break; he would have to walk off the course, holding himself together. The members in the clubhouse had the privilege of seeing him brought home on the back of the tractor after one of these collapses.

Perhaps, though, he was happiest when I began to learn the organ. I would spend hours in the dark of the church, quite scared at times, practising away without much sign of improvement, but enjoying the power all the same. Dad would often join me. This was something he'd always wanted to try and never really managed. While he climbed on to the stool and selected his stops, I would position my feet for the pedal line of the music, as this was something he couldn't manage.

I'd love to do that for him now, or run across a fairway with his three-wood.

But he's always with me in whatever I do and I often talk to him in my head, and wonder what he'd make of it all now, as the years go by.

Over the weekend, Jeannie leaves for London while I fly to Berlin to fulfil a recording contract there. The air corridors between German cities and the 'island' of Berlin are very busy in these 'post-Wall' days.

I saw Berlin first in the early 1970s when I made a radio broadcast from *Sender Freies Berlin* (Hitler had made radio broadcasts from the same building forty years before). My second visit was much later, in 1989, for two concerts with Seiji Ozawa and the Berlin Philharmonic on 30 and 31 December. I shall never forget the excitement in the city over those two days, especially the Silvester-Abend (31 December). Following the 5.30 p.m. concert a number of us went for dinner, after which we wished one another a Happy New Year. Then a group of us set off to join the crowds at the Brandenburg Gate on this historic occasion. For the last quarter of a mile we walked on a carpet of broken champagne and beer bottles. Such was the level of celebration. Crowds had been catered for. I remember the large metal portable loos for the comfort of everyone. The problem was that groups of youths had collected to sit on top of them with their legs dangling over the sides like swallows perched on telegraph wires. I pitied the souls inside who had to endure the noise of dozens of heels banging on the metal. On this night, they became well and truly 'thunderboxes'.

Thousands thronged together on the wall, hundreds more were atop the gate itself. Only much later did we hear that there had been a fatal accident. I wanted to join them on the wall for this very special moment, but Jeannie thought it unwise and held me back.

The border guards had long given up and gone home. People pressure made a nonsense of barriers and there was a free and easy passage from one side of Germany to the other through the gaps that had been created at various points along the wall. In the lights of numerous television crews young and old danced, ancient enmities forgotten. *Auld Lang Syne* rang out somewhere in the crowd, banners flew, familiar national colours joined now by the blue and yellow flag of the European Community.

The next morning I flew to Los Angeles, where my descriptions of what I'd witnessed the night before met with blank stares. The Berlin wall and Europe might as well have been on the planet Mars.

On this spring day in 1991, I find myself in the same studio I was in nearly twenty years ago. This time it's to record three duets by Berlioz with the American tenor John Aler. They form part of a compilation of solos, duets and trios. After the recording and before leaving for the airport, I take a short walk along the Kurfürstendamm, the promenading street of Berlin. I am amused to see a Chinese restaurant with the name 'Ho Lin Wah' (*sic*).

All major cities enjoy a cosmospolitan mix. In Berlin Polish Lada cars go the wrong way down one-way streets and East German 'Trabbies' 'put-put' around until they disintegrate entirely. There's a mix of high and 'clothing-coupon' fashion. There must be so many untold stories about the past two years and the pulling down of that wall. There are probably Berlin Harry Limes in the sewer system.

21 May. Returning to Cologne is rather like going home. My apartment is small, but it's where my clothes and belongings are for the moment. I'm glad to be back. Carol Vaness is glad I'm back too. She has the flat below me. Staying sane is sometimes a matter simply of being with friends. We have dinner together at a local restaurant where we're beginning to be accepted.

Arriving at rehearsal we hear the sad news that Kjell's father has died. Kjell is such a nice, mild-mannered chap and he now finds himself in a quandary. As far as I'm concerned there's no question. We're still some way from our première, and he should leave and be with his family. He'll never have another father.

We're now trying out costumes and wigs like mad. Carlo Diappi is the costume designer, as he was in Salzburg this Easter. My outfit is simply described: all black! Needless to say, as we're in Germany, leather abounds. I suspect that in the heat of southern Spain Don Giovanni might have had his tailor run him up something a little more in keeping with the ambient temperature. But here I am again in long black leather coat, trousers and boots, black silk shirt and a mane of black hair that comes to my waist with a sort of sausage hair-piece that lies across the top of my head.

To set all this off to best advantage, I will have a very pale make-up. So once again I shall give a Don Giovanni who has the appearance of having been dead for three weeks.

I meet lots of new faces in Wardrobe and Make-up departments, all very pleasant. Helmut, the wig and make-up man, is very much on top of his job.

Wednesday, 22 May. We are free all day until the evening rehearsal.

Ferruccio, ever the keen golfer, suggests a round on the course at Bad Godesberg, one of the outlying districts of Bonn. I happily agree. Well, my clubs are with me so I may as well use them. . . . He has a sixth sense for finding golf courses wherever he may be. The route to this one is not at all easy and it's two years since he was here. But he finds the way unerringly, and on what proves to be the finest day of our visit so far we enjoy eighteen holes together, though the standard of play is a touch variable. I haven't picked up a club since Houston and the skill I once had with a three handicap is more and more difficult to recapture. But I enjoy it all the same. Though golf is not new in Germany, there's still the feeling that it's for a select smart group, which makes the success of Bernhard Langer on the professional circuit all the more exceptional.

We head back rather wearily to Köln in Leporello's Porsche. I've just time to shower before the evening rehearsal.

The copper set is now toned down to resemble the pink marble it represents but I still find it an odd choice of colour. An obelisk is set at the centre of the back of the stage to create the impression of streets running from it in two directions. Naturally, this being *Don Giovanni*, we all regard it as pink and phallic. I decide not to loiter too long around it.

We're now at that stage in rehearsals when all the scenes have been blocked and we have the rest of the time to 'flesh out' the skeleton we've made. For the actor on his music-less stage, that's always an exciting prospect. Most singers, however, regard it as near enough to being the finishing line. After all, we know where to go, we've rehearsed the music. Surely with a couple of orchestral rehearsals, and one or two in costume, we'd be ready for a first night?

That is quite often (more often than not) the case. Now we have to go over and over the same procedures day by day by day. For some it's a process they've done a hundred times or more before. We're still a week and a half away from the première. Hardly surprising that frustrations and tensions develop.

There's the great worry that the whole thing will peak too soon and we'll really be ready, as opposed to thinking we're ready, several days before first night. It's a curious anomaly that, when one needs all the energy available, the growing pressure results in so much energy being spent, and this leads to worry about having sufficient rest before the première.

23 *May*. Karita Mattila is unwell and will not work at all today. We therefore sketch in one or two details, but there's already a feeling of filling in time. This changes the next day with the news that Karita is more sick than we thought and has cancelled *all* the performances. This is a drastic action for a singer. The psychological blow, the sap to confidence, is enormous. She's been to see a doctor she knows and respects. He recommends she rest her voice completely for the next four weeks. (This won't be easy for Karita, who's garrulous at the best of times!)

A spanner has been thrown into the works. A pall descends on us all – especially on the management who must comb the world to find a replacement.

I retire to the apartment, and set about painting a copy of the *Three Card Players* of Cézanne. I don't have a style with my limited experience, so Cézanne seems as good a master to copy as any – besides which he's a favourite among painters.

In 1976, suffering with hepatitis, I followed a television course on painting in acrylics, but found the medium too plastic and was frustrated with the paints forever drying on me. But the new reservoirs and absorbent papers that are available mean you can have a wet palette and the acrylic paint stays wet for several days. Today I feel inspired by the Bohemian area in which I am staying. I read that the cafés around us are frequented by several of Cologne's best-known artistic figures. At this rate I'll have to buy a beret and join them.

24 *May*. A day planned for a piano run-through in costume of the whole opera. Despite Karita's absence it is decided to carry on without her and the ever faithful Elke Newhardt dons the costume and walks through her part. Elke, who is an actress, walks a wonderful Elvira – what a pity she doesn't have a singing voice. Her role is sung from the pit by one of the male members of the music staff. Here we have opera – the gender-bender – appropriate

for *Don Giovanni*. Elke, one of Dr Hampe's first assistants, is a German lady who has spent the past twenty-three years in Australia. She is consequently a mixture of Teutonic correctness and Antipodean laid-backness and informality.

The run-through, stumble-through, however one regards it, goes smoothly. Everyone knows where they have to be and the signs are good.

Now all we have to do is find a new member of cast. Somewhere within the opera house a long list of possible replacement Elviras is produced. The world shrinks as artists' agents are contacted in Europe and America. The outcome is rather extraordinary. No Elvira is available, but a Donna Anna can be found. Carol Vaness has been contacted with the proposition that she change from Donna Anna to singing the role of Donna Elvira. She jumps at the chance. I, too, admit to a feeling of pleasure. Carol is a high- spirited lady off stage; I can well imagine the fiery nature of her Elvira – elements of *The Taming of the Shrew* come into my mind.

When we reconvene for rehearsal on Monday morning it is with refreshed vigour. At this late stage, the change-over injects excitement into what had become the day-to-day routine of rehearsals.

The new Donna Anna is Caroline James, whom none of us know, but who comes with high recommendation from Maestro Conlon. She's a young American of generous proportions and from the first it's clear that she's fully familiar with the role.

Less-than-scrupulous agents sometimes seize on such a crisis for the promotion of some budding new talent who might not be entirely ready to take over at such short notice. I well remember a situation at Covent Garden several years ago: a young lady packed her bag and was ready to step on to Concorde to take over the role of Susanna when it was discovered that, at that point in her career, she had only ever sung the role in English. Even worse is the story the producer John Copley – a fund of good anecdotes – tells of a replacement Countess for *Figaro*. The first Countess had a throat infection and cancelled forty-eight hours before the performance.

Once again the international telephone exchanges were hot with calls from London to all corners of the globe. (Just where are the corners on a globe?) All without success. Finally, in desperation, a phone call was made to Dublin where the fine Irish soprano Veronica Dunne was found to be free and ready to fly in.

This she did. Copley made the introductions and Veronica (Ronnie) began with her first aria, *'Porgi amor'*.

'That's very lovely,' said John. 'Now would you please go into the recitative – *"Vieni, cara Susanna"*, etc.'

'Oh! I don't do the recitatives,' said Miss Dunne in her delightful Dublin brogue. 'I only do the *numbers*.'

'What *do* you mean?' asked John, the truth hardly yet dawning.

'I've only ever sung the numbers.'

A moment to let this news sink home.

Copley rushed from the stage, crossed Floral Street to Number 45, wherein was the seat of power at Covent Garden, Sir David Webster.

'Sir David is not available, Mr Copley,' intoned Miss Kerr, the long-serving secretary, barring his way to the great man.

'I must see him!'

John barged in on Webster, who was occupied with the organising of various papers. Finally, when he was good and ready, he asked, 'Yes, what is it, Copley?'

'Veronica Dunne doesn't do the recitatives – only the numbers.'

'Oh dear! What do we do?' Sir David said, for once in his life at a loss.

Copley, never at a loss, replied: 'Well, I suggest *Swan Lake*.'

And so, I believe, it came to pass.

Veronica continued her career, delighting people with her lovely Irish voice and a personality that oozed Irish charm.

In Cologne everyone is falling over their tongues demonstrating their skill in delivering recitatives more rapidly than machine-gun fire. It's the trap we all fall into, in the effort to show our Italian colleagues how diligently we've studied our text.

The change-over works a treat. Carol and I have fun reworking some of the scenes we have together. Her New World approach is different from Karita's deeper, darker Scandinavian view.

Television personnel have now begun to appear as three performances will be recorded for a later showing. The last couple of days before dress rehearsal are spent mainly getting to know the possibilities and impossibilities caused by wearing our costumes. √ Can I climb down from the balcony at the start of the opera in my boots, cloak, sword and mask without killing myself? I suspect not. As I expected, James won't accept two of the principal artists disappearing for several seconds around a piece of architecture when they've just begun to sing. The risk of death by climbing a balustrade in the dark is considered the safer musical option.

31 May. And so we arrive at dress rehearsal day. The *'General Probe'* begins at 1 p.m. What to do about food is the next question. Get up late and have a mid-morning brunch? Rise early and rearrange the hours so that 1 p.m. becomes something like 5 p.m.?

In the end I behave as usual, getting up around 8.30 a.m. and lolling around the apartment until it's time to go to the theatre at midday. This works fine. I'm in costume and make-up with quarter of an hour to spare. I don't warm up too much for Giovanni, as the role is so written as to exercise the voice throughout the whole √ evening, starting with the near-conquest of Donna Anna and the death of her father and then building and climbing ever onward and upward. And so I generally leave it to sort itself out, having established that my voice is centred in the right place to begin with.

This then is the culmination of four weeks of rehearsal. The set is noisy because it's very heavy, but the show runs smoothly and the audience for this rehearsal react warmly.

In fact our fear is that everything went *too* well. Superstition again, of course, but we'd all like to feel there was a notch left still to go for the première. Instinct tells me we should have done this several days earlier when some final tweaking would have been necessary. But perhaps this is only a personal view. At the notes session afterwards, there are plenty of things to say of this rehearsal but everyone is happy with the way it went.

Now the show is ours. The producer must find his own way of untying the umbilical cord and letting it free. This must be a very serious psychological problem at times. Indeed I'm inclined to think that the desire to rehearse longer and longer before unveiling a first night is to do with a producer's reluctance ever actually to perform a work for the public at all, so that he can tinker all he likes for two or three months and then depart, having satisfied some inner craving! It leaves singers in a vacuum of course – and without any fee. Unless, that is, we started to charge audiences to sit in and watch the rehearsal process in action before their very eyes. We could save a lot of money on sets and costumes!

Our day off is the second with any kind of recognisable sunshine. Jeannie, Carol and I decide on a mid-afternoon *Rheinfahrt*. There is a great trade on the Rhine from canal boats flying French, Dutch, Belgian and German flags. So with our tickets shown, we board the good ship *Lorelei* for two hours' sailing down the river and back. The decks are crowded. Music, both 'oompah' band and German pop, blares from loudspeakers. It's not what I had in mind. A German *Brauhaus* afloat. After so many weeks of work, I'm looking forward to a party in the ballet room after the performance.

2 June. It is the day of the première and the first thing I realise is that I've done nothing about buying the customary first night presents for the cast. This is very bad. I sometimes draw caricatures for friends; this time I forgot. Too late now to do any shopping. It's Sunday and Germany has been closed since Saturday afternoon.

Traditionally, Sunday is a day I polish shoes. There's nothing more satisfying than burnishing good shoe leather and admiring the finished product. This time I add a little refinement all my own. In an effort to while away more hours, I resort to counting the holes in this particular pair of brogues. I'm at a loss to know what to do with the information.

Jeannie and I have a pleasant Sunday lunch together and walk for a while in our newly adopted locality. I write up a few notes, diary fashion, paint a few Cézanne blobs on my *Card Players* and finally it's time to leave for the theatre. There's never any way to escape the buzz of a first night, no matter where one is, or however hard one tries. A million people call by the dressing room with best wishes. I hardly have a space on my table because of the accumulation of first night presents – my guilt thoroughly compounded. Finally everyone goes to their appointed corners.

Those awful chords sound once more. Man assumes mask. He hopes that mask will not hinder man in his wall-climbing debut before the Cologne public.

A few minutes later I've safely negotiated balcony, climb-down, struggle with Donna Anna, and death of her father. We're on our way. Carol is doing great work as Elvira, it hardly needs saying. Ferruccio, underneath his smooth exterior, is feeling as guilty as I am, having also neglected his first night presents. The recitatives have an easy flow to them. Neither too fast, nor too slow – natural, as in everyday speech. For me the second major hurdle in the evening is the 'Champagne Aria'. I pace and pace before the aria trying to think and breathe in a controlled manner. Invariably my pulse is racing at this point. The speed of my writing, now, increases with the anxiety it causes. Once the aria begins there's time only to take a deep breath and see it through. There never *seems* time for a second breath in this aria – though of course in reality I take several. Tonight, I'm happy with the outcome.

The finale of Act One arrives and thankfully everything works as though by clockwork. At a point that held all the potential for disaster, the set runs smoothly.

At the end of Act One I rush through the centre door at the back of the set to make my escape. Eschewing the staircase, I leap gloriously through the air to the lower level. The shock to my system is more than it used to be fifteen years ago. I make a mental note to opt for stairs in future performances.

We take a curtain call at this halfway point. Despite the First Night audience and the fact that today is Sunday (a notorious combination), the response is encouraging.

I look to notch up four good numbers at the beginning of Act Two. Our buffo duet runs well. The trio with Elvira is nicely mocking. Ferruccio does a passable imitation of me as Don and I manage the right amount of breath control for the Serenade. The remaining aria is '*Meta di voi qua vadano*'. In the recit preceding it, the Don explains to Masetto that he's actually Leporello, servant of

Don Giovanni. He's wearing Leporello's hat and coat after all, therefore he must be. As Don Giovanni, I elect to wear a large ring with a recognisable stone, and at this point turn the ring on my finger to hide my true identity.

But I have no ring.

Somewhere during the first few minutes of Act Two it has flown off. A thought briefly occupies my mind of the bill I will face for repairs to a valuable violin in the pit below. Oh well, that's one trademark gone from this evening. I manage not to do too much real damage to Reinhard Dorn, our Masetto, in beating him up.

Now I can enjoy twenty minutes' rest before vaulting into the graveyard scene. I fill the time reading a magazine and cooling off from the previous activities. In the background I can hear the performance moving forward as sextet proceeds to aria, and so on, punctuated with some generous applause.

Rested, I await my cue to leap over the wall. Ferruccio arrives and we create, I think, a palpable feeling of tension, fear and superstition which are the often underestimated elements of the graveyard scene.

There remains the final supper scene. This I love. Why? Well, I like the joke, and fun that Mozart and da Ponte had in publicising one another's works: references to favourite pieces of the day – 'Una cosa rara', 'I due litiganti' and 'Non piu andrai' – in which they both played a part. It says a lot about these two men, I think, this youthful self-publicity.

I eat as much pheasant (chicken) as I care to and drink as much Marzemino (blackcurrant juice) as I like. Donna Elvira-Vaness arrives and our tussle goes as planned.

Elvira accuses the Don of ridiculing her.

'Ridicule you! Oh heavens! Why?' says he. 'What would you want?'

She is fooled by him momentarily.

'That you change your life,' she says, caringly.

He throws her aside with a shout of 'Brava!'

It's one of the opera's cruellest moments and lasts for only a few seconds. He picks her up by a thread, suspends her, and then drops her into the well of deepest despair. From that moment, all the world knows there is no saving him and her mission has ✓ ended in failure.

The Commendatore arrives and our 'arm wrestling' contest is a victory for him, culminating in a final scream for me.

Don Giovanni is over. (That's how it feels for the singer playing the Don, just as the singer playing the Countess believes the opera doesn't start until her rendering of *'Porgi amor'*.) There remains in fact the sextet as moral of the story, which illustrates how affected everyone else's life has been by contact with Giovanni. They each of them relate how they will spend their lives following the incidents of the past few hours.

Blackness as the curtain falls and we meet up again on stage with hugs of relief and excitement mixed. The public react warmly indeed. The 'men in black' join us for the line: producer Michael Hampe, designer Carlo Diappi and conductor James ✓ Conlon. Carlo is an Italian who speaks very fluent German, unusual in itself, but with a strong Italian accent which has a curious effect.

Wigs are peeled off, faces washed, hair shampooed and we're ready to celebrate all the hard work. It won't be for long, however, as Jeannie and I leave for London in the morning. I have an interview for Radio Three, with Rodney Milnes on the subject of Mozart and *Don Giovanni*. After all my experiences, I should have something to say. Then on Tuesday, 4 June, I have to rehearse with Roger Vignoles for a recital we'll be doing together in Munich in early July. Other than two days before the recital, this is the only opportunity we'll have to rehearse.

The party is held in a room used to rehearse ballet. Streamers bedeck the walls here and there, the ghost of some Christmas Past. Others hang from the ceiling like ancient flypapers. Michael Hampe makes a speech, thanking and congratulating everyone. I'm with Jeannie and Robert Rattray and after a couple of beers we decide to call it a day. Sometimes life is like that.

The following morning Robert collects us by taxi and we make our way to the airport. Arriving at Heathrow, we bump into Roger Vignoles going in the opposite direction to replace an ✓ accompanist at a recital in Regensburg. He explains he's left a message for me at home asking for our rehearsal to start a little later than planned, as he'll not be back from Germany until midday.

In this ever-shrinking universe, this doesn't faze any of us. We rearrange the day and go on. The world is full of musicians dashing from one airport to the next, chasing another keyboard, another hall, another theatre. And none of us would have it any other way.

The rehearsal with Roger of the songs for our Munich recital is very pleasant and, after so much opera, a welcome change. Rather like standing under a tepid shower and letting the make-up fall away as we begin to enjoy more and more the songs of Wolf and Haydn.

4 June. It never ceases to amaze me that I can get so much from the study and performance of a song. We are putting together for the first time settings by Wolf of seven very contrasting poems of Mörike. Each one is a tiny opera in itself and the imagery becomes sharper in mind the more we work together. It's study well rewarded.

Rehearsal over, I have a couple of hours before I return to Köln – this time with a smaller suitcase. I judge trips by toothpaste tubes and razor blades. A small or half-full tube of paste should see me to the end of this next session, and one set of blades should be just about right. You may well ask: 'Have you ever thought of buying stuff when you get there?' But that's not the point. As a regular traveller, there's enormous satisfaction to be derived from managing to organise the last day of the stay to coincide with the last dreg from the toothpaste tube, the final clean shave. I love orderliness. I suppose it's silly, but we all have our quirks.

The second performance of any opera is always the most dangerous. A relaxation sets in after the hullabaloo and anxiety of a First Night, and here in Köln there's no exception. But the pitfalls are there for us to recognise and we're careful in endeavouring to maintain the tension of the première.

Two days later (my 'Cézanne' now nearing completion) we begin rehearsals for the television cameras. What is generally required of us is that we stand closer together in certain scenes in order that we can be properly framed by the camera shot – rather like assembling for the group wedding photograph. It's not as strenuous as we had first feared. No singing is required, as a cassette was made at the time of the Dress Rehearsal of our singing. This plays over us as we mime our way through the two acts. Some of the live 'off the record' commentary as the cassette plays is better than the original, but not for public consumption.

Whole blocks of seats have been lost to accommodate five or six cameras in the theatre. They are positioned at points in the house to allow for a variety of angles. With the set-up here, it's like looking at the old-fashioned football forward line ready for attack. Three middle forwards and two wings. For a moment I put Giovanni aside and pretend to be a goalkeeper facing the old Sunderland line-up I knew so well in the early 1960s.

I used to have a drawing-board, and during my school years it became covered in the graffiti and doodles of a wandering-minded schoolboy. Over and over again I wrote down the names of the players of the Sunderland football team who were my heroes. I had no skill as a footballer, and so it was necessary, in the soccer-orientated school I attended, to find an alternative outlet for my sporting energies.

I became involved with rugby – never rugger. Anyone who used the word 'rugger' was in danger of becoming a regular visitor to the local accident hospital. Saturday mornings would find fifteen (sometimes fewer) of us stalwarts, with an odd assortment of kit, heading off to various venues for adventures into the world of rugby, which usually resulted in a trouncing. We couldn't play at home as there was no rugby field. (I'd spend hours after school kicking a rugby ball over association goalposts, trying to imagine the uprights we never enjoyed.)

In the afternoons, after our morning of rugby, a further group of us often assembled in Park Lane, Sunderland, for a mug of tea and a pie before trekking over to Roker Park for three o'clock, to be dazzled by the talents of Montgomery, Ashurst, MacNab, Mulhall, Crossan, Anderson, and (most of all) our hero, Charlie Hurley.

A macho exterior was all-important to me in those days. Being a choirboy had previously led to several bloody noses and accusations that I was a 'Jessy'.

*

In our contracts, a period of time was set aside for TV rehearsal. It seems now that a public performance extra to the ones for which we're engaged has been arranged without our knowledge. Michael Hampe insists it is not necessary for us to sing, as the exercise is a technical one for the benefit of the cameras. Our Spanish TV director, José (endearingly, a Ken Dodd look-alike), has other requirements: namely, that it is essential that we sing. We agree to abandon the discussion in order that the two directors can sort out their misunderstandings.

My *faux Cézanne* is now finished – I think. I'm quite pleased with the result. If I had any talent at all, I'd want to emulate this man. I set off for an afternoon's walk, taking in several Romanesque churches I've a desire to see. Though approximately three-quarters of Cologne was flattened by Allied bombing in the Second World War, the restoration has been on a vast and successful scale, with some grey exceptions. There appears to be an admirable policy here that visitors are reminded that they are in God's house, and not a museum. The disrespect that abounds these days from Salisbury to Rome makes me angry. Great architectural follies make me angry too. Next to the wonderful warm pink Church of Maria Himmelfahrt, which dominates the area just away from the twin-spired *Dom*, someone was allowed to build a huge black-windowed carbuncle. Once inside the church, my anger disappears. Here is rococo of the most wonderful form. A high Perpendicular nave with vaulting leads to the radiance of the altar and reredos. Elsewhere the church is decorated in white and edged with a gorgeous plumbago blue. The side aisles are beautifully panelled in a natural oak and the believer has a choice of dozens of confessionals. I am fascinated by ritual and pomp and I love this church. One can sense the closeness of a Supreme Being and feel peace in a place such as this. It's not overpowering. More a tasteful Disneyland that is saying: 'Come in. Welcome. You're safe here.'

A telephone call when I return to the flat. Michael Hampe informs me he believes they've reached a satisfactory agreement and that the TV recording will proceed. From here on things are on a much more even keel. The differences between us have been aired and we can now concentrate on doing the job.

Now it's a question of resting and eating properly to see us through the next few days of hard work. Carol decides we need a good pasta diet with plenty of tomato sauce, and lots of water to drink. American singers invariably know what's best. They're in possession of all the latest homeopathic and vitamin pills as well as anything else that promises a better life. The latest addition is a product that enriches the calcium content of the body.

I once sat with several colleagues at a table in the cafeteria of the Met during rehearsals for *Billy Budd*. All the Americans knew exactly what their cholesterol level was – or where they were at, in American parlance. One by one they revealed their statistics. To this day I have no idea of my own, but then we do things differently in England, and generally ten years after America.

But I have no objection to Carol's regime and we take it in turns to choose which pasta and which vegetables. We endeavour to maintain some form of domesticity far from our homes – particularly far for the Californian Vaness. She's wonderful company and we talk about all kinds of subjects. Much fun is made of my various occupational therapies, particularly the tapestry I'm attempting. A man with sewing in his hands is not Carol's idea of a man.

A friend of mine in the medical profession in America, an anesthesiologist by trade, also enjoys tapestry work. Some years ago, he'd sat down on an aeroplane bound for Europe. Shortly into the flight the lady seated next to him showed signs of wanting to embark on a lengthy conversation. Like most people in this situation, he didn't want this, and cut off communications with her by bringing out his latest tapestry project.

After a few minutes, her curiosity could not be contained. 'I hope you don't, er . . . mind me remarking,' she ventured, 'but what you're doing there . . . well . . . you're a man . . . and, well . . .' Finally she came to the point: 'Don't people remark on what a strange thing it is for a man to do?'

To which my medical friend replied succinctly, and in a dry Californian drawl: 'My analyst says it stops me from masturbating.'

'Oh, stewardess,' screamed the woman, 'this man is offensive. Please find me another seat.'

Carol and I enter into great discussions about whether we sit in her apartment or mine to cheer the day. In mine, we can talk or not as the case may be uninterruptedly for hours. In hers, she is constantly having to answer the telephone to speak to friends in New York and Milan, family in California, rehearsal planners in Glyndebourne. She's just one of those people around whom many people revolve, and to whom telephone companies are eternally grateful.

The pasta regime suits me at any time and works well for us over these next few days. The following two performances are also filmed for television. From the three performances to be recorded they'll be able to make a very good whole. We bid an amicable farewell to our television colleagues with a small party given in the rehearsal room. I have a glass of water, say my adieus and leave after five minutes. The last performance is in forty-eight hours.

I have a final shopping spree in town, in the frenzied fashion that assails one at times like these and that I recognise from previous experiences. It amounts to the folly of buying a pair of English-made golf shoes in a German shop that is doing its best to pretend it belongs truly in Bath or Cheltenham. Cricket caps and bats adorn the window.

Jonathan Friend is at this evening's performance. He's the Man from the Met. At one time in my early Northern life, we laid store by the Man from the Pru. These days, my career is in the hands of such men as Jonathan, who casts for the New York Metropolitan Opera Company.

I'm well enough rested for this last onslaught. Altogether, and strangely, given the closeness of the performances, the overall standard seems to be higher now than at the beginning. We've all done it so much by this time that we can afford to loosen a little and explore one or two new paths. We have a certain amount of last-night fun, even in this dark piece, and I leave the Cologne public with a scream which I hope will be remembered for at least a short while to come.

Following the performance, hugs and kisses all round. Ferruccio leaves early tomorrow for rehearsals at La Scala. Kjell goes home to Oslo. Caroline goes to London and Milan for auditions at this early stage of her career. Andrea Rost, our Zerlina, and her husband and child set off in an old Volkswagen early the next morning for the long drive to Budapest. I wish them luck! Carol and I stop off for a Big Mac before going to our apartments. We sit in McDonalds wondering what Callas and Onassis did in similar circumstances. Perhaps they had a Wimpy. Such is our glamorous life.

Early the next day Carol leaves for Glyndebourne and performances of *Idomeneo*.

I have one more performance to fulfil in Munich, before a two-week holiday in Africa.

Chapter Four

THE BARBER IN MUNICH

MUNICH is ever-welcoming. A second home. I'm happy to say they're pleased to have me there in a variety of roles whenever I'm free.

This time it's a one-off performance of *The Barber of Seville*. The *Barber* Figaro is a role I've sung many times before, but one day of rehearsal is not a lot to cover the production, with no time to rehearse musically. Ronnie Adler, faithful Ronnie, the resident staff producer, is on hand to show me the details of the set, and where I'm to go and when. We work from 11 a.m until 1 p.m., on 19 June, the day after my last *Giovanni*.

I have to admit to tiredness, but am trusting to guile to get me through.

The tenor, Bob Tear, is here, to my surprise. He's an old friend and we've been quite close over the years. I watch him briefly on stage rehearsing the world première of Penderecki's *Ubu Rex* in which every second word appears to be *Scheisse*. I note that he's giving one of the tortured, interesting souls for which he's justly renowned as an actor-singer. I spend several moments trying to spot the music.

After a quiet supper at my hotel and an early night, I feel rested. Top notes – Gs and As – are in order for Figaro. My voice appears to be in good shape, much to my surprise after the screamings and rantings of Don Giovanni. All the same, I can't help but entertain a thought that I'm asking rather a lot of myself – and my

'I swear I'll die to win her love once more.' As Eugene Onegin,
realising too late what he has lost by rejecting Tatyana.

The Marriage of Figaro
With Three Susannas: Dawn Upshaw (playing Susanna as ingénue, in Salzburg); Teresa Stratas (giving the professional maid, at Covent Garden); and Marie McLaughlin (portraying the earthy servant, at Covent Garden).

As Four Counts: still wet behind the ears in 1970 (Welsh National Opera); suave and sophisticated in the 1990s (Covent Garden); dressed as a Barbara Cartland lookalike in a genuine eighteenth-century waistcoat (Florence); and enjoying the luxury of the Berlin and Vienna Philharmonics for his music-making (Salzburg).

My roots in the north east of England
Golf at Seaham – with Ryder Cup Captain, Dai Rees (1962). In
Newcastle for an honorary MA – with a proud mum and dad; in
Durham, receiving a D.Mus. from Dame Margot Fonteyn.
My painting of Vane Tempest Colliery (detail).

My family
My son, Stephen, with his wife, Julia, in Disneyland. My stepdaughter, Francie – during a spell of work in Zululand. Rob – my pilot stepson. With my wife, Jeannie, and Stephen. At Buckingham Palace after receiving my CBE.

Billy Budd: 'Billy in the darbies', in the English National Opera production.

Doctor Faustus: With Graham Clark as Mephistopheles. The first staged production in England of Busoni's masterpiece, at the ENO, was directed by David Poutney and designed by Stefanos Lazaridis.

Barbieri di Siviglia: The 'Magritte' production by John Copley at Lyric Opera, Chicago. With Frederica von Stade as Rosina.

Cunning Little Vixen: A rehearsal break at Covent Garden. With Lilian Watson as the Vixen and conductor Simon Rattle. Stuart Hopps (left) did brilliant work on the animal movement.

Iphigénie en Tauride: At La Scala, Milan, in Gluck's opera. With Carol Vaness as Iphigénie.

Pelléas et Mélisande: Awaiting the arrival of Mélisande. Covent Garden.

Die Zauberflöte: Papageno – at Welsh National Opera, as an Indian; at the Metropolitan Opera, New York, in feathered suit.

audiences – by undertaking such a contrasting role with so little preparation.

Strangely enough, it does me good to get away from Mozart, however briefly. Rossini and his *Barber of Seville* don't hold the attention for long, but they provide a delightful little sparkle of nonsense, in contrast to the discipline imposed by Wolfgang Amadeus. I enjoy the performance very much.

It's a shock to walk on to the stage and sing the *'Largo al factotum'* with so little preparation, rather like living out my worst night-mares. Finding a light in which to be seen is my first task and not an easy one. That accomplished, I settle myself down to do my best to blend in with the other members of the cast. My natural strength, coupled with a considerable amount of experience of *The Barber*, see me through. Otherwise it wouldn't be possible in these circumstances.

I first sang Figaro in *The Barber of Seville* with Welsh National Opera in Cardiff in 1969. Welsh National Opera was to be the venue of many of my 'firsts'. At the time, I thought I'd never ever learn the role – so many notes and almost as many words!

I'd auditioned for the company under the encouragement of James Lockhart, a teacher of mine at college, and newly appointed Musical Director of the Welsh Company. They'd liked what they heard and offered me some small roles, which quickly grew bigger, far out of proportion to the amount of experience I'd gained in the meantime. Soon I was singing my first Count in *Figaro*, my first Schaunard in *La Bohème*, my first Papageno in *The Magic Flute*. The biggest moment came when I was asked to sing Billy Budd for the first time. I had serious doubts about that, and everything else I took on. Was I ready for it? I'd arrived at WNO with no experience at all. . . . Jimmy Lockhart squashed my fears by informing me that they'd never ask me if they thought I wasn't capable.

And so with his musical encouragement, and later that of Richard Armstrong, and the guidance of lovely, gentle producer John Moody, I began my first baby steps on the professional stage. Those three years spent with Welsh National Opera were as fine a preparation as anyone could hope for.

*

After the performance I greet several familiar faces at the stage door. A lady I recognise hands me her usual collection of cakes and chocolates. (If I'd eaten all the goodies she's given me over the years I'd conform much more to the singer image.)

Back through the Midsummer's Eve rain to my hotel and a sandwich supper. Now I'm on holiday. I allow myself a bottle of beer from the mini-bar of my room – the first for quite a few weeks.

My flight to London leaves at 7.55 a.m., and I arrive in good time on what is now Midsummer's Day. The rain is pouring down, but it doesn't matter. I leave with Jeannie and Frances, my step-daughter, for a long-planned two-week holiday in Africa that same evening. The change in climate and, most importantly, the thrill of watching animals and birds will be the perfect antidote to the work already done, as well as relaxing me in preparation for all the work that lies ahead.

Chapter Five

AFRICAN INTERMISSION

23 June. John Matterson calls for us at 7 a.m. at the house of our friends the Joneses in Johannesburg. We head for Lanseria airport. On the way we collect Sunday newspapers for the staff in the Botswana safari camp, who are otherwise out of touch with the world. John's 'Bushdrifter' company Cessna 25 KDH, known to John (and soon to us) as 'Katie Darling Heart', is brought out of its hangar and loaded with our few bags – room, too, for a case of wine, there being only four of us in this six-seater. Two hours into our flight towards Maun (Botswana) the oil temperature gauge is reading high. We obtain a reluctant permission to land at Orapa, the diamond-mining landing strip and camp owned by the de Beers company. It appears the engine has overheated. John makes contact with an engineer who can get hold of a part and be on a plane coming in from Gaberone. He arrives at 2.15 and works for over an hour sorting out the problem.

We leave for Maun knowing we must stay there overnight instead of our planned camp at Jedibi. Crocodile Camp has space and we stay there by the river, a short ride outside of Maun. Jeannie and I have a rondavel 'en suite' whilst Francie and John must trek to bathroom and loo. This is my first night under a mosquito net.

24 June. Woken with tea at 7.30. Breakfast of back bacon and eggs and coffee. The description befits a civilised boarding house in any small town, but Maun is the back of beyond. John is still trying to arrange for the return of the engineer to his base at Gaberone. We drive to the airport through 'suburban' Maun. Life is spent in mudhuts and rondavels. Basket-making is going on as we pass by. Goats and chickens abound. Not many dogs. There were more, but it seems the Korean road-gang that worked on a new modern tarred road here not long ago devoured most of them.

It's a bright day and within minutes we enjoy a smooth take-off.

Soon afterwards we are over the swamps of the Okavango Delta. We're with the eagles and vultures. A hammerkop flies by – at our height. John asks our permission to go lower. We spot elephant, zebra, giraffe, warthog, lechwe, wildebeest, tsesebe, and a large herd of buffalo, which we 'buzz' only a few feet above their horns.

After landing on the dirt strip at Jedibi, we leave immediately for a drive. Before long two elephants come into view. Shortly afterwards we see three lions resting in the shade of an acacia tree, a male and two females, one of which is particularly large.

I have no camera, and am enjoying the freedom this allows me.

A Batteleur eagle flies low overhead. Its distinctive beak is red. Above it – far above it – a dozen vultures wheel effortlessly in the hot air like a slow carousel. We head for the camp and lunch, passing a small herd of impala in the shade of a most wonderful baobab tree. The tents here at Mombo Camp have all 'mod-cons'. Shower, loo and basin – almost Czech and Speake! Two Great White Heron fish slowly in front of our tent whilst a little further in the distance graze two more lechwe antelope.

Later a wood fire smells homely as we await supper. The wait is worthwhile – especially for a dessert of cream-custard pudding which would not have been out of place at the Sharrow Bay Hotel. After eating, we sit by the fire and listen to the sounds of jackal, hyena and hippopotamus, none of them far away. Here, one doesn't venture on a stroll after dinner.

25 *June.* During the night buffalo and jackal have left evidence of their passing presence in camp. Our shoes survived outside the

tent. This morning the buffalo graze on the plain in front of us as we enjoy breakfast. A packed lunch is prepared and we set off in the truck towards our new adventure.

Out of the blue John spots the ears of two cheetah half a mile ahead of us. They're lying in the shade of some low scrub. I simultaneously spot a secretary bird, but there are no takers for it with two cats in our sights.

We make slow progress towards the cheetah who allow us within two hundred yards of them before leaving to find less disturbed shelter from the blazing sun. After some time to allow them to settle, we trace them once more and manage to get within fifty yards of them. We watch for more than half an hour, when they decide to move off.

Their gait is reminiscent of that of very relaxed – I suppose laid-back would be the modern expression – sprinters, supreme in the knowledge that, when needs must, they can extend themselves and outrun anything on earth. Bigger and heavier, these two males, than I expected. They take half an interest in some buffalo and a family of warthogs. But their main preoccupation this morning seems to lie in posing for us.

We arrive at a wet flooded area of the delta, rich in bird life that includes pigmy geese and whiskered terns. Just around the corner at a more sheltered inlet, a huge crocodile suns itself on the bank whilst another swims, log-like in appearance, only its eyes visible above the surface. It shares its pool with a hippopotamus. There are snake-birds (Anhinga) and open-billed storks to add yet further colour.

How odd that we make a small fire and brew tea at the appointed hour!

We set off slowly back to camp, pausing to observe striped mongooses playing in and around an anthill. A beautiful Melba finch catches the early-evening light as it flits from bush to bush. The bird chorus that comes with sunset is incredible. There must be hundreds of thousands of many species, all singing together. I recall my first visit to Botswana, when in the course of one day we managed to spot and identify nearly one hundred and fifty different bird species.

The smell of wild sage is all around. One can live with the minor discomfort of an itchy nose, for beauty as natural as this.

26 June. Francie wasn't feeling well after supper. Jeannie has gone to spend the night with her in her tent.

Left on my own, I open up the flap at the front of the tent, leaving the mosquito gauze between me and the wild world outside. Moonlight bathes the plain. I begin to sleep, snug in my track-suit. Am I dreaming or is it reality before me in the shape of two large buffalo? I can see their silhouettes not ten feet away from me – there's no sound. Sometime later – it feels like 4 a.m. but I have no watch to prove it – something wakes me. I raise my head slowly from the pillow and try to focus on the scene outside. Three lions are passing by – a male and two females. They stop and seem to stare in at me. As dark shapes they could be looking in the opposite direction. But I believe not. They are ten yards away from me – no more.

Everything has been distilled into this moment. I feel at perfect peace, and, though they represent an immense strength and savagery, I have no fear, only awe-struck respect. Those few moments, twenty or thirty seconds, have made this whole undertaking worthwhile.

I couldn't give a damn about music now.

A call for breakfast at 7.30. I shower and put aside shaving. En route to coffee and rusk I try to identify the spoor of the night before. A lion roared at 7 this morning, just as it did yesterday. It's nearby, just beyond the staff camp. At breakfast, Karen, who runs this camp, talks of the buffalo who snorted at her tent in the night. She shooed them away, like a couple of friendly Jerseys.

I'd wondered whether they were a dream – now I have my answer.

We pack our dusty belongings – the few there are. They're piled into the truck and we say our farewells. Alan drives us the 'pretty route' to the airstrip which gives us the opportunity of marvelling at the colours of the crimson-breasted shrike. If one tried to represent this red in a painting it would be regarded as phoney, so strong is the hue. The plane, KDH, is intact, though there are signs of a hyena visit. Alan says goodbye and drives down the strip to clear it of any stray animals – yesterday there were sixteen giraffe at this very spot.

In my bag is a Bushman doll which took my fancy at Mombo. I offered to buy it, but Liana, our landlady, told me to take it as a souvenir. I shall treasure it. It's a girl, made of various batiks, of red and black, with enormous breasts. Pride of place will be found for this simple but lovely thing.

It's difficult to estimate time without a watch – we all left them behind deliberately.

At Maun we wait for John to do his bits of paperwork in the famous Duck Inn, a sort of Rick's Bar of Botswana, where khaki-clad refugees of the world's rat race hang around waiting for their trips to the bush, seeking endlessly their escape and the wind-down process. There are many German families here, and no doubt we shall meet the Japanese ere long.

Formalities completed, we take off once more and plot a course for Zimbabwe and Victoria Falls. More red tape. The immigration officer – one M.E. Mondo – can't believe I have no money on me. He reads the details of my passport, and with a smile asks if I shall be singing here in Zimbabwe. 'No,' I reply, and he begins to search in several very dusty drawers for a piece of paper which will declare that I shall not be working whilst visiting the country. Quite why I've been singled out I'm not sure – perhaps the Zimbabwe branch of Equity is particularly strong.

A battered red Datsun taxi takes us the short journey into Victoria Falls town. 'Beware minefield' signs remain at the side of the road, leftovers of the recent war.

The Victoria Falls hotel is a legacy of a colonial past and, but for the garish luminous colours of shorts and eye shades of the modern guest, very few of the old traditions have changed here. It is an enormous contrast to the simplicities of the Okavango camp. The Falls are thunderous. They are awesomely impressive in their power. The air is saturated with the pulverised droplets as millions and millions of gallons of water tumble down. Several rainbows fill the air. One of them stretches round in a huge arc almost completing a circle. But the mist of water is so dense that each element of the bow disappears. How apt the native description of the 'smoke that thunders' – *Mosi – oa – Tunya*. Above us the sky is only blue. It's cold in the wooded area above the Falls, which is soaked like an Amazon rain forest; a few steps away the land is dry and drought-ridden.

Tomorrow morning, courage permitting, we intend to go on a white-water-rafting expedition along the Zambesi. This evening we look forward to a 'braai' in the hotel grounds.

As well as the taxis that abound between hotel and airport, the other favoured form of transport is the donkey cart. In Maun, too, this was the case. The carts come in various shapes and formats, the most refined, perhaps the most affluent, pulled by a team of six donkeys in two rows. There was even one with seven, if I managed to count correctly. I suppose there's sense in that. Donkeys have a reputation for stubborness, so the greater the number employed the greater the odds on getting some kind of co-operation from them. That is, until the day they form the donkey collective and their joint stubbornness brings everything to a standstill.

27 *June*. Today is the day we go white-water rafting. Following a Continental breakfast, the hardy rafters assemble by the swimming pool. We survey the raftmen who arrive, bronzed and fit, all in T-shirts, every bit the beach bum's uniform seen the world over. Their leader addresses us on the need to wear life-jackets and to remove all but the most essential articles of clothing. We are advised to secure shoes tightly and to fasten hats to our life-jackets by lengths of string provided.

We now have a clearer indication of what lies ahead. An indemnity form is produced. We are obliged to complete and sign this, freeing the Zambesi Rafting Company of any responsibility for us in the event of . . . whatever.

Transit vans transfer us to an open truck of a type that probably did its best work in the Second World War. It takes us on the bumpy journey to our starting point. Here, several hundred feet above the river, we are shown how to secure the life-jackets and our hats. My immediate thought is that I can't breathe and that this degree of tightness is surely unnecessary.

We begin our descent in blazing sunshine. Half-way down the steep gorge we stop for a cup of tea by a pool. A team of Zimbabweans is there to provide the refreshment. They live, it would appear, in clouds of smoke, partly from the camp fire and partly from the leaves of Dagga that they smoke. Pressing onwards and downwards we arrive at the river, where four large Avon rafts await us. The river is quiet at this wide turn in its course, making a large pool.

Our main party is assigned a raft rowed by Brian, along with two African assistants, one qualified, one a trainee. After a little time getting to know one another – Charles, a passenger from Cape Town, completes our party – we practise the various techniques required on confronting a rapid.

Sitting poised in the bow of the boat, John, Charles and I prepare to 'highside', the move that puts our combined weights suddenly forward in order to counteract the surge of the oncoming wave. In my middle-aged enthusiasm, I fail to return to my start position and disappear over the bow of the boat into the waiting Zambesi. In one move I have become a *klutz*!

A fine start, Stanley!

I'm the cause of some hilarity as I struggle back aboard. We jostle and parry for positions in the gentle current which takes us ever nearer the first rapid – No. 11 on the river.

We watch the number one boat and its skipper Jock go safely through it and find we're next in line. Slowly we approach the rim.

A moment later we bob over and are on our way. We've chosen the most dangerous route. From our left comes a huge wave. We are now at the bottom of a deep trough. All the highsiding in the world won't see us through this tidal wave. It's too late. It picks up the raft and tips it over like a leaf. We are all in the water. For a moment I'm under the boat (a nightmare) but quickly orientate myself to emerge on the outside. I find the handrail but the string of my hat is entangled with the boat's painter and is starting to strangle me. The string snaps under the pressure and my hat is gone. For a second I ponder whether to go after it. Sense prevails. Hanging on to the boat seems a better idea.

But there's no sign of Jeannie or Francie.

The most awful dread comes upon me.

After what seems like minutes and can only be seconds, Jeannie emerges along the side of the raft. She's panicking about Francie. I scream to reassure Jeannie that I'm sure Francie's all right. Now I'm glad my jacket is as tight as it is. There's no sign of our skipper Brian. Or Charles. Only our qualified African is there, atop the raft, trying to right it. John appears from the other side, gets on to the raft and lends a hand. Finally they succeed in getting it the correct way up.

Our African trainee is also missing.

We are hauled aboard like so many dying cod, and shake ourselves free of excess water. Jeannie is pale. She has been struck on the side of the head, by the oar perhaps, and is looking very timid and shaken.

There's still no sign of Francie, Charles, Brian and the African boy.

We recover as best we can and make it to the nearest sheltered bank. Now we see the others, Francie included, coming to us from further downstream like a family of drowned rats. They are, it seems, none the worse for their experience.

After the exchange of our various adventures, we settle down in the boat once more. Jeannie and Francie are without shoes or hats – victims to Rapid No. 11. It occurs to me to turn back, but the thought of crocodiles lurking on the river banks keeps us moving forward.

The adventure continues. We are one man light now as our African trainee has assessed the situation and fancies his chances better in one of the other boats. Another raft flipped at No. 11 which goes some way to restoring our fading morale. We pass from very tranquil moments to others of great energy and activity when anything is likely to happen. Numbers 12a, b and c are safely passed, as is unlucky 13. We rise manfully to the task at the front of the boat and there's a great boyish thrill jointly enjoyed at beating the enormous waters. Further rapids go by. I check on Jeannie who is developing a large bruise on the right side of her head. She's also complaining of a headache – not surprisingly – and is looking very pallid.

We've been at it for two hours now.

No-one could ever prepare you for the danger of this activity. On other rivers there's a lengthy training period prior to setting off and everybody always wears a safety helmet. Not here on the Zambesi, however. A crocodile is pointed out, sunning itself on the rocks at the side. What a consoling sight from this small boat! We safely negotiate 14, 15 and 16 and are now becoming supremely confident.

Another lull in the river's activities allows us to discuss our technique for the final three rapids. The first two pass without a hitch. There'll be no trouble at No. 19 at this time of year, with this 'medium' volume of water. (When it's lower, we learn, it can be really treacherous.)

Famous last words. We approach 19 nonchalantly. It begins well and we're almost home before we're tossed into the water once more. Perhaps we were 'out of sync' with our highside. Whatever it was, this upset has come as an awful shock.

Francie has lost contact with us once more, but I soon spot her, bobbing safely and half-smiling, some way downstream. Jeannie is alongside me rather anxious for Francie. I'm able to reassure her. Ahead of me I see the remainder of Rapid 19 and a wall of water growing ever higher.

John, Jeannie and I are now clinging to one another in a chain, and one by one we manage to haul ourselves on to the just-righted boat, seconds before the next wave hits us. We'd thought we were home and almost dry, and could have done without this second ducking. Apart from the physical strain on our systems, it is a psychological blow. Our skipper Brian is in shock – he'd only just finished telling us that no one flips at 19. Now he begins repeating the words in a kind of trauma.

We drift rather disconsolately to the shore.

A lunch of salads and bread has been prepared ahead of our arrival, in the shade of several grass awnings. Stories of conquests and flips are exchanged. New friendships have quickly been established under the catalytic effect of white-water experiences. Some concern is expressed about the bump on Jeannie's head. There's a pair of Swedish doctors from Göteborg in the party and they prove helpful.

After a couple of hours of lunch and siesta, we start our 700-foot ascent out of the gorge to the promised cold beers and cokes. It's slow going. None of us is very fit and we've been through a fairly traumatic experience. The sun is very intense and Jeannie feels the need to make several rest stops. Slowly we're getting there. Encouragement comes from all quarters. Hooting comes from the top where beer rather than coke is already flowing.

Twelve feet from our goal, Jeannie slumps against the rocks and slithers to the ground in a faint. As she goes down, she's already diagnosed that she's not suffering from exhaustion, but from delayed concussion.

The Swedish pair, named Brink, are quickly on the scene. She is made to suck ice, and cold compresses are applied to her neck and arms. From nowhere a stretcher has been constructed out of canvas and spare oars and she is carefully managed to the top, rather as though she'd fainted in a football crowd, and into the shade of the truck. She describes her hands as tingling and her legs are in a cramp. We get into the transit van with her and, along with the Swedes, Brian, John and a couple of other helpers, are soon on our way to Victoria Falls hospital. Some simple tests are carried out on her whilst we describe, as well as possible, the day's events. The local doctor sensibly decides that she must stay here under observation for the night. Francie, John and the rest of the group leave.

28 June. We are able to spend a comfortable night together, Jeannie in one bed, me in the other, in a small private room. A baby next door is suffering from malaria. The cockerels of the nearby village begin their dawn chorus. There must be dozens of them. Tea is brought to us at what feels like 6.30, but is confirmed as 7.30 by the arrival of the train, hooting some distance away.

An Indian lady doctor arrives at about 9.30 and proceeds to examine Jeannie. She's not entirely happy about releasing her, but I believe the comfort of the hotel will do more to revive her than the services of this pleasant but small, poorly equipped hospital. Only aspirin and panadol are offered as painkillers; there's no X-ray facility.

We are shown the bill for services rendered. We owe the hospital fifty-five Zim dollars – about eleven pounds; needless to say this constitutes a princely sum in Zimbabwe.

At the hotel we anticipate a restful day in contrast to the one just gone.

I set off in search of something to draw. How lucky to find at the station an old steam engine hissing away promisingly, having just watered. It's a strange configuration, with one of those sloping extensions at the front full of bogeys and pistons. It sets off to do some shunting around the station sidings. It's a lovely sight and sound, this relic of the steam age, No. 377 'Udwai'. As I return to the hotel, its whistle blends harmoniously with that of the birds.

Later John and I explore. Beyond the shops and the market building, we walk into the bush. We find warthog droppings, and just a little further on those of buffalo, impala and elephant. We're no more than five minutes' walk from bank and post office and the wild is already here. Track after track goes off into scrub bush. Keeping the sound of the Falls in earshot is our compass. We cross the line of the Zimbabwe National Railway whose rolling stock still bears on its windows the engraved inscription RR – Rhodesian Railways. Only the paintwork of the carriages has been changed from the old days. We'd examined some of the coaches earlier – they're not dissimilar to one in which John used to live. The old first and second class coaches are beautiful. Lots of varnished wood-fittings and dark green leather seats that serve as sleepers for the evening. They're well cared for and would not be out of place in a London Gentlemen's Club.

29 *June*. Woken with coffee around 7 a.m.

Earnest English trainspotters are identifiable on the station even at this hour. They're in uniform – open-necked Bri-nylon shirt, sleeves neatly rolled, grey flannel trousers and socks and sandals. This morning the train is late, to the chagrin of all the Johnny Morris look-alikes. I decide on breakfast and from my table hear the disappointing sound of yet another diesel. Trainspotter-man returns. His trousers are on the short side, owing to his increasing portliness and a waist-band that reaches to just below the arm-pit.

I photograph Jeannie's bruises for the record.

Today we fly to Lake Kariba. The runway at Fothergill Island is a dusty track beyond which lies a small inlet with a suitable jetty to tie up a boat. When we arrive we have a treat to look at – a lovely boat and a lioness lying by her kill.

Africa!

Viking is magnificent. What have I done to deserve this? Sung a lot of notes is the answer. Jeannie and I have a double-bedded cabin in the bows – I stop short of calling it a stateroom. We cast off, in the direction of a vast herd of buffalo that had caught our eye from the air.

Munich could be a million miles away.

Later in the evening I take a pee from the water-level decking of *Viking* when it occurs to me a crocodile could easily take me now, *Jaws*-like, and no-one would ever know.

30 June. Up-river, we see coucal, water-buck and crested barbet. At one spot there's a profusion of euphorbia and agave and, flitting around the bright flowers, scarlet-breasted sunbirds. My first sight of a Goliath heron – how aptly named. It stands still as a tree stump, incredibly tall. Finally disturbed, it rises in flight, and from some distance I can hear the flapping of its huge wings, taking it to seclusion in the next inlet.

Eggs and bacon await us on our return.

Later, at Buma Hills a number of elephant and water-buck decorate the lake edge. There are five adult elephants and two young. The antics of the babies occupy us for a long time. Though separated in age by some months, these two enjoy a form of play that is perfect proof that wild beasts also have time to pursue activities other than those geared to their survival. They take it in turns to bump into one another, which always results in the bumped one slithering gloriously into the mud bath. Late in the day fishing lines are made ready and John, Francie and I set off to catch whatever we can. A beautiful sunset is almost complete as we rejoin the boat. There's a brilliant red sky and the colours this produces in the wake of our small craft are extraordinary – it's an aquamarine kaleidoscope, with a wonderful luminous quality.

Dozens of nightjars feed on the insect life in the fading light of our bay.

1 *July*. This is our last full day on the boat. Jeannie and Francie are ready to leave – for them this is time enough to be cooped up. The bush, Africa, its wildness, are not compatible with this luxury boat life.

John thinks he has seen some antelope on the shore line. I'm sceptical as he points to an area a long way off and already some distance behind us. We set off to satisfy our doubts about his spotting ability. As we come nearer it's clear that he was right. From that great distance he'd recognised the profile of a group of three beautiful sables, as lovely an animal as can be seen. They allow us to drift closer to them with our engine now cut off. After a while they wander elegantly away. Two females and a young male – gigolo! Their swept-back antlers catch the sunlight, and the mix of white, black and auburn of their coats is extremely attractive.

We'd seen only one sable previously, a shy specimen in Okavango that was under threat of poachers. Our guide on that occasion, Fish, vowed that if anyone killed that animal he would kill him. I had no reason to doubt him.

I won't ever forget the cheetahs or the lion night-visitors. Francie compared moments of the holiday to a religious experience. Such is the magic of Africa.

Chapter Six

ANCORA LA MUSICA

A T the completion of a two-week African holiday filled with adventure, Jeannie went on to stay for a further week with her father in Natal whilst Francie and I returned home to London.

Holidays are fine in the music business, so long as one is not required to perform a day after returning. I allowed myself four days before a recital at the Munich Festival. But it became apparent that all was not well with me by the Sunday afternoon, the concert being on Tuesday, 9 July. Fully rested, I was nevertheless experiencing what was either a cold or a severe bout of hay fever.

Roger Vignoles and I went on rehearsing the programme but by Monday I had to make a decision. There are certain venues and certain audiences with whom I am familiar. The Munich public know me well for my Giovanni and Count Almaviva. But I was not prepared to 'crave their indulgence' while I wheezed my way through a programme of Haydn, Wolf and Britten. I most reluctantly cancelled. They would have to hear me at a better time.

This left me with a couple of free days before my next appointment. Munich again, the opera house, the familiar Rennert production of *Don Giovanni*.

There is a history to my singing this role in Munich. Originally I was contracted, several years ago, to take part in a new production to be prepared by Maximilian Schell. That plan faltered and the next candidate was Jean-Louis Martinoty. His designs weren't acceptable for the theatre, whereupon Wolfgang Sawallisch, the

Music Director of the Bavarian State Opera, approached me during some concerts we gave together in San Francisco in April 1985.

'How would you feel,' he asked, 'if instead of a new production, we brought together this cast and rehearsed for three weeks in the old Rennert production? You would be perfectly justified in withdrawing under the circumstances,' he added.

I said that, with proper preparation and the chemistry created by a completely new cast, this might be a very interesting way of saving the situation. Withdrawing was the last thing I could think of – it never entered my head.

And so we rehearsed all those years ago and the result was a phenomenal success which saw the twenty-year-old sets save the Staatsoper a huge amount of money. Tours to Japan and Spain followed.

Rennert, of course, died some years ago, but his productions in Munich have been faithfully reproduced year by year, with unfailing devotion by the resident staff producer, Ronnie Adler.

There are familiar faces in the cast for this 1990 Festival. Stafford Dean is my Leporello and Ann Murray sings the role of Donna Elvira. The rest of the cast consists of Julia Varady (Donna Anna), Hans-Peter Blochwitz (Ottavio), Angela Maria Blasi (Zerlina) and no less than Kurt Moll as the Commendatore. I say 'no less than Kurt Moll' because he is one of the giants of opera. He's a very big man who sings mainly German repertory, his mother tongue, and is possessed of one of the greatest bass voices I've ever heard.

What luxury.

During the *Giovanni* rehearsals, a crew from Bavarian Television plan to follow me around town and theatre for the next couple of days to make a report on the English Don. For this they require me to enter a porcelain shop to enquire after a small piece of Meissen for my wife. Hardly original, but the stuff of which such programmes are made. We also spend a little time in the English garden, where they film me quietly seated in a corner sketching the tower of a nearby church. The English garden is known for its nude sunbathing area, and I'm rather pleased to find I'm not needed there for any candid shots.

The most worrying and demanding scene for the film requires me to sing a song that I would have included in my recital three days ago had I not had to cancel. I've endeavoured to find an accompanist for this, without success, and so I've elected to play for myself.

The only other time I've done this in public was on stage at Covent Garden at a Jubilee Gala for the Queen. As there was no room in the pit on that occasion for the harpsichord, it was wheeled on to the stage at a given moment, and Anne Howells as Rosina and I as Figaro accompanied ourselves in the recitative that precedes the duet *'Dunque io son'* from *The Barber of Seville*. As the spotlight came on, and the television cameras hovered, I looked down, I recall, at my hands and watched my fingers as they swelled to the size of prize-winning Cumberland sausages. And, after all that, William Mann wrote in *The Times* the following day that Anne Howells and Thomas Allen had *mimed*, quite acceptably, the harpsichord continuo. What cheek!

Here I was again, in a similar situation, but this time my effort would be recorded. I'd chosen my song: Haydn's *'She never told her love'*. I prayed that my fingers wouldn't secretly swell to provide me with a mess of split notes, while hoping more than anything that the camera wouldn't dwell overlong on my hands. Fingering was never my strong point.

Because of all the various cuts and angles required for a film, we shot the song several times. At the end of it all I feel I have become reasonably proficient, though I've never dared to ask any accompanists for an opinion.

Saturday, 12 July, sees the first *Giovanni* safely through. The theatre in Munich has a cosy, unintimidating ambience and the acoustic is excellent. When I wish to whisper a line of recitative or produce some very quiet singing, as in the Serenade for instance, there is never any feeling of not being heard. If only Covent Garden were like this.

That evening I begin to be bothered by some sort of infection in my right ear. It would appear the inner ear has some swelling and my hearing is impaired. It's also becoming painful trying to sleep and to open my mouth as wide as I'd like. I'm puzzled.

Sunday morning I spend once more with the television crew, this time in the foyer of my hotel where they set up a corner for an interview. This is carried out by a young lady called Annette Hopfenmüller. On German television she's associated with pop music, but there's clearly a lot more than that in this lady's background. Her questions are searching and extremely interesting, and at the end of the session we all seem to agree that something useful has been recorded which will serve well for the completion of the programme. My 'profile' will take up about twenty minutes of an arts programme entitled *Capriccio*, which will concentrate mainly on Munich and the Festival.

After the interview I make a dash to the airport for a plane to London.

It looked at one time as though I'd have to travel to Edinburgh the same evening to begin recording *The Magic Flute* with Sir Charles Mackerras the following morning. But the schedule has changed and I'm able to spend a night at home in my own bed, travelling to Edinburgh on Monday morning instead.

The discomfort in my ear is now worse, and Jeannie has telephoned on my behalf to make a date to see a specialist in Harley Street before I leave for Edinburgh. By now, late on Sunday, it's beginning to feel as though the canal in my ear has closed up altogether and the pain has become intense.

In a schedule as busy as mine, life is reasonably simple as long as everything goes according to plan. The problems arise when something untoward, such as an ear infection, happens just before a scheduled recording. Then there's one hell of a job to find the hours in the day to deal with the difficulty.

The doctor is able to tell me it's not serious – in fact, *otitis externa*. He inserts an alum-soaked lint into my ear as best he can. I leave for Edinburgh, hearing less all the time.

15 July. On this, the first day of recording , I meet many old friends. Sir Charles I've known for years. We've worked together for television, recording studio, opera house, concert platform; there isn't much left for us to share together except cabaret. The producer of the record for the American Teldec Company is James

Mallinson, who was responsible for the *Figaro* recording made some years ago in Vienna under Riccardo Muti. The cast here in Edinburgh features more members of the 'club'. Tamino is a friend from New York, Jerry Hadley; Barbara Hendricks sings Pamina; June Anderson, Queen of the Night; and Robert Lloyd, Sarastro.

The project takes place in the Usher Hall, and, as far as I can discover, is its debut as a recording venue. It's a barn of a place. But huge areas of the stalls are covered with sheets of plywood and a softer, more acceptable acoustic is thus obtained. It's a pleasure, too, to be here with the Scottish Chamber Orchestra, who play Mozart so sensitively. We last worked together on a Mozart aria recording in 1984.

My first day of work consists of two major chunks of Papageno's role – the birdcatcher aria and the suicide scene. I call to mind Derek Jacobi playing Claudius: I have to hope that the character who threatens suicide today will resemble and match his earlier self whom I haven't yet recorded, just as Jacobi mastered the problem of going back and forth in age to portray Claudius coping with varying degrees of stuttering.

After the musical session we have a certain amount of dialogue to record before I can be released to return to London. I have to get through this as quickly and as successfully as possible, as tomorrow I must sing a further performance of *Don Giovanni* in Munich. At the back of my mind I'm worried about missing the plane or being delayed for some reason. The Austrian baritone, Gottfried Hornik, is on hand to guide us along the right paths with our dialogue. His help and advice are invaluable.

I regret that I have no time to enjoy Edinburgh, which is one of my favourite cities. I dash away to London, and the following morning leave on an early flight for Munich. My hearing is still impaired, but the pain is somewhat less, thank goodness. I rest at my Munich hotel for as long as possible and leave at 6 p.m. for the second performance of *Don Giovanni*.

Though my ear is still blocked, I can hear well enough to be in tune. What is worse affected, however, is the sensation which is my normal reaction to the sound I make when I sing. It's as though I am hearing everything from the other side of a dividing wall. If this – God forbid – is what the start of deafness is like, then I want none of it. Whenever the question arises – 'If you were to lose either the power of sight or your hearing, which would you choose?' – I have no hesitation in opting to retain my hearing.

Apart from the hearing problem, I feel very fit. The performance is enormously enjoyable. I learn to appreciate more and more Professor Sawallisch's seemingly relaxed but in fact controlled way of conducting. For these performances he also plays his own harpsichord continuo.

In 1990 Dr Sawallisch and I performed *Don Giovanni* with this same company on a visit to the Teatro Liceo of Barcelona. In our dressing room area, the temperature rose to 45 degrees centigrade. The heat in the theatre itself was much the same. And yet, at the end of the performance, when the good professor walked on to the stage to join us for our bows, he looked immaculate. Not a hair out of place, his shirt exhibiting no sign of perspiration, his cuffs showing a perfect couple of centimetres below the sleeves of his tail coat. The performance wanted nothing for excitement, yet he was able to summon it all up, in that temperature, without any outward sign of distress. I find that remarkable.

The following day I return to London and later to Edinburgh to resume the recording. This time I carry my golf clubs in the hope that the added luxury of a little spare time might be available to me.

We work slowly through the various numbers of *The Magic Flute*, continuing until late in the evening to complete all the dialogue that has to be covered.

We keep ahead of the schedule and I'm delighted to find that Sunday morning is free, allowing me time for a rare round of golf. I hope in the afternoon to see the outcome of the Open Championship on television. Jeannie has joined me and we meet up with our friends, Alick and Susetta Rankin. Alick is a member of the Muirfield Club. Not far out of Edinburgh and just off the Berwick-bound A1, Muirfield lies in a tract of great golfing land and is the jewel amongst many fine courses. The weather is perfect and the views of the Kingdom of Fife across the Firth of Forth most beautiful. To my amazement there's hardly anyone around when we arrive. Today my swing seems to work for me and I rise to the challenge of the course. I'll never set a record but it always pleases me when I can see the remnants of the standard by which I used to play. We enjoy a club lunch – for which Muirfield is well known – among about two dozen of its members. It need hardly be said they are all men; for there are no lady members at Muirfield. Nor is there a professional or a shop. Such traditions have taken centuries to acquire. Alick points out one particular member, a small dark man, resplendent in his brogues and knee breeches – the perfect Scottish gentleman – except that this particular Scot is an Italian lawyer who makes the trip from Milan to Muirfield every weekend. Such are the fascinations – and lunacies – of golf and the golfer.

By the following day, Ian Baker-Finch has spent a night relishing his Open victory; I've picked up a rare Scottish suntan; and we complete the recording. Jerry Hadley churns out story after story, entertaining us at the post-recording dinner.

22 July. Jeannie and I leave on a morning flight for London. We now have a couple of days to get ourselves organised. We are to spend the summer in Salzburg, at the house in Reitgutweg which we left at Easter.

The weather was wondrous in Scotland, but in Salzburg they've been experiencing a lot of rain. The city is swarming with visitors for this summer season. Not only visitors for the Festival but also for the pretty houses and metal signs that are such a feature of the Getreidegasse, a narrow street now so packed it would be difficult to get from one end to the other in the course of an afternoon. I make a point of staying out of town unless absolutely essential.

Our early rehearsals are held in a building called the Lehrbauhof, which lies in the shadow of Salzburg's most prominent local mountain, the Untersberg. Lehrbauhof – literally the building teaching place – is just that: a rather spectacular building used as a training centre for apprentice builders to learn their trade. One rather disturbing sign, however, is soon apparent in this rainy season. Water trickles steadily down the inside of walls and windows, forming great pools just to the side of our working area. But that's a small quibble, and greatly outweighed by the advantage of working out here in this beautiful spot away from the bustle and noise of the town centre.

Bernard Haitink is here and in good spirits, looking forward to being able to concentrate entirely on *Figaro* without the distraction of additional concerts – as was the case at Easter.

Michael Hampe is back to produce us in our work, but he, on the other hand, has also to prepare productions of *Così fan tutte* and *Don Giovanni*, and how he'll find the time is surely a problem for an advanced computer.

The only cast change is in the role of Doctor Bartolo, in which we now have the Greek bass Dimitri Kavrakos, an old friend from Glyndebourne and Covent Garden, in place of John Tomlinson who is in his now regular Wagner season at Bayreuth.

The view from the house in summer is different from the one I came to know so well at Easter. The house I painted beyond the bottom of my garden is no longer visible. It has disappeared behind a screen of greenery. The birds are also different. My first shopping trip saw me with my usual bag of sunflower seeds for the garden birds. Now from the terrace something new can be seen. I spot three varieties of woodpecker. And a bird I don't immediately recognise. A flick through my reference book produces the answer. I'm watching my first nutcracker. An impressive bird the size of a small crow or large jay, it spends its day searching among the hazel trees for its favourite diet. Humans need a metal contraption to get to the food inside that hard shell; I can't help but marvel at the strength of this bird's beak in doing the job so efficiently and so untiringly.

It is now 2 August, and the weather has worsened from what was already incessant heavy rain. After the morning rehearsal, I set out to return to my rented house for lunch. About a mile away from home I come across diversion signs. Something is amiss. Indeed, I can go no further with the car, and decide that the only way I'll have lunch at home today is by wading through two-foot-deep fast-flowing flood waters. After taking off shoes and socks, I roll up trouser legs and plunge in. A knotted handkerchief on my head would complete the pretty picture.

After lunch I return to the car by the same means. There is

raucous laughter as I arrive in my dishevelled state for the rehearsal. At the end of the afternoon rehearsal, I have to leave the car some way off, to go bare-legged through this coffee-coloured flood.

The weather remains unsettled and all over the town fire engines and emergency vehicles are out to deal with the problems that have accumulated. At a house just a few hundred yards down the hill from me, Anthony Rolfe-Johnson and his family have been battling with sandbags to keep the waters at bay. Sir Georg Solti, von Karajan's successor, is stranded and has to be air-lifted to his performance by helicopter.

Two further days into rehearsal we have a pleasant morning working together. But in the late afternoon we resume with the news that Ljuba Kazarnovskaya, our Countess, is not feeling well and won't be rehearsing today. The next day, 3 August, things have become rather more serious and we are informed that she will not be taking part in the Festival at all. It seems that the Festival issued an ultimatum. One never, as a mere artist/employee, hears all sides of such gossip but by all accounts Michael Hampe was not pleased by the actions taken and the way in which the situation was handled.

Shortly after this, we hear that Pamela Coburn, the American soprano, has been engaged as replacement Countess. We've been lucky in this: she had only just set foot in America when she was called back through immigration with a request to take an immediate return flight to Europe – from whence she had just arrived (she lives in Munich). All credit to Pamela for being prepared to fill in under such trying circumstances.

She is very experienced in the role of Countess Almaviva. I sang it with her only once previously, in Hamburg, but I've no doubt she'll be a wonderful replacement.

The next few days are spent recapping in order that Pamela can catch up with our work but there is really no problem. Michael's production is orthodox and she must have been through similar moves and situations a hundred times before. Our first stage rehearsals with the orchestra are rather different from those of the

Easter Festival. For the summer we have the luxurious sound of the Vienna Philharmonic, an orchestra used to playing operas from the pit. Indeed they seem to have an eye on the conductor and an ear on the singers – the skill of true accompanists. Their sound has a more transparent sheen than that of the Berlin Philharmonic and, while both are supreme orchestras, the general opinion seems to be that Vienna have the advantage when it comes to playing Mozart.

Bernard has discussed various points with me and we're approaching the Act Three aria rather differently. It's faster and has much more energy. This works for me and blends well with my playing of the Count. The beauty and genius of Mozart triumphs once more. I believed I'd explored every avenue of interpretation for the Count by now, but no sooner did I allow myself to think that than a hundred new ideas came to light. Small details, maybe, but points that nevertheless prevent any kind of weariness or stagnation from setting in.

Dress rehearsals are rather interesting in Salzburg. So desperate is the demand for tickets for performances that people will settle finally for a dress rehearsal and, in order to make less of their disappointment, will then dress up as for an evening show. . . . The sight of several evening dresses mixing with dirndl and holiday denim is even more incongruous than that of black-tied and begowned Glyndebourne-supporters leaving Victoria Station on afternoon trains.

There is a much more comfortable feeling this summer than I remember at the Easter Festival. The shadow of von Karajan has been weakened by the arrival on the scene of many other musical personalities. Bernard, too, seems in more relaxed spirit than at Easter.

By way of relaxing after the rehearsal, Susanne Mentzer (Cherubino) has opened her house to various colleagues who are in town. It's an occasion for us to contribute something towards an informal party. I've put together my thick onion tart which has become something of a calling card for such gatherings. Carol Vaness has brought along a chicken dish, Susanne a delicious fruit salad. There's never a shortage of food when singers get together, nor any lack of variety.

Ann Murray's son, Jonathan, is there with his nanny. He explains he's going to see his mummy later in *Così fan tutte*, all correct and very grown up. But they're all rather unusual, these travelling-circus children. During our performances Ben, Susanne's son, who is a very special child, sits quietly in the wings with Wendy, his nanny and minder, while mummy entertains 2,500 people as Cherubino or Zerlina, then he greets her and goes with her to her dressing room when she leaves the stage. He makes it all look as commonplace as if he'd been playing in a sandpit with his friends. What an extraordinary life they have.

Sam Ramey is there in between *Giovanni* performances. We've known one another since Paris in the late 1970s and there's always something to hear about, a story to tell. This is a very special time for me: the two days between dress and première, when I can relax and catch up with friends like any normal human being. It doesn't last very long and is therefore that much more precious.

The following mid-afternoon we await the arrival of friends from England who have holidayed in France and Italy and are slowly making their way home. Carol Guise, the opera fanatic of the pair, has known me as a singer from *Billy Budd* days in Wales and has since become very close to us. Jamie, her husband, not originally a music man, will listen to anything now – so long as I'm in it! And indeed he does seem to enjoy opera, though I suspect he might prefer to be out somewhere catching a salmon. Having settled them into their temporary home, we dress for a party to be given that evening by Philips Records at Schloss Leopoldskron. The party is a way of Philips saying thank you to some of its artists for years of work and to Mozart for his all-too-few-years on this earth. The Schloss is probably best known as the house in which Christopher Plummer lived as von Trapp in the film of *The Sound of Music*. It is, consequently, on the tour-bus route. A storm, a Salzburg special, is brewing as we arrive at the main entrance and before long the subdued lighting of the interior is being enhanced by massive lightning bolts which flash down towards the ornamental lake behind the house. It's a truly operatic scene.

10 August. First Night is a buzz of anticipation. Jeannie, Carol and

Jamie come with me to the theatre and leave me rather quickly to enjoy my nerves alone.

Gerhard fixes my hair and make-up in his usual fastidious manner and a new dresser, Walter, fusses over my costumes. I'm feeling fine. The voice is in just the right slot, and everything resonates as it should.

And so it goes. Act One: fine; Act Two; lots of fun with the replacement Countess (Pamela Coburn) remembering everything she's rehearsed; Act Three: a sexy duet with Susanna (Dawn Upshaw who always tries to find something new) plus the aria full of all the gusto and energy we'd decided on in rehearsal; Act Four: spirited. Great success. Very relaxed and hugely enjoyable.

A word here for Antonio, the gardener, as played by Alfred Kuhn. His voice is exceptionally resonant. It really is extraordinary even to hear Alfred speak. As he enters my dressing room and begins to chat it's as though someone has switched on a loud-speaker, such is the cutting power of his voice. He's a wonderful person, a delightful colleague and worth a lot of anyone's time.

Sandy Oliver has played Don Curzio once again and the dressing room he shares with Alfred is a place to go at the start of Act Four when I have a little time to myself and need to laugh. I put up even with their smoking for the value of their company, and that's saying a lot.

Sandy tells the story of the Scottish lady who enters a singing competition in her home town. The adjudicator has come from Edinburgh and is rather astonished to read that she has chosen to sing Lady Macbeth's air.

'Miss McBride,' he says to the little thing in twin-set and pearls and newly permed hair, 'I see you'll be giving us Lady Macbeth.'

'That's right,' says Miss McBride with a voice reminiscent of *Dr Finlay*'s Janet.

'Well,' says he, 'you should know that many a celebrated international opera star has been sorely intimidated by the enormous technical problems and difficulties inherent in this piece of music.'

To which Miss McBride, clutching her handbag to her front, and perhaps tweaking the perm, replies: 'No' me.'

After the show we troop off to celebrate at a nearby restaurant, which has prepared, as a special favour to me, one portion of Salzburger Nockerl. The problem with this dish is that it takes tremendous nerve to accept it graciously as it is carried ostentatiously to one's table with all the ceremony afforded the haggis in Scotland. A high soufflé the size of a small bed, it creates interest and talk whenever it appears. No self-respecting gourmet would be seen in the same town with one, I suspect. On the other hand, one shouldn't leave Salzburgland without trying it. The fruit base is delicious.

Now there are two free days during which time we can show Carol and Jamie a little of the area. This is something we've not often enjoyed. Mostly our trips abroad separate us from friends, but this time we're thrilled to be able to have them with us for even so short a time. The weather is now settled and we can visit all the places we have grown to love. It's also good practice for our next visitors. An aunt and uncle are coming for a week's stay, and immediately afterwards more lovely friends from London. I'm beginning to sound as though we're running our own version of *Sound of Music* tours.

The second performance happens on 13 August and is again well received.

14 August. A taxi picks us up early to take us to a train bound for Munich. Thence by air to London. The same afternoon I'm due to rehearse with Roger Vignoles for our recital at the Aldeburgh Festival on 15 August. Salzburg, with one direct schedule flight per week, remains difficult to reach by air. We fly either via Zurich or via Munich, and the journey can take between five and six hours. Zurich is a huge international junction. The previous time I made this connection I sat quietly in a corner, pretending to read my book, while enjoying people-watching, a sport to which many habitual travellers are addicted. One particular lady caught my eye. She could hardly have done otherwise, as she paraded by me on at least six occasions, her jewel-encrusted arm supported by a small middle-aged man – I would guess Italian. 'Support' might have been the lady's middle name. Built as she was, cross-bred through Gina Lollabrigida and Victor Mature via Sophia Loren, her figure-hugging skin was eighty-five per cent on view. From the waist up she wore what could only be described as a petite black bra, several sizes smaller than Nature required. This lady was enormously courageous, with lashings of what one can only call *chutzpah!*

I think of her now – as we make our journey via Munich – and wonder whether the pair of them are still searching for their connection.

By the time I get home I feel that no good will come of trying to work after this length of journey.

Jeannie and I quickly repack and set off to drive towards East Anglia. Friends who live forty-five minutes from Aldeburgh will be looking after us. Roger and I meet at the Snape Maltings on the morning of the recital.

What a contrast this short visit proves to be. Summer is the time of music festivals, but the shape and variety of them is really rather extraordinary. Two days ago I was in the thick of the glitter of Salzburg. Here, at Snape, I wander around the old buildings, watch wooden boats being built, enjoy a pub lunch, and hope to see a bearded tit somewhere out on the marshes. People stroll by in relaxed mood and light summer Laura Ashley frocks.

Our rehearsal goes well, and the concert that evening, though requiring a lot of concentration from me to keep *Figaro* out of my head, is very satisfying. Roger and I enjoy a happy rapport with the audience and perform several very specific encores. The first one comes by way of a request from that doyenne of English singers Joan Cross, who is sitting to my left in the front row. We follow this with three of Britten's folk songs, with a respectable interval for applause in between – they are encores after all. '*The foggy foggy dew*' is a particular favourite of mine. '*Come you not from Newcastle*', for me, is near enough to home to make no difference. '*Oliver Cromwell*' is the last word (literally) in encores.

The outsider can be forgiven for thinking that singing is singing is singing. But just as there are field and track events in athletics, so different categories of singing can be classified. The hundred-metre sprinter, for example, trains with the objective of providing all the explosive power and speed he can muster over a vital ten seconds. In singing, there are certain moments that require just such an explosive quality and usually an accompanying large volume of sound. An example is the aria *'Di quella pira'* in Verdi's *Il Trovatore*. An aria such as *Manon Lescaut*'s *'In quella trina morbide'* requires a calmer, more controlled approach; here energy can last for a longer period of time because of its less explosive nature. This might be likened to the requirements of an athlete for an extended run over ten thousand metres. The nature of breathing varies, too. Slower, less frantic breaths, in keeping with the mood of the aria, for *Manon Lescaut*; while the breaths in *Trovatore* are 'snatched' in the shorter gaps that are available.

In recital, as opposed to opera, the singer paints pictures from song to song as the programme proceeds. Some of them are pale watercolours – particularly in the French repertoire – and others powerful statements by a Picasso or a Klimt. The quality of voice is carefully chosen to interpret in sound the various moods of the poems set to music. I try to have a very clear aim in my mind of what picture is being painted. I also have to know exactly what type of race is to be run at every moment. Otherwise the whole becomes a mish-mash of musical styles to no-one's satisfaction.

The working of the human brain is an extraordinary miracle. On this occasion in Aldeburgh I've had to concentrate particularly hard on every aspect of the songs. This is because I've just arrived from the white heat of Salzburg and I'm departing again tomorrow. But, if called upon to do so, and even at very short notice, I know I could launch into another two or three recital √ programmes and another dozen operas.

The daily routine of working as a singer, and in at least four languages, can produce some fairly astonishing statistics.

At the outset, I had an 'O'-Level understanding of the French language and slightly more than that of my own. Learning roles with a language coach was an experience which brought out in me the desire to converse in the languages in which I was singing. Mastering languages didn't happen overnight; but a day eventually dawned when a light entered the room and I realised I was finally properly in touch with the foreign texts.

With a large repertoire of songs in English, it's also important to me to work on the language that is my mother tongue, in order to wring out of it all the value and subtlety that it has to offer. It is easy to assume that because a language is one's own less care need be taken. I would argue the reverse.

Jeannie drives me home to London after a light supper, as I have to return to Salzburg in the middle of the next afternoon, to be ready for the next *Figaro* and the arrival of Aunt Elsie and Uncle Albert. They've been to Austria on several package holidays from their home in Sunderland, but this is the first time they'll have been into the opera house for a performance.

I have to set some time aside on Saturday morning, 17 August, for working out a shopping list, so that my amateur efforts in the kitchen will meet with approval over the next few days of family visits. While Jamie and Carol were with us, I took great delight in showing them the Kleines Festspielhaus and the Felsenreitschule, that extraordinary theatre that has a back wall of arcades hewn out of the mountain. A canvas roof folds back and a stalls area lifts by means of steel cables lowered from the ceiling. All these thing were in operation when we called by, so it became rather like a second festival performance for them.

Jeannie has stayed in London. Her son, Rob, a Second Officer with Cathay Pacific, is due in England for a few days and naturally she wishes to see him, not having done so for several weeks.

The performances are now in full swing and running like a well-oiled machine. The sets, beautifully designed by John Gunter, have been constructed by marvellous craftsmen. Doors and windows fit perfectly and there's never any fear that a handle might come off or a door stick when it should open.

On one occasion in Houston earlier in the year, I banged vigorously on a securely locked door, ordering Susanna to come out at once. To my horror I watched the door quietly swing open for me, ruining the entire plot. There was nothing to do in the circumstances but to close it as quickly as possible and hope as few people as possible had seen.

Robert Rattray has arrived. He brings with him the information that a projected plan for Los Angeles next year has had to be scrapped because of money problems. This leaves me free to return to Salzburg for repeat performances of *Figaro*, provided that the powers-that-be haven't already recast the role. There would appear to be no end to this year of Mozart celebration. But I'm pleased, as the production has now begun to work very well, and it will be fun to be here to repeat it next year and, I hope, to uncover more new ideas.

22 August. By way of something completely different, today is the day put aside for completing the Berlioz song record for Deutsche Grammophon, which we began in Berlin in May. The venue is the Church of St Konrad on the shores of the Wolfgangsee near St Gilgen. When I arrive, Cord Garben is already buzzing around the piano and checking microphones. He is a jack of all trades, a recording producer in his own right, and has very strong ideas about the placing of the mikes.

We have five long songs to record and the work is quite arduous. But the project goes well and in four-and-a-half hours we've completed the task in hand. One would imagine this peaceful place to be the perfect setting for quiet concentration on such work. But one would be wrong. The countryside has its own traffic problems and our afternoon is interrupted frequently by the sound of tractors, lawnmowers and, worst of all, the local refuse collection.

The following evening our last batch of visitors arrives by train from Munich. Tim and Susie Leon and Gaynor Churchward have elected to fly from London to Munich and to take the train to Salzburg. Rain begins to drizzle down at the Hauptbahnhof as I watch them get off the train and head towards me, all three dressed in trench coats. The hiss of steam from the locomotive is the only missing element – that and a romantic Rachmaninov theme. They look as if they've just been dropped from a Lysander and are on some secret mission fifty years too late.

My aunt and uncle, spending their last night with us, seem a little overwhelmed by the high energy of these newcomers. But all of us – seven in this crowded house – enjoy our supper together. I look forward to the next two or three days. Susie, Gaynor and Jeannie were colleagues in the clothes world at one time and know each other very well. Susie is great fun and comes out at times with the most outrageous statements. As for Gaynor, well, she's just one of the world's great human beings and I love her dearly. They enjoy their visit to the opera the following evening.

24 August. We plan one of our favourite routes which takes us to the top of a mountain near St Koloman. From there we would have views of the Dachstein Glacier and the full range of the Tennengebirge. Wild flowers grow in profusion. Earlier in the month, I'd seen my first Apollo butterfly here, a huge white creature with aeroplane roundel markings in red on its wings.

Jeannie has begun the morning with a slight headache and towards the summit of our climb announces she doesn't feel well. Soon she is exhibiting symptoms which she'd already suffered on two occasions since our recent visit to Africa. Has she picked up malaria while on holiday? She is shaking uncontrollably and becoming very distressed.

We return to Salzburg as quickly as possible, and Gaynor comes with us to the large Landeskrankenhaus (hospital). And it is there Jeannie stays for the next three days, being tested and observed, as strange symptoms ebb and flow. She receives marvellous treatment. But they don't seem able to identify what's wrong, any more than doctors in Africa and London could come up with a sure diagnosis.

Sunday evening, 25 August. I happen to be present when two young doctors come into the room to announce that, as a result of blood tests, they have identified malaria. This is reassuring news as, up to now, everything has been surmise and conjecture. I go to report to our visitors, who are also relieved to have the thing confirmed.

Returning to visit Jeannie at the hospital on Monday morning, I find her less happy than when I'd left her last evening. She explains why. This morning the professor consultant has been to see her and he is not prepared to accept the diagnosis of malaria as there hasn't been any accompanying fever. He begins to look elsewhere for the explanation. By the end of the day the answer seems to be concussion, which she has been suffering as a result of our boating accident on the Zambesi River several weeks ago. Concussion can wreak its havoc after several months of dormancy, it seems.

Our visitors leave on the same afternoon and I resume visits to the hospital.

Tuesday, 27 August, is the last performance day for *Figaro*. After the farewells and arrivedercis at the curtain calls, I go once more to the hospital to report a successful completion of the opera series, and hoping to see a cheerful face.

There is nothing worse than the helplessness one feels when watching anyone (but more particularly a loved one) going through the distress of some mysterious complaint. Watching Jeannie's condition worsen, as I did in London and again in Salzburg, was one of the most frustrating experiences of my life. All I was qualified to do was offer a warm, loving hand and words that might calm, knowing that if the illness turned out to be something even more serious I could only sit and wait as nature took its cruel course. The workings of the human body are a miracle, and Jeannie's suffering made me appreciate, even more, the bond she and I have, and its importance in our two lives.

I recalled dashing from Cardiff to be at my mother's bedside when she suffered her first heart attack in the late 1970s. My father was already there, of course, when I arrived.

After many minutes, he turned to me with tears in his eyes and said: 'I don't know what would happen without her.'

At moments of crisis, I think of my father and those words, and many thoughts flood through my head.

Sometimes I regret that I was not raised within a family where even delicate subjects were a matter of discussion and debate. We didn't talk about important things. So many families don't. But towards the end of my father's life he and I began to talk much more freely and openly than I'd ever have thought possible. I'm relieved so greatly that we did, because he then became so many other things as well as a wonderful dad. He became to me a true human being as well as the parental figure I'd always respected.

I've tried, in the past five or six years particularly, to create the foundation for such a relationship with my own son and I believe we are now beginning to reap the benefits. It is my fervent wish that my two stepchildren, Rob and Francie, will also feel that same sense of freedom with me.

28 August. Jeannie's unsteadiness, her lack of balance and general 'whooziness', seem now to have left her and she is happy for me to be calling first thing in the morning, with everything more or less packed. The next day sees us taking leave of the old house that has been our home for Salzburg 1991, and that evening we are safely back in our own London nest with the doors firmly closed behind us. Getting home for even a short time – in this case, two-and-a-half days – is a treat to be relished.

Tomorrow will be a new start and a new quest to discover the cause of Jeannie's problem.

I have two days left in which to prepare for the Edinburgh Festival, where I am to sing the same recital I gave at Aldeburgh two weeks previously, and to think about what I need to pack for two months in Los Angeles.

Our London garden is minute but it gives us enormous pleasure when we're at home. The flowers are still alive, thanks to Maria, our wonderful Portuguese housekeeper. The prize goes jointly to a Handel rose given to us as a wedding present, a *hosta Sieboldiana* (my own choice) and a *fremontodendron Californicum*, which clambers happily up our west wall at an alarming rate – currently ten feet. Strong winds broke it in half earlier in the year, but it's back now where it was, and seemingly stronger than ever. Its sticky yellow flowers are an enormous attraction to all kinds of life, so it provides interest on many levels.

Stephen and Julia, my son and his fiancée, come to dinner. We chat about a subject that interests father and son – who's winning at golf. Stephen's golfing ambitions are the big thing in his life, and he tells me how he's progressing.

Out of the blue he announces that he and Julia will be getting married next September, around the time of my birthday. About two days later I react. The news was slow to sink in; but now that it has, I'm happy for them both. They're very young but have known one another for a number of years. I must now make a conscious effort not to cluck around them like a mother hen worrying over how they'll manage. They've chosen to marry and so must have taken into account the various demands that follow in the wake of such a decision.

Before supper I'd shown them my latest efforts at painting. I'd spent a large part of the time in Salzburg on a picture of some allotments in Dawdon, part of Seaham, my home town. It's a scene with terraced houses, gable ends, rows of leeks and the pigeon 'crees' which are so much a part of the allotment scene in North-East England.

There were great things about Seaham. It wasn't beautiful – the town had grown up with no reference to anything but the successful hewing and hauling of coal from deep under the ground and its transportation from the nearby docks to the fireplaces and furnaces of faraway places. Line after line of workers' cottages had gone up to accommodate the workforce. Folks struggled for a living, and their plight became the cause of many a celebrated politician, including Ramsay MacDonald and Emmanuel Shinwell.

Byron – Lord Byron – was married disastrously to the local squire's daughter. He didn't seem to notice the plight of the community, seeing only the horrors of the North Sea, of which he wrote: 'Upon this dreary coast we have nothing but county meetings and shipwrecks; and I have this day dined upon fish which probably dined upon the crews of several colliers lost in the late gales.'

It had been incongruous to look out of the window at forests and the Untersberg while I worked on a subject so far removed from Austria, though so much part of my own memories.

Drawing, and more recently painting, are now an important part of my travelling life. My golf clubs were with me in Salzburg though never used. The golf bag, however, served the dual purpose of carrying not only clubs but also my dismantled easel. I'm nothing if not resourceful.

My dilemma now is whether to inflict upon the young couple one of my masterpieces as a wedding gift. There'll have to be some considerable improvement before I feel confident enough to do so. At least it will give me something to aim for – my own Academy Summer Exhibition!

To Edinburgh once more, and the finale of Frank Dunlop's reign over the Festival.

A morning recital in the lovely Queen's Hall with lots of familiar faces dotted around, including that of my old Physics master and first singing teacher, Denis Weatherley.

Denis has watched me develop from schoolboy baritone and member of the 'broken-voiced choir', as he used to call it, to the position I've now reached.

In 1959, which seems like another century, preparations began for the annual school concert. There would be a couple of choruses from *The Messiah*, the brass group formed from members of a local colliery band at Dawdon, a recorder group and a first-former with '*O for the wings of a dove*'. Other volunteers were sought, and I arrived home one evening and began a search among the old books in the piano stool for something to sing. Why I chose '*Simon the Cellarer*' I shall never know. It's a song made popular in earlier years and sung by gentlemen singers of mature experience. I was barely out of short trousers. But *Simon* it was – Mam thought it sounded 'lovely' – and a few days later I presented it to Mr Weatherley. He chose me to take part in that concert and accompanied me at the piano. The same evening I also played an organ solo – the *toccata* of the renowned *Toccata and Fugue in D Minor*. I was studying the organ locally under the school music master, Oswald Fox, but that evening Denis clearly saw more potential in Tom the singer than in Tom the keen-but-slightly-deficient organist.

Denis had heard something unusual in my singing and began to teach me to sing during school lunch hours.

When the time came some years later to decide what to do with me, it was obvious I'd lost interest in pursuing the idea of reading medicine at St Andrews University (apart from anything else, I detested Physics and Chemistry), and my headmaster, Mr Graham, who had never before encountered a problem such as myself, took a sensible course and made enquiries of Professor Arthur Hutchings at Durham University.

And so, one day, dressed in the maroon and gold of my prefect's uniform and armed with my score of *The Messiah* and a couple of songs, I took the bus to Durham and located the Music School on Palace Green where I was to meet the good professor.

He was not there.

Fate has damned me at the first trial, I thought, though I didn't then express it in quite those words.

I left the Green to return to the bus station. An oldish man, coming towards me with two friends, stopped me with: 'Are you a singer, young man?'

'I'd like to be,' I replied.

'Hutchings,' he said. 'Come with me.'

Back we went to the Music School.

He heard me sing Handel and Schumann's *Two Grenadiers*, and said he'd be in touch with my headmaster.

True to his word, a few days later he'd arranged an interview for me at the Royal College of Music with Sir Keith Falkner.

I was on my way.

That's more than thirty years ago. I always feel that Denis can claim the right to have discovered me. He still looks very well – an undiminished twinkle in his eye. I've no doubt he's still possessed of that lovely, rich, fruity bass baritone voice for which he became so well-known in the North-East. His rendering of '*Keep yer feet still Geordie Hinny*' and '*Wor Nanny's a Mazer*' were favourites with all us schoolboys.

The afternoon plane takes me back to London once more. Once home, I spend the rest of the day putting away Edinburgh and taking out Los Angeles.

The tightness of conflicting schedules has meant that I will be two weeks late joining rehearsals in Los Angeles. My contract is for a new production of *Madama Butterfly* and a further *Don Giovanni*.

With the exception of the recitals, almost all my year has been taken up with Mozart. I'm looking forward to being sullied by the lush sounds and excesses of Puccini's music, which will come, I admit, as a refreshing change.

I leave with misgivings. Jeannie is not one hundred per cent fit nor back to playing the tennis she loves so much. But she's determined I should go as planned and not lose any more time and she's in good hands in London.

Chapter Seven

A LITTLE PUCCINI

L OTS of shorts and baseball caps on the Los Angeles flight.
These journeys often seem interminable. Eleven hours is
not the longest flight in the world by any means but there comes a
point when I could cheerfully abandon ship. I do my best to sleep
through the experience.

The house I've rented in LA is in Beverly Hills and is very cosy. A
perfect getaway from the madness on Sunset Boulevard. There is
intellectual activity in Southern California, but it is so outweighed
by narcissism and hedonism one could well be led into believing
that nothing goes on out there that isn't film, restaurant or car life. I
like to lurk behind a book, just people-watching.

My first day in California is without rehearsal, it being Labour
Day – a curious irony!

Peter and Jane Hemmings are giving a lunch party at their lovely
house in Pasadena. They are English. Peter was for many years
with Scottish Opera before spells with Australian Opera and the
London Symphony Orchestra. A Union Jack flies from their new
pole to make identity easy. Staff members, cast and wives,
husbands and friends are all invited. Dozens of us sit in the
sunshine by the pool enjoying the hospitality.

The first night of *Butterfly* is only a week away. Maria Ewing is to
sing the role for the first time. The Cuban-American tenor, Jorge
Pitta, is singing Pinkerton in performances two to six, but Placido
Domingo will be flying in to sing the gala-opening first night.
Meanwhile we rehearse with Jorge.

3 September. I have a morning walk-through of my role (the American Consul, Sharpless) in preparation for the evening Piano Dress Rehearsal. By that time I expect to be wholly in the grip of jet-lag.

Once again John Gunter has done a wonderful job. The set is one large invention – a house, a garden and a hillside, the whole enclosed in a red Japanese lacquer frame. With lighting beautifully designed by Pat Collins, the stage picture is one of enormous beauty, a huge Japanese painting brought to life. The house is on a considerable rake with three slightly different living levels and the usual assortment of sliding doors (shojis) to confuse poor Suzuki. Suzuki has several lovely lines to sing, but not enough to cloud the fact that her main jobs are to spend long periods of time on her knees, serving tea, and to see people in and out of the house through the correct gaps in the walls – thankless tasks.

Ian Judge is the English director of *Butterfly*. We've known one another from several stage-door and back-stage conversations, but this is our first time of working together. Ian's career has revolved largely round the Royal Shakespeare Company, but in the past few years he's been able to indulge his passion for opera. He's a Lancashire lad from Southport, and we cause great confusion by playing the fool in circus acts recalled from Blackpool. We clown our way through pantomimes, lapsing from time to time into the technique of mouthing in the manner of mill workers the juicy bit that lies at the end of a piece of gossip. Les Dawson was, of course, the modern day exponent of this Norman Evans-'Over the garden wall'-humour. 'Did you hear about her up the street – been seen with him at. . . .' It never fails to make people laugh, even here in tinsel town.

During the week a headline caught my eye in the *LA Times*. It said simply: 'Murder plot verdict' but further reading makes the story more interesting. It seems a lady in Houston became overly ambitious for her daughter and, in order to secure her place on the high school cheerleading team, engaged the services of a hit-man to murder the mother of her daughter's nearest rival, thus unbalancing the rival and ruining her chances in the cheerleader stakes. The murderer, I read later, was sentenced to fifteen years in prison. Ever fascinating, America is at other times deeply disturbing. Watching news reports and various lobbying groups representing the National Rifle Association is, for me, one of the upsetting aspects of this society. The debate on the right to bear arms becomes more poignant when, several weeks later, a disturbed man, a 'loner', enters a diner in a small Texas town and murders twenty-two people before taking his own life. The following day the Senate declined a call for the restriction of the use of automatic weapons. For further enlightenment, I can watch on several TV channels the daily grilling of Clarence Thomas. America is washing its dirty linen in public.

Placido has arrived, reasonably fresh from a concert in London, and we spend a couple of hours seeing him through the production.

This is not the normal run of events prior to the première of a new show, but Ian was aware of the situation from day one. Placido, as artistic consultant to the Los Angeles Opera, needs to make an appearance on stage as well as in the boardroom, and this is the only way in which it could be made possible on this occasion. He admits that it is many years since he sang the role of Pinkerton, but with his vast experience I don't think he'll have much trouble. Monday's Dress Rehearsal does, indeed, run smoothly, Placido producing beautiful tone even after so long a flight the previous day.

Madama Butterfly is, in my opinion, a work of genius. It may be my favourite of all operas – and I dare admit this in the middle of √ this Mozart year.

I love the part of Sharpless.

It's a role not greatly beloved of many baritones, mainly because it has no great aria. But, like a number of other baritone roles, such √ as Lescaut in *Manon Lescaut* or Marcello in *La Bohème*, there's an enormous contribution to be made in underpinning the emotional impact of the story.

From Sharpless' first entry, with his rather offhand, ambivalent attitude towards this arranged marriage, we can watch his growing involvement as he realises that Butterfly has rather more substance than her name would suggest. Not for her the 'one-night stand' with Pinkerton that he, like so many of his kind, has assumed. Her marriage to the American means the adoption of a new name, new customs, a new religion. Pinkerton sees none of this. It remains the concern of Sharpless.

Act Two provides the potential for one of the most moving half-hours in all opera. Sharpless reads Pinkerton's letter aloud to Butterfly, with increasing difficulty. She rushes off – and brings back a blond child, the product of her brief union. The music that accompanies this moment is an emotional bolt of lighting. Every time we reach this point I feel that my legs will give way beneath me.

It is easy as an opera singer to become very involved in the emotions of whatever scene is being played. At Covent Garden some years ago, during the performances we gave of *Butterfly*, I watched Anne Mason, who was singing Suzuki, begin to weep at the tragedy unfolding before her. I wasn't surprised. Yoko Watanabe, singing the title role, was remarkably touching and I was affected myself in exactly the same way as Anne. But we had to steel ourselves against these feelings, otherwise the illusion would be lost and we would no longer be able to sing. The lump that one experiences in the throat in real life, if permitted to form on stage, somehow becomes free and infectious and the singer in whose throat it lodges is in danger of being strangled.

Anger is another of the dangerous qualities to interpret. Too much involvement, ranting and raving, and the voice is lost. The facial grimaces and tensions of body that one genuinely feels at such times must be reproduced for the stage, but without including any destructive over-emotional element, otherwise the game is over. Producing the necessary voice to be angry, cold or sexy is largely a question of experience and technique. But, in truth, if I am in the frame of mind which is right for the character and if I am absolutely clear in my head about the intention of the scene, then my voice will come out with all the colours on it proper for that mood.

There are two free days before the First Night. Tuesday, 10

September, is my birthday. Jeannie has packed four or five parcels which I am now allowed to open. I wish she were here to watch me do it. I spend the evening by the sea with friends at Newport Beach, admiring some of the wonderful old yachts that are still sailed in this part of the world. There're few things finer than shining varnished wooden hulls with creamy white sails above, drifting quietly by on a balmy evening.

The première on 12 September is an evening filled, as ever, with tension. We perform for a glossy, silver-and-gold audience whose attention is caught up by our stage efforts. The conductor is the American Randall Behr. He's a dedicated professional musician and I have tremendous admiration for him, his integrity and the way he conducts this difficult score.

The party following this Opening Night of the season is held outdoors in the area between the Dorothy Chandler Pavilion and its sister theatre, the Mark Taper Forum. Naturally, the theme is Japanese and we pass between red arches and over miniature bridges to assigned tables. A big band plays loudly in the manner of big bands, which is something of a shock after the drama and sadness of *Butterfly* minutes before. The mood is good. We appear to have been successful, though I suspect it would be party-time no matter what.

I'm home by midnight and wind down in front of my bedside television, having found *The Entertainer*, with Olivier, Bates and Livesey giving their best. I hope Ian Judge finds this too – he'll be able to mouth the words Lancashire mill-fashion. Before going to sleep I telephone Jeannie with news of the evening and hear from her that she's booked her ticket and will be with me in a week's time.

Two days free now to paint, write and study before the next performance.

We go to the ball game. Most of the *Don Giovanni* cast has now assembled, and the sportive ones plus one or two others – ten of us in all – set off to Dodgers Stadium to watch the local team play the Cincinnati Reds. I am inclined to support Cincinnati as they share the same red and white colours as Sunderland, my football team. There the similarity ends.

I travel the short journey with the American bass, Kevin Langan, who will be singing Leporello. En route he expresses concern that our party's three cars will have difficulty in finding parking together. His fear proves unfounded. There is an immense amount of space for cars, as one would expect in this car-centred town. The stadium is set among the hills that overlook downtown Los Angeles, and were it not for the smog the view would be stunning. I'm struck immediately, walking to the turnstiles, by the people coming to the game. There's a cross-section of society, comprised of all the ethnic groups that make up the population of this multi-racial, multi-lingual town. And nowhere do I experience the segregation of rival groups of fans that is the curse of English – and now European – soccer. The all-seat arena is well lit by enormous banks of white lights. Pre-match activities include raffles and fund-raising events for local chapters of the Red Cross. Orderly lines form for the assortment of foods that are available. Entering into the spirit of the occasion, I opt for the Jumbo Dodger Dog.

The finer points of baseball leave me confused. It's rather like girls' rounders. I'm not yet ready to debate the subject on the terraces, nor do I think it's the nearest thing the Americans have to our cricket, as is often supposed. Twice, I find myself trying to explain cricket's beauty, but such is the cultural and geographical gap that I opt instead to enjoy the game going on in front of me.

What strikes me as an outsider is the infrequency of contact, bat on ball. This season, the Dodgers signed up the skills of the great Darrel Strawberry, for the not inconsiderable sum of eighteen million dollars. Mr Strawberry barely makes contact with the white pill all night. In fact, I'm not sure that he even scored a point, though I may be mistaken there – I did say I hadn't mastered all the subtleties of the game. Sitting somewhat to the side of play, midwicket as it were, I was well pleased to watch the ball travelling at an estimated 90 to 100 miles per hour – a sight that can only be described as awesome.

I harbour a desire to swing a baseball bat one of these days. Then the bubble will be burst. For no longer will I be able to delude myself that within me lies the greatest untapped baseball talent the world has never seen – someone to rival Robert Redford in *The*

Natural. 'The Geordie di Maggio' of North-Eastern baseball – perhaps I'll live contentedly with that idle thought.

Jeannie arrives on a British Airways flight. She's not yet in the best of health and I'm hoping that California sunshine and a restful time here will help her to a full recovery.

Friends – the hosts who have looked after my welfare on the last three visits to Houston – have come to see us. After the *Butterfly* performance on Saturday, we re-group for dinner at a well-known Los Angeles landmark, the Pacific Dining Car, which has for many years operated a twenty-four-hour service of food all-year-round. The attraction for me is to enter the lost world of the American railroad dining-car. I look for the ghosts of Robert Mitchum and Farley Granger. It was once a favourite haunt of Frank Sinatra but I don't see him this evening.

Sunday, 22 September. Jeannie and I elect to explore the San Bernardino mountains, the Mojave desert and Death Valley. It's a hot day and the freeway is bumper to bumper, so we head north on Interstate 15 towards the mountains. In no time at all the landscape has changed. The road takes us through boulder-strewn gorges and passes. This is the America that seems never to alter – Lone Ranger country, where man on horse still takes priority. An enormous plastic Trigger, looking to my eyes like some giant, recently completed Airfix kit, stands rampant at the entrance to the museum built in the form of a huge cavalry fort which is named after Roy Rogers.

Buildings become more and more sparse and the scenery now resembles any take in any Western film. A 'Desert Information Center' provides us with details of some of the animals and plants we are likely to encounter in the miles of desert that lie ahead. Here, we ask the ranger about the habits of coyotes. Returning from a late supper, delayed by the traffic jam that is Sunset Boulevard in the early hours of the morning as people cruise this weird and wonderful thoroughfare, we had seen a wild coyote calmly crossing the road in front of us. He went unnoticed by hundreds of people in search of more exotic game. The ranger told us that such is the water shortage here, that the coyotes come down from the hills to find refreshment in the city. The temperature is in the mid 90s. A fairly flat terrain is broken occasionally by an outcrop of enormous rock. Joshua trees spring up in great groves lending a proper identity to this form of nature. And yet around the next corner we fall upon a small township by the name of Calico. A familiar red neon sign invites me to a welcome glass of beer with hash browns and two eggs sunny side up. We eat Sunday brunch at Peggy Sue's Diner listening to a juke box playing 1950s favourites. Marilyn Monroe stares from a hundred posters. If, theoretically at any rate, Mozart had not the hours in his lifetime to write all the notes he is supposed to have written, how then did Marilyn find time to pose for all the photographs that were taken of her?

Calico has its saloon, its court house, its sheriff's office, its undertaker, its smithy. To these have been added, by a recent entrepreneur, a candy store, a Western photo studio, leather and embroidery shops, to say nothing of popcorn and burger stalls. It's unspoilt despite these additions and the layout gives a good impression of what life must have been like in these tiny outposts a hundred and more years ago.

The audience has clearly enjoyed this evening's performance of *Butterfly*, helped by the surtitles that are commonly used in opera theatres these days. Some of them are showing their appreciation in the manner of sports fans; they are 'hootin' an' a-hollerin'. Somehow, the agony that Pinkerton and I are trying to represent on stage at the sight of the mutilated body of Butterfly has not been fully absorbed by that section of the audience. Is this enthusiastic but noisy reaction the shape of things to come?

Rehearsals for *Don Giovanni* have now begun. Apart from the Australian Donna Elvira, Rachel Getler, and me, it's an entirely American cast. The production in Los Angeles is that of Jonathan Miller and it has already been seen in London and Florence. Dr Miller is not here to oversee the work himself but his ideas are in the hands of his English assistant Karen Stone, whom I know from Covent Garden.

The sets and costumes are by Robert Israel. The street scenes he creates are reminiscent of some early John Piper designs, though painted an unforgiving grey. It will be easy to give an impression of shadow and furtiveness within these alleys and doorways.

The performances are to be conducted by Lawrence Foster, with whom I have worked on several occasions. He hasn't arrived as yet, so for the time being we are in the hands of Randall Behr, conductor of *Butterfly*.

There is no need for me to worry about being bored by yet another beginning of yet another *Giovanni*: this one starts with a difference. After Leporello's usual protestations about his life and work, Giovanni rushes on in his shirt tails, one leg in his pants, one leg out. We are in the realm of *flagrante delicto*. My first task is to negotiate my naked leg into my breeches and then both legs into boots. I recognise the big, red, warning signs – POTENTIAL DISASTER. Singing is one thing, but standing in the wings worrying about getting through the first ten minutes without making a fool of myself is something I could do without. But nothing ventured, nothing gained. I keep an open mind.

Our Donna Elvira is singing the role for the first time and comes to rehearsals with lots of ready-formed ideas. Unfortunately, these do not always match the ready-tried ideas of the Miller production. Time has to be spent on adapting her views, so that we can steer more closely in the direction Karen would like us to follow.

Don Giovanni or *Il dissoluto punito* is described by Mozart and da Ponte as a *dramma giocosa*. In most productions one is dealing with either one or the other, but seldom successfully with both together. To me, the *giocosa* element does not lie in slapstick but (as in all the best comedy) in the funny situation that erupts at the peak of an otherwise dramatic or moving moment. The appearances on the scene of Donna Elvira throughout the opera act as a catalyst for such humour. Giovanni has eavesdropped on the cries of self-pity that come from this shapely, anonymous creature, and is duty-bound to seduce her, only to find she is a past love of several passionate, tempestuous days spent in Burgos. He hopes that

Leporello will be able to crush her desires once and for all with the infamous catalogue of women. Instead, she swears to bring Giovanni to his senses and to her bed, in a pursuit that is a continuous thread through the opera. Her next appearance undermines his seduction of Zerlina and shortly afterwards interrupts what she reads as his seduction of Donna Anna. Each time she appears, her presence adds a new layer to the *giocosa* element of the piece. But she is, behind this humour, always a tragic figure. The singer acting the part of Giovanni can take several cues to produce a raucously comic situation or a deeply tragic, or chillingly dangerous, one. These moments have to be finely judged – a mistake can make a nonsense of the work.

When I'm in America, the only television I always watch is *Cheers*. This half-hour show is based on the lives of individuals who patronise a bar in Boston called 'Cheers'. The characters are wonderfully well drawn, and none more so than the owner (or former owner, depending on when you see the show), Sam Malone, as played by Ted Danson. Here *is* Don Giovanni. The true Lothario, with total, unshatterable confidence in his irresistible power over women. His astonishment at a moment of rejection makes American television worthwhile. If ever I direct *Don Giovanni*, the image of Ted Danson as Sam Malone will be there in the forefront of my mind. That would be one interpretation.

Meanwhile, in a rehearsal room devoid of any atmosphere and in front of the assembled company, I'm expected to conjure from nowhere the extraordinary drawing-power of this man. In the process, I may look rather remote and self-possessed, but this is a necessary part of the preparation and, in my experience, it works. Opera singers rarely concentrate on acting in rehearsal to the same degree as one would in the straight theatre. I'm as guilty as anyone. Yet, on those occasions when I've been aware of not simply 'going through the motions' but instead of reaching far beyond to a plane where I am no longer aware of my surroundings, the result can be shattering.

Three times this year something strange has happened at rehearsal as a direct consequence of this. During Act Two of *Figaro*, after a recitative between Count and Countess, Bernard Haitink didn't bring in the orchestra to begin the subsequent trio. He apologised for having become absorbed in the play. In a Los Angeles *Giovanni* rehearsal, I got Zerlina into my eyeline and caused her to fluster and forget her words. The same thing had happened at the same point in the music with the Zerlina in Köln earlier in the year. I'm convinced that this recitative is written in a way designed to hypnotise the girl. This is an element that is important to Giovanni and that is often missing. He possesses a mystic power that can create disquiet in his intended victim.

I never cease to express my wonder at the genius of the Mozart/ da Ponte collaboration in representing so brilliantly so many qualities of so complex a man. It's October now, and I have almost nothing but Mozart before me until early March. Always a staple of my musical diet, Mozart has left me almost saturated in his bicentennial year. It could have been worse, of course. We might have been celebrating with great chunks of Donizetti or Bellini. Few composers could survive exposure on the scale that Mozart has recently enjoyed.

As earlier in Houston, no one can lay hands on a pair of proper eighteenth-century button-and-buckle shoes with a decent heel, even though we're close to the immense resources of Hollywood. I've made a mental note to bring my own in future.

Nor have costumes been delivered from the last home of this production in Florence. Instead, the outfits I wore in Houston are sent. The Houston production had Giovanni gradually deteriorating to tramp status, but his first costume, to convey the contrast with his final degradation, was of white satin with ostrich-feathered tricorn hat. Understandably, there is some reticence about such a suit of lights in this very different reading of the piece. Robert Israel has to search stockrooms to put together something more fitting.

The last week of rehearsals involves us in a tiring routine at the end of which I invariably find myself asking the question: 'Why do we use up more and more energy and resources the nearer we approach the first night?' One answer is that we are in a sense lighting the fires under a boiler that will heat and produce the steam that will give the force to that first performance.

Monday begins with two two-and-a-half-hour sessions, with the orchestra. These rehearsals we call *Sitzprobe* in that this is the time when we can forget all the movements in the stage book and concentrate wholly on music. It is literally a sitting rehearsal and that is exactly what we do as we sit in chairs awaiting our turns to sing.

As yet the opera company has no permanent orchestra of its own. The services of the Los Angeles Chamber Orchestra are called upon to do the work in the pit. They play very well, having been under the music directorship of several well-known conductors in their time, including Sir Neville Marriner, Gerald Schwarz and, most recently, Iona Brown.

Tuesday, 1 October, is the day of a stagger-through of Act One with piano only. This lasts from 7.30 p.m. to 11 p.m., plus an hour for fencing practice beforehand. By the end we've learned something about Act One and a great deal about fighting with swords on stage.

The struggle between Giovanni and the Commendatore is in the hands of Anthony De Longis, billed in the programme as 'Fight Choreographer'. He has been dragged from rehearsals of a different sort in a film studio. Concurrently with our *Giovanni*, he's training Michelle Pfeiffer in the arts of the bullwhip, which she will be asked to put to good use in the next *Batman* film. Despite all our hints, he thinks Miss Pfeiffer may be too busy elsewhere to join us in our operatic efforts. Anthony is a fine product of the land of opportunity that is America. He acts – that goes almost without saying – but when 'resting' has several other strings to his bow, of which teaching martial arts is the principal one.

For our rehearsals he wears round the head a bandana that gives the clue to his involvement in various disciplines of Oriental origin. I believe he's also a skilled skier and marksman – I gleaned this from what I read on his selection of T-shirts. Clearly he's very skilled not just at fencing but at understanding the requirements of a fight that has to happen within a certain musical framework and that also has to read truthfully.

This stagger-through of Act One turns out to be just that. Much work has yet to be done on the basic moves we have rehearsed.

Everything feels different now that we are on stage and have the set. Even the set is by no means fixed. Some walls don't operate to create new scenes as they did in their previous theatre, and certain modifications will have to be carried out.

I have problems with costumes and props. As originally intended, Giovanni arrives on the scene in some distress, desperately attempting to get into his trousers and make his escape. My first efforts at this are disastrous. The shirt tail catches in the zipper and I can't fasten the hook that keeps me respectable for the rest of the scene.

I proceed to my next trick. Leporello (Kevin) hands me my right boot, liberally doused with talcum powder in order that it should slide easily over my foot and on to my leg. Either my pants are too tight or I'm not as well co-ordinated as I ought to be. I finish in a heap on the floor. Kevin is still optimistically holding out the left boot.

But this is a rehearsal and the second time around I fare better.

During the course of the past two weeks in the rehearsal room there'd been the opportunity for some healthy arguments. We'd spent quite a long time over the supper scene and Jonathan's idea of the controlled, level-headed way in which Giovanni handles the situation. Giovanni welcomes the ghost – it's a ghost in this production, not a stone guest. Nor does the arrival of Donna Elvira fluster him – he calmly sets about peeling an apple. Interesting, I thought to myself. But at the back of my mind I was already hearing the rhythmic pounding that goes through the second half of this scene and that has to contradict this control. That rhythm – relentless, hurtling towards the fateful moment – says more about the end of *Don Giovanni* than the filmic scenario of a man quietly peeling a red apple or holding debate with a ghost.

From those rehearsal room discussions nothing was finally settled, but I vowed to try my hardest to resist my instincts in order to go with the ideas that Karen had suggested to me.

There are times when small things begin to niggle me and then I become very restless. What lights my blue touch paper is to be told categorically that something cannot happen, that something is wrong. I've no doubt that this is a fault on my part.

I have an argument across the pit about the sword I carry on to the set for the scene with the peasants celebrating with Masetto and Zerlina. At the end of a lengthy recitative, the couple have 'their first row', after which Giovanni makes a very pronounced threat to Masetto. Now, I know he doesn't require a sword for that, but if a sword hangs at his waist, then it is the simplest thing in the world just to indicate it and remind Masetto of the danger. In the recitative with Donna Anna Giovanni offers any protection he can from the strength of 'this' hand and 'this' sword – presumably the sword that hangs at his side, and not the one kept in a cupboard at home.

I detest waffle. To be told that the producer chooses not to see it in that way has sometimes lead me in the past to wonder how much more the producer chooses not to see in order to circumvent an awkward corner that suits his interpretation not.

This confrontation leads to lengthy discussion in my dressing room. Karen makes her points on behalf of Jonathan Miller, and Robert Israel, the designer, gives me a lesson in dress codes for the Spanish gentleman of the eighteenth century. I counter that if we were truly observing dress codes then no one was properly attired, as I have yet to see evidence of a gentleman with a hat.

Eventually we all laugh over what has been a small matter.

'What if we make a compromise and I have a swagger cane rather than the sword?' I suggest.

'Would you like that? It's a good idea,' says Robert.

'Have you time to rehearse with it?' asks Karen.

'Yes. No problem,' I say cunningly – hoping I won't live to regret my words.

From this cane-swaggering, foppish Giovanni I'll have the spring-board to charm Zerlina and Donna Anna, and threaten Masetto, Donna Elvira and Leporello. The cane could be a good solution. Danger from the unlikeliest of sources. There's something rather wonderful about the eighteenth century. The manliness of a Don who has the camp mannerisms of a dandy. This Don disguises the potential for terror and unpredictability.

The piano run through of Act Two that follows is a much smoother affair.

Our early evening warm-up for the fight scene has become a well-tried ritual. The few skills I manage to learn as a swordsman are extremely useful. This is just as well since my opponent on this occasion is Louis Lebherz, a large man who doesn't move with the grace of a dancer, and I find myself parrying heavy blows that will only become heavier when the curtain goes up on our première.

Jeannie and I are enjoying our little cottage in Beverly Hills. The owner lives in the adjoining main house. Nancy Herrera Cooke by name, she's led a most interesting life and has a wealth of background in the cultures of South America and India. We awake each morning to the sound of mockingbirds, blue jays, crows and hummingbirds. Hummingbirds feed on the nectar of the pale pink hibiscus flower that grows by our front door. I never cease to marvel at these delicate creatures. How can such a frail little thing survive on these tiny wings? I've watched them on slow motion film, going through an extraordinary series of twists and gyrations to keep their bodies in the air.

Someone has invented a petrol-driven machine that blows away fallen leaves. An army of Mexican 'blowers' scour the wealthier suburbs with such machines strapped to their backs. I imagine wars breaking out as leaves are blown by one operator on to the patch of another.

This is the week of slow build-up, culminating in the opening night. Next is Piano Dress. Even at this late stage, we are interrupting our run-through in an effort to sort out remaining bits of business that require work.

Lawrence Foster won't truly have the reins on proceedings until tomorrow evening when the orchestra join us. I always regard this as rather curious. The conductor has taken a back seat so far, in order that the director has full control. Tomorrow it will be the conductor's turn entirely to control the rehearsal while the stage director sits in the gloom of the theatre biting nails and peeping between fingers, as his precious production slips from his grasp into that of the music department. It sounds counter-productive. Two forces, one representing the stage and theatre, the other music. Time and again, they appear to be at loggerheads. A lot depends on the temperament and personalities of the individuals concerned. Frequently there are mammoth slanging matches as one dinosaur wrestles with the other. Many conductors won't take a back seat at any time.

On this occasion there are no primeval battles. Conservation of energy is now first priority. We have rehearsed here all those weeks to give only five performances. Barely time, as you can imagine, for much of the development that one associates with a long run. I still feel the need to explore further.

The finale of Act One is something of a surprise in this setting. I don't know where he finds the money, but Giovanni's house is full of the rustics he has invited, the three maskers, Anna, Elvira and Ottavio, and an odd assortment of aristocratic hangers-on who seem to be permanent residents. Apart from the peasants, everyone is dressed much better than the Don himself. This is the result of the non-arrival of Giovanni's costumes from Florence. His clothes have been cobbled together from at least two *Figaros* (Houston and LA). In my effort to rationalise this problem, I shall pretend that the Don is making an outrageous statement such as: 'You're welcome to my home for dinner, but I'm eccentric and you'll have to take my fashion statement as you find it.'

Dress rehearsal day is upon us and clearly we are intended to regard this as something akin to a performance. With the First Night just two days away, and bearing in mind the effort required to perform this work, I am tempted to adopt the singer's favourite technique of marking some of the scenes. But the house is packed and we feel morally obliged to give of our best.

In all honesty, I do believe it's healthier to sing out with good voice than to mark improperly. Marking for singers varies. Some adopt an almost totally silent routine. Others adapt the role they are to sing, bringing all the high notes down an octave and the low notes up. It's often hard to recognise very familiar themes. On this occasion I'm feeling strong and opt to give it 'the full poke', as one colleague describes it, though I know full well that nothing will substitute for the adrenalin that will be available to me in two days' time, when it's a real first night.

I'm enjoying myself. The scene with the Commendatore goes so well the fight receives a round of applause.

The Hogarthian figure I now inhabit, complete with walking stick and lace 'kerchief, is a powerful one. He's an obvious pivotal force in the drama. Everything runs extremely smoothly. Too smoothly. There seems nothing left to add for the première, but I know only too well the folly of such a statement.

One slightly disturbing factor through the evening has been the effect of the surtitles. Determined to enjoy themselves, the people in the audience find humour in almost every situation. It's very difficult knowing how to react. Should one wait for the laughter to die? Which may not, of course, coincide with anything humorous being enacted on stage at that moment? Indeed, some of the more desperate and tragic scenes seem to cause hilarity. The solution may well be in the hands of the surtitle operator. If he mistimes a cue, then of course we lose the synchronisation and for a while at least have a potential disaster on our hands. At least we don't have the 'hootin' an' a-hollerin' that accompanied *Butterfly* – yet!

Nancy Herrera has come to *Giovanni* for the first time in several years – the last man she heard in the title role was Ezio Pinza.

Following two quiet days in which I find time to catch up on some painting and correspondence, we get to First Night.

I used to have a rigid routine before performance. Lunch was a steak and potatoes. After that I would go to bed with the radio tuned to *Woman's Hour* on Radio 4, followed by the afternoon play. Halfway through the play I would be fast asleep and two hours later up and about and ready for the theatre. Now I'm taking a different approach. I still have lunch, but no steak. Pasta and vegetables have replaced red meat. No retiring to bed either. In the heat of the California afternoon it seems much pleasanter to sit in the gentle warmth of our guest cottage and become more and more absorbed in painting. In no time at all the hours have been whiled away without giving in to all the awful tensions I generally suffer.

The drive to the Dorothy Chandler Pavilion takes anything from half an hour to an hour. I have to be at the theatre an hour before curtain to go through the fight one last time.

Anthony puts us through a quiet warm-up routine before we try the cuts and parries of the fight proper. It's become second nature now and the hours spent in preparation have been worthwhile. All I hope now is that Louis, the Commendatore, doesn't suddenly lose his head in the heat of the moment, settling all the old debts of British sovereignty with one blow.

There are cards, chocolates and flowers in my dressing room. No matter how I might want to play down the glamour of a first night in an attempt to remain calm and in control, this first sign of celebration would put a stop to any pretence. Time has to be spent opening envelopes, reading cards. At the end of all that the nerves and butterflies I know so well have returned just in time to add their own special qualities to the occasion.

Bill, my dresser, is a marvel. He is telepathic. I think about having a glass of water and one magically appears in my hand.

'Would you like some coffee?' he enquires, just as I was about to ask for some.

Jeannie sits with me until she senses it's time to go. This is something she's always done instinctively. She knows there's a point where she can be of no further support or comfort to me and she leaves quietly to take her seat. I'm grateful for her understanding.

Now I'm on my own with my thoughts.

Giovanni evenings are unlike any others. There are the first chords again. Gloom descends upon me. I prepare my costume to make it appear that the pants have been hastily pulled on. The shirt tail flaps behind me, the side fastening is loose.

In the dark of the wings Donna Anna, the Commendatore, Leporello and Giovanni meet with toi-tois and kisses, the 'Do Well' wishes of the opera theatre. Chari, the stage manager, calls places and the performance is under way.

I needn't have worried, following our successful Dress Rehearsal. This first performance has that expected extra element in it that is the X-factor of most first nights. The fight is clean, neat and successful. Arias go well, ensembles too, and I feel very buoyant. At moments like this I can admit to feeling enormously privileged. Here I am in this theatre, involved with this magical music, asked to play one of the most fascinating characters of world culture. It's not a bad life really, when it goes well.

The final scene has me dragged to hell by six dancers made up to represent some of the many ladies I've wronged in my life. They're grey and haggard. Bloody, too. Straight out of *Macbeth*. Our final tableau presents a sight awful to the eye and my scream as I depart this life for warmer climes meets with generous applause from the audience.

It would be permissible to have a stand-in to do the screaming for me, such is the care we have to take not to damage our throats. But I could never countenance handing over to anyone else the dramatic and terrifying climax of hours of work building up to this moment. The trip back to the dressing room would leave me feeling desperately unfulfilled. Not to scream would be rather like going through the trials of courtship and caring that lead to marriage, arriving at the ceremony, and asking one of the groomsmen to look after the bride that evening, as you had rather worn yourself out. I suppose the sexual analogy is an obvious one for Giovanni.

Performance day once again and I embark on the more or less usual routine, getting up not too early, pottering around with a leisurely breakfast while catching up on world news on television, and painting. I can forget everything when engrossed in the process of trying to define a colour and how to achieve it on my enamel dish. For the moment I've put aside a book I've been reading. Its subject is drawing and the author Ruskin. Ruskin took the line that painting is so difficult it cannot be treated flippantly, and indeed that no-one should just launch himself casually into drawing. To continue reading this heavy warning is not the kind of thing I need at this moment, though at another time I can well understand his point of view.

I arrive at the theatre to the hum of a performance in preparation. Twenty minutes are spent in a rehearsal room where we go through our fencing exercises and remind ourselves of the fight yet again. David needs another twenty minutes to do my simple make-up and to put on my wig. Bill sees that I'm suitably dishevelled to begin the opera – shirt tails to the wind.

There are those few nights when things seem just to come together. The left foot goes where it's supposed to in harmony with the movement of the right arm and the voice sits in the place the notes should be coming from. That may sound untechnical but it means that one's senses, instincts and co-ordinative powers are properly in tune. Tonight appears to be one of those nights. I'm happy. One of the loveliest moments in the opera is the silence – the long silence, longer than in any previous production I've played – before the intimate words that herald the seduction of Zerlina. I look forward to this as a yardstick each evening. It comes after Masetto's aria *'Ho, capito, signor si'*. Giovanni and Zerlina are left on stage alone for the first time. In sizing up the prospect – namely her – Giovanni need do nothing but observe the girl in silence for as long as he dares. For her, it's extremely disquieting, which is exactly the effect he desires. Tonight I dare to go very long with that pause – not for the sake of breaking records but because the Don chooses to spin it out making Zerlina more and more unsettled as he circles her, before pinning her down like some lepidopterist, ready to secure a new specimen to his collection.

The final moments duly arrive and we hear very generous applause from the second-nighters.

We now have one day free. It takes me at least a full day after *Don Giovanni* to restore my resources. Was it always that way, or is the passing of time beginning to have some effect on me?

Just as the first performances were as I described – bliss – with each constituent part of me in some sort of harmonious under-standing, so tonight I am rather less co-ordinated. It may or may not be discernible to the public, but it affects me. My left foot moves forward disjointedly with my left arm. I feel like one of those awkward conscripts who were the bane of many a sergeant major.

Second and subsequent nights are often that way. It's a sort of reaction that sets in after the build-up. Frequently the result is a performance that has 'gone off the boil'.

With two free days, Jeannie – now fully recovered from her white-water adventure – and I make a visit to New Mexico. This means taking a plane to Albuquerque where we collect a hire car for the drive to Santa Fe. Even the airport here is inspired by the adobe buildings that are indigenous to the area. The colours are that beautiful combination of pink terracotta and a very particular shade of turquoise. The landscape is barren: few trees in the desert, and we're at a height of seven thousand feet. The sky is wide across a vast horizon and what cloud there is looks as if it were just dotted in the sky for artistic purposes by Magritte. The cloud certainly doesn't have any rain in it. No wonder the area is so favoured among artists, health freaks, people seeking a better rhythm of life, and, more recently, hot-air balloonists. Festivals here bring together balloons in all the colours of the rainbow and in all shapes and sizes, varying from delivery vans, whisky bottles, and champagne in buckets, to Santa Claus, clowns and dinosaurs.

We opt to drive the extra sixty or seventy miles to Taos to visit the Indian village about which we'd read. I'm glad we did. The American nation is made up of many different tribes. A walk down any street in any American town provides one with shop names that come from Europe, the Far East, the Pacific. But what one sees little of in this vast land is the 'Red Indian' or, to give him his now-preferred and recommended title, the Native American. One tends to hear tales of a rather depressed, lazy people whose menfolk have nothing better to do but get drunk every day. I could also be writing about the Australian aborigine. But they're there, these victims of colonisation, and this short visit gives us the opportunity to see for ourselves at least the nature of the Pueblo Indian at his home in this part of New Mexico. It costs money to enter his village – five dollars per car. One also has to pay to see Portmeirion in North Wales, so one should not think unkindly of this small outlay, which also serves the purpose of allaying any fears one might have had of appearing to be insensitive snoopers. Incomers such as ourselves are an important part of the economy of this tribe.

Adobe buildings have been here in one form or another for nigh on a thousand years. They're a pure form of structure – plain walls daubed with the hardened earth upon which they stand. Originally without doors, entrance was gained to a house by a hole in the flat roof reached by means of a ladder. Doors have now appeared

144

but the ladders are still a feature, leaning against the building, casting incredibly strong shadows against the earth walls. Straw is visible in those walls, part of the primitive formula that holds the structure together.

The day is bright like a crystal.

A mountain, sacred to Indian ritual, stands as backdrop to the Pueblo. Christianity came five centuries ago and a simple Hispanic mission church stands as symbol of that faith. Part of its walls are painted white. As far as I can see it's the only time this colour is used and it has the effect of making the church look like an iced gingerbread biscuit. The old native religions are also still practised here in the Pueblo, but very strict rules prohibit any outsider from being a witness to the ceremonies.

There are some wonderful words of *Parra Wa-Samon*, in Comanche Indian: 'There are things which you have said to me I do not like. They are not sweet like sugar, but bitter like gourds. You said that you wanted to put us upon a reservation, to build us houses and make us medicine lodges. I do not want them. I was born upon the prairie where the wind blows free and there was nothing to break the light of the sun. I was born where there were no enclosures and where everything drew a free breath. I want to die there and not within walls. I know every stream and every wood between the Rio Grande and the Arkansas. I have hunted and lived over that country. I lived like my fathers before me and, like them, I lived happily.'

Taos has become one of those places I stick in my memory with a promise to return whenever possible.

The next performance is a matinée beginning at 1 p.m. There hardly seems time to have breakfast before singing. Indeed, should I bother with breakfast? Or will I run out of energy? I feel indecisive as if I had jet-lag. I opt finally for a true American brunch at an establishment renowned for this. I go from there direct to the theatre. The show is back on an even keel.

After the performance, we happen to get into discussion with some business people unacquainted with the way of life of singers. They think that we're all paid vast sums of money from some rich man's bottomless well, that we travel first class, have wonderful suites in hotels and luxury holiday homes provided free of charge. This is not to mention the liveried servants who wait upon us at home and abroad, see that the bath water is at the right temperature and prepare food which won't interfere with the delicate balance so important to our orchid-like existence. . . .

Time for some home truths.

I have an agent in London who serves several purposes in my life. He acts as a *poste restante,* so people can find out where I am in the world, what I'm doing and when. Theatres, opera companies, orchestras will telephone him to enquire after my services. He informs those people and others of my availability for any particular season. Other agents based in Paris, Vienna, New York, representing my interests in these various countries, will also be in touch with similar enquiries. All agents have to be paid, and usually in the form of various percentages from my earnings.

Let us suppose I am engaged by a German opera house for a new production of *Figaro.* Their management will make an offer of a fee, which my agent and I discuss, and eventually agree upon. This sum then appears in a subsequent contract. The opera house will provide me with funds to get to the first rehearsal and to leave after the last performance. Managements in Europe offer a normal economy fare. In America most theatres also offer economy or coach, but because of the distance involved, particularly to the West Coast of America, I argue for a business class fare – not first class, as I've no wish to cripple the economy of the Arts and I'm not greedy. This is everything I receive by way of payment.

I have to find somewhere to live for what may be a period of two months or more. It should be warm, so that I don't run the risk of colds and ill health. It should be near my work-place. Opera houses have a habit of being in the centre of a city, the area around which everything revolves, and prices tend to reflect this. Consequently a flat or room in such a situation can cost quite a lot of money. I have to provide every meal I eat when I'm away from home. Absolutely all outgoings have to be paid out of the money already negotiated.

Even more strenuous are the demands on some of the women.

The strain on marriages is always very great, as a singer's life is not unlike a politician's. Many of my female colleagues have young families. It does not take much imagination to guess how little is left in their purses at the end of a month in, say, Geneva, with normal living costs doubled or tripled by the added burden of nanny and charges in tow. My admiration for them in pursuing their careers in the circumstances knows no bounds.

There is no singer alive who is not capable of producing something reasonable in the kitchen. Necessity requires it. The business of surviving in a strange city, of finding where to shop, where to eat, which doctor to go to if necessary, are everyday features, before he or she even begins the only part of life for which we are trained – that is, to sing.

Too well-paid? Too high the fees? Never.

One can, of course, point to the highly publicised arena of entertainments at which one or two singers make a block-busting appearance – for a huge sum. Elizabeth Taylor was the *exception* when she received an outlandish fee for her part in *Cleopatra*; yet actors, film stars and singers are often grouped, like cattle, under the mistaken assumption that none of them even leaves home until a contract has reached five or six figures.

I can speak on behalf of most of my colleagues when I say they are singers because of some very strange gift with which they were blessed. Their work is arduous, both physically and mentally – excessively so, in some cases. Whatever success has come their way – be it celebrity status or material gain – is hard won and richly deserved.

Larry Foster announces that he will have to cancel his last two performances because of family ill-health in Europe. This is unfortunate, but we are sympathetic and wish him well on his departure. Randall Behr is now lined up to take over in the pit. He'd conducted rehearsals before Larry arrived and I'm perfectly happy to go on stage without further fuss and preparation. His tempi are faster. During his first performance the fight goes by as though it wasn't there. The 'Champagne Aria', notorious for fast speeds, finds him more relaxed and I'm not as pushed as I expected to be. At the interval Chari informs me that Randall took three minutes less than Larry. It doesn't sound much, but in ninety minutes of music it makes a huge difference.

But we enjoy the show and Randy's professionalism shows once again in his careful preparation for this and in everything else he does.

The following morning there's a message to ring David Hockney. I'm delighted to do so. Though I've never met him, I've seen him around on several occasions, the first time at Covent Garden when he made a brief appearance on stage at the end of a 'Friends of Covent Garden' party at which I sang. I've looked at his work over the years, read his books and remember seeing a very good television film about him. He's long made his home in California.

We join him for lunch at his house in the Hollywood Hills where he's working with the producer John Cox on his designs for *Die Frau Ohne Schatten* for Covent Garden. It's clear that they're having a whale of a time playing with what is, to all intents and purposes, David's train-set. An area at one end of his vast studio is taken up with a scaled-down stage. Perched on the front of this is a small-scale model of the Royal Opera House, identifiable by its gilt proscenium arch and Victoria medallions.

The panel in front of all of this has an array of rheostats that can turn the lighting within these little theatres up or down as required. It means that, a year ahead of schedule, David has designed his sets and can light the entire opera here and film it on video, to demonstrate to management and technical departments how his concept should look from start to finish. This avoids the awful experimental process that goes on into the middle of the night – trying a bit of green here, a bit of pink there – at a point in the life of a production when it is already far advanced. It sounds simple – you might call it visionary – and it's intelligent and forward-looking, making use of materials already available to anyone involved in lighting and design in the theatre.

Lunch is a delightfully simple experience. We sit in his all-purpose primary-coloured living-cum-dining area. It hardly needs saying that there's a pool outside. Cut-out fish dangle beyond the

Three accompanists
With Roger Vignoles after a
recital at La Scala, Milan.

With Graham Johnson at
Roslyn Hill Chapel, nearing the
completion of our Schubert
recording.

With Geoffrey Parsons and
Felicity Lott during rehearsals
for Wolf's 'Italienisches
Liedenbuch' at Harewood
House.

With my agent, Caroline Woodfield, in Tiburon, California.

Working for Jim Henson: I 'guested' in the series *The Ghosts of Fafner Hall*. Here with Fugetta Fafner.

Poring over a Mozart score with Claudio Desderi (Leporello) and Giorgio Strehler, the Italian director at La Scala, Milan.

The threatening profile of Don Giovanni (La Scala, Milan).
Cross-dressing: Jeannie found my Giovanni costumes extraordinarily heavy.

As Don Giovanni: With Richard van Allan (my first Leporello, in Peter Hall's Regency production); with Edita Gruberova as Donna Anna; with Stuart Burrows as Ottavio; and with Elizabeth Gale as Zerlina. Opposite: Final scream: Glyndebourne and Milan.

Decline and fall: A 'Prince Charming' start for the Houston production
of *Don Giovanni*. (Leporello is played by Tim Noble.)
Much seedier in the supper scene.
Police profile: the make-up, the bald pate, the concealing wig.
The true Don revealed (opposite) as he descends to hell.

Another interpretation: the first act finale in the Gunther Rennet
production of *Don Giovanni* in Munich.

window. Suspended from the branches of trees, they are painted in day-glo fluorescent stripes. At night you can imagine you're lying underwater watching the fish go by. Alternatively, we are the occupants of a humanarium, the fish the visitors to the Hollywood zoo.

The time spent with the model theatres means that too little is left to indulge my natural curiosity. I know the studio walls were covered in a variety of paintings; the shelves contained pots of assorted brushes; and compilation photographs were dotted here and there. It's a fascinating work-place and I am intrigued to see David going about the thing he knows and does so well. Whenever I spend time with a person who has enjoyed artistic success in whatever field, I feel rewarded. I am an interpreter. I am absorbed by people who are creators or originators.

Our stay in Los Angeles is now ended. The final performance is full of those little extra moments that creep in when we are aware that we're leaving and wish to put our mark on the work. Risks are taken, musically and dramatically. I've been looked after by Bill, one of the best dressers I've ever encountered. Farewells have the hope built into them that we'll be able to repeat these performances on some future occasion. The easel and personal belongings that I unpacked weeks and weeks ago must now be repacked for our return to England.

As a parting bonus my stepson Rob has arrived in Los Angeles and Jeannie and I are able to see him for a few hours before we set off on the flight home.

Chapter Eight

EUROPE CALLS

I travel North for a BBC film that requires me to recall childhood memories in a place that was once familiar to me and was an important part of my early life. This is a departure from my normal routine that I really enjoy.

There are lots of changes in Seaham Harbour, my home town, where I'll be meeting the BBC film team. Rock House, where I've asked them to film, was known to me as a child through my father. Here he was accompanist for the local male-voice choir and later a glee club of mixed voices. We spent many happy evenings here; I remember watching my first performance of *Hobson's Choice* in the hall. Like all places one revisits after many years, the hall is much smaller than I recall, but it's been beautifully cared for by the local community association and there's clearly a pride in the place. J. B. Priestley wrote about this hall and the community centre in *English Journey*.

I heard many good local singers here in the glee-club concerts my father ran, and, before that, in the male-voice choir. There were men such as Bob Blackwell and Jack Foggin, but the best of them all was a tenor. By name, Jack Wick, he, like my father, had only one leg, as a result of injuries from the First World War. I think he saw himself as a bit above singing in such groups, and he was undoubtedly right, though he deigned to sing in our church choir at Dawdon. His voice was as sweet as that of Stuart Burrowes and he'd have enjoyed just as much of a reputation, at least on the concert platform, in different circumstances and at a different time.

I wander round the area that was Dawdon Colliery. The two huge towers of the winding gear still stand but everywhere else teams of men are employed in taking apart what has stood there all this century. Sparks and flashes from oxy-acetylene burners are a clue to the steady dismantling. The coal industry has finished here. Two other pits combined their resources briefly, but the oldest of those, the 'Nack', has closed, and now for a short time only 'Vane Tempest' remains. Huge flattened areas will then be made free for reclamation. It will be pleasanter to look upon green meadows than upon the black mountains that are the result of man's labour to produce the nation's fuel. But I wonder what will become of the community that has known only coal for over a hundred years. It's a sobering thought and only time will tell.

1 *November*. I'm now in Munich for *La Bohème*. Normally Munich to me has meant *Don Giovanni* or *Figaro*. But it's been some years since I sang Marcello and I'm happy to have this opportunity.

It is often assumed that baritones are the wallflowers of opera. But I love playing these parts. The challenge is to depict them as fully fledged characters who are as important to the plot as some of the flashier roles. Marcello, in *Bohème*, provides support; he's the stalwart painter at the centre of everyone else's drama; he's the constant. Sharpless, in *Butterfly*, is a kind of moral baton, finally berating Pinkerton for his less-than-commendable behaviour. In my opinion they're both seriously undervalued. The exception is perhaps poor Albert in *Werther*, a chartered accountant if ever there was one. Eugene Onegin is gloomy, made so by the nature of the life he leads, uninterested in anything that confronts him until, too late, he realises the quality of the woman who, as a young girl, expressed her love for him. Then he explodes with a passion that is shattering in its power and made worse by its fruitlessness. Billy Budd, too, not a saintly figure, but a man, is flesh and blood, with the fatal flaw of a stammer. He is a light among his fellow crew members; it is his strength and integrity which cause his downfall.

These are among the baritone-voiced characters who people the operatic stage and bring to it colour and excitement – but then that's easy for me to say.

*

The complications of *Bohème* are many. It's all too easy to regard such a hackneyed old piece as something that any company can throw on at the drop of a hat. The truth is that the stage business required of Act Two alone – which lasts no more than twenty minutes – can well benefit from the attention of long hours of rehearsal over several weeks. I have known productions – John Copley's at Covent Garden, for instance – where each member of the chorus had a well-defined character to play in that short act. Each child and chorus member contributed to the picture of Parisian pre-Christmas bustle, at the centre of which the Bohemians operate. Done well, it's brilliant. Done badly, it can lead, if not to disaster, then to an evening of considerable dissatisfaction where there should be only warm pleasure.

Here Act Two proceeds relatively successfully but in the close confines of the garret of Act Four there hasn't been time for us fully to grasp the requirements of the set. The only thing that will help us avoid the most awful of entanglements is our collective knowledge and experience of the piece.

To remind anyone who may have forgotten: the youthful euphoria of love has waned. Rodolfo and Mimi have been apart some time, and her health has deteriorated alarmingly. Marcello's hysterical lover Musetta bursts into the garret to announce that Mimi has collapsed on the stairs. Mimi is brought in and everyone notices her sad decline. She is helped to the bed. . . . On this occasion, it is as though someone has tipped the garret on its end and the six characters are huddled into one corner, Mimi bed-ridden at the centre. Schaunard, the musician, then announces to all of Paris in no uncertain terms that the lovely young tuberculoid, not a metre from where he stands, has but thirty minutes left her. A little forethought, and he could have taken anyone but Rodolfo aside and quietly passed on this information.

Wickedly, I indulge myself in a fleeting scene which passes quickly through my mind. I tell Mimi that she misheard Schaunard: 'No, dear, he didn't say you'll be *dead* – just that you look nice on the *bed*.' And I tell Rodolfo: 'Of course she's going to be all right – what do musicians know anyway? It's just that pale new make-up she's wearing.'

4 November. Paris. I'm staying near Les Halles, a wonderfully cosmopolitan area. Richard Rodgers' Pompidou Centre is round the corner, Notre Dame across the way, and the concert takes place in the Forum des Halles, a relatively new complex close to the Châtelet Theatre.

Roger Vignoles and I are to give a song recital. The programme is a mixed one of Italian songs, Schubert, Wolf and several settings of American and English songs. Roger has flown in on the morning of the recital, having played in London the night before. The audience is warm and friendly. I recognise some faces that always seem to turn up whenever I appear in France. It has been a short visit but rather a useful one in that it encourages me to want to come back to this city to which I had an allergy at one time in my life. We have sung some songs and laid some ghosts.

Home to London briefly. A rehearsal with Roger at my house in preparation for our next three projects. Over the next nine days I have three more recitals as well as a repeat of *Bohème* in Munich. To make life more difficult, each of the recital programmes is different.

The first is a recording in Berlin of two half-hour programmes for the station *Sender Freies Berlin* – the same studio in which I recorded Berlioz earlier in the year. It's always interesting to return to this strange place. I'm continually astonished to look at the map and note how far to the east Berlin lies. I search for signs of change. I don't have to look far. The wall that was so solid and permanent has gone, as if by magic, and with it have arrived the problems that these two Germanys now face. I wonder, as does everyone else, whether they can meld, or whether they will be as politically immiscible as oil and water after so much time living under such different doctrines.

One thing hasn't changed. The studio of *Sender Freies Berlin* is the same 1920s building it always was, protected as a national monument. SFB served a very important purpose in those Cold War years. It broadcast its Free Berlin programmes for the benefit of all and received rich backing to ensure that the voice of freedom was always heard over the wall. Now there is no longer any need for the voice and the finance has dried up. It looks as though our song programmes will be among the last to be recorded in these historic studios.

Roger and I finish in Berlin and catch an afternoon plane to London. It's important to try to spend a night at home. The following day Jeannie and I set off by car for Roger's home, where we have our final complete run-through of *Winterreise*. We're performing it together for the first time at Harewood House on the following evening.

In September 1990 Roger and I recorded this great Schubert song cycle but I'd never elected to perform it in public. This was to be the occasion. For the past year the songs have been always by my side. There have been weeks when I didn't look at them, but I always felt that a moment might arise when I'd need to delve, and so they were always there. The twenty-four songs have become stronger and stronger visual images, and my feelings about what I wanted to do with them have become more and more crystallised. At this stage in my life I now feel ready for *Winterreise*.

There's a very strange phenomenon with which I have to live: the moment any performance is complete it is already of the past. I know that whatever preparation I've made for this 'Winter Journey' and its twenty-four songs is valid only until the evening of 15 November. After that, the journey goes on. The next interpretation will be different for a variety of small reasons of which I know nothing at present. Then that one will be gone, and so on, until I stop singing, I suppose.

Winterreise is harrowing, enlightening, perceptive. It's a work of such greatness that, like a Mozart opera, it can never pall. It's there in my being, now, and everything that happens to me will have a bearing on how I perform it next time.

Harewood is a homely stately home. George and Patricia Harewood work hard to keep it that way. We couldn't have chosen a better time to be performing this particular programme. On this mid-November morning Yorkshire has a rime over it and the sun blazes down on a diamond-clear day with no warmth in it whatsoever.

The room in which we give the concert has been newly decorated and restored to its original designs. The wall to my right is hung with an extraordinary display of Italian Old Masters. Longhi rubs shoulders with Bellini, with Titian, Veronese and the Spaniard El Greco. Roger and I both agree that not since a recital we gave amidst the Turner Collection of the Clore Gallery have we felt so challenged.

Such days as these seem to pass five times as slowly as others. The afternoon drags on until the final forty-five minutes I allow myself for dressing. The occasion makes me meticulous. So many songs, so many words. The moods to be found. Do I know where I am when the journey starts, where I'm going, and where I shall be when it ends? I may as well stop nagging myself with these questions as the only way to deal with them is to present what I have prepared and to trust that it will hit its mark.

In the splendour of one of the Harewood ante-rooms I have a long sip of water before stepping out.

The first word of the first song has to tell what I'm about. '*Fremd.*' I am a stranger.

Like a painter, I've selected a colour for this and I hope the others will follow on its spectrum.

Seventy-five minutes later I've met the hurdy-gurdy man.

The evening is over. I can remember little of it. My legs – around the knees – have gone through a series of feelings of tension and numbness. Now they just ache. (At least, on the opera stage, I'd have had some exercise.) But the anxiety and hard work are worth it.

This piece is an opera. It's a complete setting of winter, with the cold and harshness one associates with that season. But interspersed are dreams and memories of times past, of warmer seasons, when life was happier and a young woman loved a young man. Then, winter came. The darkness in the house that night is all enveloping and thick.

In the morning a mist covers the parkland and the frost lies once again on the grass. The house has a perfect setting – in its park and in Yorkshire. It wouldn't look right in Berkshire or Sussex. Before leaving, we spend a couple of hours with Patricia looking at the bird collection in which she takes so much interest. She's reminded of her Australian roots each morning in the most attractive way. The kookaburras are installed in a cage nearest the house, and there they sit on this cold November morning – apparently as at home as they would be on the other side of the world.

In the back of my mind is the thought that the long year will soon be coming to an end. I knew, because of forward planning, that Harewood House would lead to Birmingham, and then home. The thought of my own surroundings fills me with pleasure – partly because they are still familiar to me. Any longer on the road and possessions would begin to be strangers.

21 November. There are changes to the programme for Birmingham. This time we open with Schubert songs about the sea and fisherfolk, moving then to a large group of songs by Hugo Wolf. That completes the first half of the programme; the second half consists of the six *Shropshire Lad* songs by George Butterworth, Billy Budd's soliloquy and folk-song settings by Britten and others.

We weren't prepared for the joy awaiting us in Birmingham. For years, artists have returned to these shores complaining of not having a concert hall of the likes of New York, Madrid, Vienna, Berlin or Munich. It would appear we now have one. There, in the middle of the tangled web that is Birmingham, great things have been achieved. Due largely to the loyalty Simon Rattle has shown towards the city's Symphony Orchestra and to the international success they enjoy, Birmingham has looked at itself, dusted itself off and, with astonishing will, produced the money to provide a conference centre and world-class concert hall. Being there is rather like controlling the Starship Enterprise or awaiting the arrival of an Encounter of the Third Kind. Space-age technology means that a singer can produce the quietest of tones for a capacity audience of over 2,000, and still be heard, and can also delight in the clean beauty of the lines of this ultra-modern hall.

We have a most enjoyable evening and one to make us feel proud that Britain has managed to produce such a world-class facility.

Home afterwards to my house, and home, too, to Covent

Garden where I am to begin rehearsals for *Figaro*, followed by a
new production of *Don Giovanni*.

Chapter Nine

YEAR'S END AT COVENT GARDEN

25 November. This *Figaro* is already four years old. The production is that of Johannes Schaaf who has come back to see to its revival – now with several changes of cast. He will also be directing the new *Don Giovanni* as well as the revival of his *Così fan tutte*. The scheduling of rehearsals for these three mammoth works should keep a band of computers happy for several minutes.

It's strange to come back to an old production. The set has been brought out of store, from wherever it has been kept under wraps, and is rather the worse for wear. Much depends on the smooth working of bolts, locks and doors in *Figaro*; someone will have his work cut out before the set reaches the stage. Though we have three weeks' planned rehearsal, what with the cast changes and the slow, meticulous way in which Schaaf works, we'll not have much spare time.

Sadly our Susanna, Marie McLaughlin, is indisposed in the first week. Her understudy is given the awesome task of filling in for her, but the mad Scottish spirit of Marie isn't there and we miss this. Felicity Lott (Flott as she is universally known) is the Countess. Though she has sung the role many times before, this is her first appearance in this production.

For the first few days the going is very laborious. Schaaf is bogged down in a process that can best be described as Mediterraneanising the Countess. I suspect he hasn't dealt with someone of the coolness and smoothness of Flott, and he'd rather like to see her spill some blood in uncovering the nature and temperament of the lady he's looking for. Is Schaaf also preoccupied with the enormity of his own task over the next two months? It will be difficult for him to devote sufficient time to the two revival productions, *Così* and *Figaro*, when, from the discussions we have together, it's apparent that his mind is very deeply occupied with the staging of a new *Don Giovanni* over five weeks of rehearsal.

In most productions of operas with recitatives, one is constantly urged to get a move-on. It's not unheard of for a singer to risk a glance towards the pit only to receive an impatient gesture from a Maestro anxious to get on to the next section that involves him with his orchestra. At such moments artistic truth has to take a distant back seat. This *Figaro* is exceptional in giving time to dwell on the recits. The rehearsal process is none the less tedious. Words and timing that were so interesting first time around now appear to have no natural flow.

There is a lack of enthusiasm that is almost tangible. Schaaf is dwelling on the finest details without letting a single moment pass. The cast is doing its best to recall the details of a very difficult *Figaro*. The time spent now, in repeating over and over again tiny moments of the first scenes of Act One, will cause a log-jam in the planning of rehearsal time for the other three acts in the following two weeks.

Mozart's *Mitridate*, written when he was just fourteen, is receiving a new production at the same time. I fill in a spare half-hour with a peek at the Dress Rehearsal. The massive scarlet set is impressive, the initial stage-picture stunning in a way that one associates with that wonderful cleanness of image and design that comes from the Orient. At the centre of the stage, dominated by scarlet walls, burns a small flame. Perched behind that, a beautiful, red-tailed eagle. This, for me, is the ultimate scene-stealer. I would never object to being upstaged by such a magnificent creature. It sits attentively at the centre of things, a creature with innate dignity. I'm reminded of T. H. White's book *The Goshawk*, and of the vigil a man must undertake to enjoy even the most meagre working relationship with these birds.

We progress from rehearsal room to stage and piano rehearsals. Jeffrey Tate is conducting, his first *Figaro* at Covent Garden. Now our days are spent largely on stage, but partly in the chorus room where we work solely on the music and refine the various dynamic requirements of ensembles and arias. Twenty years ago there was a fashion for heavy decoration of the repeats of arias and for the liberal use of *appoggiatura*. Some still follow this trend, but in our case excess has been abandoned in favour of a more selective approach.

Schaaf's assistant, a fellow German, is known to us all as Harvey. His name is Hans-Werner, and in German the two initial letters of his names when spoken in quick succession sound like 'Harvey'. The two men are gradually developing a double act. Harvey's job is to remind Johannes of what he originally produced. Occasionally he will also remind him of how much time he's losing, but he dares to do this only on rare occasions.

These occasions, however, are becoming more frequent. We've few days left now before the Dress Rehearsal, and certain sections of the opera have not been touched.

I've developed a cold.

My voice disappears into regions of me that have never been so nether. There is simply no chance of my attending further rehearsals until it has cleared. It would do me no good and none of my collegues would thank me for spreading my infection. I use my days at home to catch up on some painting. I've decided I'll give each of our children a picture for Christmas. Stephen's is already completed. He gets the allotments and council houses in Seaham. Francie, my stepdaughter, fell in love in Zimbabwe and her picture is of the railway station at Victoria Falls. Rob's painting is the one that needs work; and follows several miles after the style of Edward Hopper – a café diner in Houston, Texas. Since Rob was at university in Dallas, this subject seems appropriate.

Painting at the top of my house occupies me for hours. Finding the right textures and tones is wholly absorbing. It annoys me that I have to suffer an awful cold before I'm able to enjoy this pleasant pursuit. Why do I call it 'a pleasant pursuit' when I know it's become a hugely important part of me?

After five days, the awful symptoms disappear. A newspaper report shows the country laid low by Beijing flu. Is that a sign of the times? Decades ago we knew of the more generalised Asian flu. Now, with the slackening of restrictions, we've tracked the virus down to Beijing. Perhaps the next epidemic will have a street and house number.

Johannes is happy to have me back, in good health once more. He probably suspects I needed time away to recharge my batteries. We have a roguish way of regarding one another.

Producers understandably become irritated when a cast member causes problems. My approach is to get on with it and catch up on my work as quickly as possible. Johannes would like us to set up camp beds and keep ourselves on stand-by twenty-four hours a day. That way he wouldn't need to bother with the details of a work-schedule. He's already running from one rehearsal to another.

Johannes has many depths. He can say things which take me by surprise. We'd been discussing a feeling, a sense of abandonment, in *Figaro*, when he related an experience from his own life when he'd been on a trek through a jungle in Indonesia. The party consisted of himself and a guide. They lived on whatever the guide could trap, kill or lure. In such circumstances, the sense of dependence on another person becomes overwhelming. None of the skills one has learnt for life is sufficiently refined to provide for this moment. Listening to him, I began to wonder what exactly Schaaf's story is. I've no idea how old he is – how can you estimate the age of a giant troll? He could be sixty, or he might be fifty. There is no shortage of energy and stamina, which is just as well given his workload. But the impression is of someone restlessly inquisitive, someone who's gone to all kinds of faraway places to experience a variety of wonderful happenings. It makes it interesting to be in his company. He can be infuriating, but always returns to a belly-laugh that comes from something in his great spirit.

He is something of a raconteur, and gregarious by nature; he seems to me to glow when in the presence of ladies even more than at other times.

161

II

I hate the tiny cells that are the new dressing rooms at the Opera House.

The door opens on to a narrow little corridor which barely allows the passage of a flowing robe. To the left or right will be a toilet and shower room and beyond a small square space provided with a little dressing table, an upright piano and a comfy chair. This is one of the few places in the world where I seem to suffer from a mild form of claustrophobia. My routine is to put on the basic essentials of the costume and then fling aside the doors to let in some air, or even finish dressing in the corridor. God alone knows how an inmate of one of H.M.'s sanctuaries must feel, 'banged up' twenty-three hours a day.

When I began life at Covent Garden twenty years ago, we used the original dressing rooms much nearer the stage and shared them with the ballet company. Now those rooms are used exclusively by the ballet and we are privileged to have these new-block monstrosities. They have all the charm of a hastily erected American hotel-chain and none of the atmosphere of theatre tradition of the old ones. Perhaps I'm talking about the lack of years and years of accumulated grime. Much has been said and written about the squalor backstage at the Opera House, and indeed it is considerable. But this holiday hotel has not been the answer to anyone's dreams.

The costumes are laid out for me. Familiar pyjamas of Act One, hunting outfit of Act Two, formal 'scrambled-egg' of Acts Three and Four. The pyjamas amuse us all as much as they did when they first appeared. They're enhanced by the use of a dressing gown of beautiful blue silk which adds to the picture of a man who has just risen and at the sight of Susanna on this, her wedding morning, is about to rise again.

Flott and I reminisce. We remember the Munich *Figaro* with the tiny Susanna. Now we have Marie as Susanna who, with much less 'theatrical' excuse, could be mistaken for her mistress in the dark.

Nostalgia is a popular indulgence in this theatre. The place is full of folk who are as successful at telling anecdotes as they are at singing. Flott and I are busy creating legends out of the Munich experience, not a year after the original event.

Bob Tear as Basilio wears a wig that is an extension of his own Benedictine tonsure. But it's much seedier and, combined with black cassock covered in stains of unmentionable variety, presents a character the Count could well afford to do without in this household. He looks like the accumulated left-overs of a long-burning candle.

Lucio Gallo as Figaro has rehearsed throughout in his glasses. Johannes likes the rather studious and vulnerable appearance this gives him, and Lucio has agreed to sing the role bespectacled. By so doing he will no doubt provide new material for critics to ponder over in their columns.

I'm happy back on the stage of the Opera House. In a few days we shall enter 1992 and the twentieth-anniversary year of my debut here as Donald in *Billy Budd*. Donald is one of the crew of *HMS Indomitable* to which Billy is impressed. As well as learning Donald, I was asked to understudy Peter Glossop as Billy Budd himself. Once again the brain seemed to have little problem in compartmentalising the music for the two men and keeping them separate. I'd prepared both roles on my own at home, sitting at the piano with Donald in the morning, and, by way of a change, with Billy in the afternoon.

But these days I'm like many other singers and often resort to the tape recorder to help me commit new music to memory. I find it enormously helpful, and of course something I can do when travelling or sitting quietly in an apartment. As a respite from study I switch to orchestral music, and for a real change take great pleasure in listening to singing of a very different type – Nat King Cole, Ella Fitzgerald, Billie Holliday, Sinatra and, my favourite, Barbra Streisand.

I well remember my first stage rehearsal and the joy of seeing the House lit from the stage. It was difficult to restrain a tear at the beauty of that first sight. The cream and gilt, the dark plush of the upholstery and, most of all, the shades over the candles that illuminate and warm the various levels of the theatre. It's something that I appreciate more after an absence. Each time I return I am slightly changed. Along the road new lessons have been learnt and, I hope, further refinements made. I feel I might disappoint those in the House who know me best if I had failed to move on a step or two every time they saw me.

Living in London, with the deep wealth of an English heritage, is both a blessing and a curse. Development in the interest of future generations is hindered because of the close proximity of listed and conserved buildings. Consequently, space is restricted and further growth to the Opera House stage is virtually impossible. Not for the Garden the luxury of a Salzburg or a Metropolitan with sports-field-sized storage facilities. Repertoire has to be planned years in advance, not only with a view to which singer or dancer is available but bearing in mind the logistics of whether sufficient space is available to store *Nutcracker* alongside *Boccanegra*, *Figaro* with *Giselle*.

At the prompt corner a panel that would be the joy of any model railway enthusiast is the point from which each ballet and opera is controlled and artists' calls are made. To the side of that is a prop room in which can be found the smaller items that constitute the minutiae of any show. At times it serves also as a room for quick costume change. Behind that are smaller docks where lighting gels and various other odds and ends are kept handy.

There's a small memorial in the form of a photograph and plaque to the stagehand Greg Bellamy, who was killed in an accident on this spot on 31 March, 1989.

At the back of the stage, the elements of the scenes of the current production share space with several others: a huge mill wheel for *Fanciulla del West*, the giant Christmas tree for *Nutcracker*, the massive head of an *Aida* sphinx.

Above all this is a forest of battens, cables and lights interspersed with painted cloths. These are housed in the fly-tower that is a feature of any theatre. It's alarming to lie face-up on stage and look up at this great mass of machinery. It's not for the faint-hearted or those of an over-active imagination.

Below the stage is the conglomeration of stage engines that allow the various bridges to rise and fall, so giving the different levels that can be available to make up a stage picture.

In the old passages and staircases of the 'OP' side of the stage are the old wardrobes and the long-established armory – a small Tower of London with equipment sufficient to supply a small army. Huge dock doors on this side open on to the airy spaces of the still elegant Floral Hall, an immature Crystal Palace, used now for the storage of stage sets and equipment.

It's a fascinating place, this theatre.

I love its elegant pillared exterior and the womb-like warmth of its interior. The stage crews are men I've known all the years I've worked here. They have their favourites and their less-than-favourites. Some are ballet men, some opera; for others it is a job like any other. But the majority have a feeling that is rooted deep in the history of the house. That's a comforting thought and not at all over-romantic.

Reg Suter, a big man with many years' service, runs the stage crew with a quiet authority, but mention the name Verdi and Reg will launch into an encyclopaedic lecture on the merits of this his favourite composer. So involved is Reg with his subject he formed a society some years ago, calling it 'Amici di Verdi' in further tribute to his favourite music. Concerts, lectures and visits he organises with passionate zeal.

16 December. Dress rehearsal day, two days before our First Night.

Traditionally we begin at 10.30 a.m. It's not always easy to produce a beautiful *legato* line – or any other, for that matter – at this time of day. Everyone feels the same. The saving grace is that the duty house manager normally makes a front-of-curtain announcement that this is not a performance but a dress rehearsal, and that some of the artists may choose to mark their parts.

'Are you singing out this morning?' comes the question. 'I'll see how it feels. I'm not really feeling too wonderful,' is the standard reply. But invariably, after the clearance of overnight frogs and gremlins, a better feeling is achieved and before long everyone is in full voice. It's not easy to resist. Singing is a heady experience. Marking is not really in anyone's interest, provided there's sufficient time to rest and recover between dress rehearsal and first night. Clearly on this occasion we're blessed with a cast of healthy artists. No-one feels the need to cosset and harbour their talent and in no time at all a full-blown performance is under way.

But it's not really a performance. It lacks danger, that special quality that comes of the build-up to seven o'clock and the paying audience. It lacks good-luck-sending, champagne, flowers, cards. The pressure is not the same.

In a recording studio a little red light flashes. Prior to that moment, the free-and-easy spirit of music-making is all-pervading. When that light goes on, something is lost. The next note uttered or played or struck is for posterity, and a little voice has said: 'Back off, go for a slightly easier option. Play safe, be correct.' By then it's already too late and that extra element of live performance with its built-in risk has vanished. There are few exceptions to this experience.

Act One is a warming-up time for me as Count. The first trio is a good stretching exercise for the voice and determines from the start whether the voice is sitting in the right place for the rest of *Figaro*. Ideally, I like to feel the voice being slightly heavier than normal at this point. It's good for me to know that I can put more weight than I normally would on the whole octave and a half below what we know as Middle C. If that is in order, then, in my experience, my voice is well set up for the long evening ahead.

Act Two is a series of slanging matches, with my wife, with Figaro, with Susanna, with the gardener. It finishes, of course, with the Count in full flight in anticipation of the court hearing of

Act Three that will see justice done and Figaro married to Marcellina. The entire act is a masterpiece of construction. The Countess makes her first appearance and is clearly an unhappy lady. Her husband, who wooed so boyishly and genuinely in *The Barber of Seville*, now overlooks her. She expresses her feelings to Susanna, who suggests a plot devised by Figaro, who for his purpose will require the services of the young nobleman Cherubino. The Count arrives abruptly to find his wife's bed-chamber locked against him for no obvious reason. Once she has opened the door he stalks her room, dangerously suspicious – and hugely hypocritical. The chauvinist subjects his 'almost guilty' wife to rigorous cross-examination. Excuse follows excuse as each probing question is parried in the nick of time. The excitement builds from scenes involving one singer, then two, then three, four, five, with the act ending in utter turmoil.

Johannes' production shows the Countess at the end of her tether. Among the powders, smelling salts and perfumes on her dressing table there is a half-drunk bottle of wine – one suspects several 'empties' may lie hidden under her bed.

The Count has just returned from hunting on his estates. If all that one reads of hunting is true, then his blood is certainly on the boil and he's in a very dangerous mood. This is the time when singing becomes dangerous. It would be easy to be carried away and to represent that mood on the stage simply by being angry. What is difficult is to learn from the process of being genuinely angry and then to make that into a technical exercise. That way one finishes the act with one's tonsils and vocal cords still in their proper places and not spread liberally around the stage.

Act Three is another gem of musical creation. The duet for Susanna and the Count with which it begins is one of the loveliest Mozart wrote. (Like *'La ci darem la mano'*, the duet for Don Giovanni and Zerlina, the straightforward clean beauty of the lines cloaks an undercurrent of enormous eroticism.) Marie and I play cat-and-mouse games. She leads me 'a merry dance'. It's a wonderful small scene to play, and (like the Giovanni duet) the better for being played with simplicity. Once it becomes too explicit, I always feel the game is lost.

The scene leads quickly on to the Count's aria. There is always a reason for the placing of an aria in a work. In this case the Count, having been led by the nose by Susanna a moment before, then overhears her plotting with Figaro. He realises immediately the trap into which he is walking. Mozart therefore wrote this aria in three sections, the first being the Count's initial reaction to what he's just heard and the question-and-answer session that this causes in him. Having drawn the conclusion that Figaro cannot win his game, he moves on to a more structured central section in which his own jealousies are made known, namely that a mere servant can have knowledge of the woman he loves. He rues the day he gave away the *droit de seigneur*. Finding this situation intolerable, he goes into orbit with the third section of the aria. Now he's boiling.

When I reach this point it's as though I'm being supported by huge bubbles, I'm floating over the surface, feet off the ground, I'm transcendent. This is to be the Count's triumph. The exit from the stage is one of supreme confidence in his victory. He enters the room in which the hearing is being held, certain in the knowledge that Figaro will be defeated and forced to marry Marcellina, leaving Susanna free and the relationship of master to servant fully restored.

The rest is history, of course, the thump of the Count's fall resounding over two hundred years of artistic endeavour. We can only guess at the colossal impact of that moment when the play, and then the opera, were first presented at a time when the feudalism of the *ancien régime* still held, but dark clouds were on the horizon.

The rest of the morning falls easily into place, as is often the case after Act Three. The rehearsal is followed by a notes session, which we attend out of a sense of duty. But the truth is that after expending that amount of energy in the course of a dress rehearsal we're generally too distracted to absorb any of the information that is being offered.

17 December. The day between dress reheareal and first night is normally sacrosanct, but on this occasion I'm involved in a charity concert to be given at the Guards Chapel near Buckingham Palace. Though the First Night is very much on my mind I'd agreed to this evening months before and it would be unprofessional to cry off now. In any case it serves to keep the voice 'warmed' for the following evening, and as my contribution is one short Christmas song by Michael Head, I'm hardly likely to exhaust myself.

First Night. 18 December. Today is one of those lovely, invigorating December days. The morning is spent at the piano going through a few songs of Hugo Wolf that will be part of a recital series in the coming season. They serve as a guide to today's vocal health. Satisfied that there is a voice there for the evening performance and that I won't have to make that awful telephone call that means cancellation, I can enjoy the rest of today's routine.

Yesterday's short concert went successfully – the little song not putting me under any strain other than looking out at a sea of hundreds of faces. I expect they were wondering what I was going to offer; but I felt convinced that they wanted to see me fall flat on my face – at least musically. Where does all that paranoia come from? I ask myself. And where could my voice disappear to overnight?

Figaro tonight will be fine, I keep on reminding myself, as I go for a walk in the warm December sunshine. A long-time addict of Radio Four, the Home Service as I still prefer to think of it, I listen to the radio in the house almost incessantly. That and cooking lunch seem to go well together. Pasta as usual today. Starch for the energy it will give me for the four hours of *Figaro*.

Though not new, this *Figaro*, now enjoying its second revival, is still a first night. A buzz of anticipation around the theatre when I arrive an hour before curtain. Nevertheless, the atmosphere remains fairly relaxed among my colleagues. Bob Tear and I exchange a few pleasantries before suggesting we'd both prefer to be elsewhere. On cue, we deliver what is required of us. The voice seems to be sitting in the right place with plenty of the weight it needs for this role.

Johannes' last note to me, '*Don't say anything until you need to,*' makes sense. Of course it applies to the recits since the 'numbers' have music attached to give us our moment to speak. Having performed in *Figaro* so often, I'm in danger of replying with a kind of Pavlovian response to any given cue. Johannes is right. The piece must be freshly invented each evening. But it's not enough to leave gaps simply for the sake of doing so. If the intention of the artists is right then the pauses and breaks in the dialogue will have a natural organic feel to them and not the machine-gun ratatat-tat effect beloved of so many producers. The recitatives then will not be criticised as too slow, because they will have an intrinsic truth.

Lucio is enjoying a very successful debut as Figaro, aided by the 'knowingest' of Susannas in Marie. Flott presents no southern fury of a Rosina. As one who has so often interpreted the Marschallin, she gives a Countess reminiscent of that particular Straussian lady. Flott has style, and it's interesting to watch her find her way into Johannes' rather unconventional reading. There can't be many other productions in which she's required to take to her bed with migraine and succumb to the temptation of a good bottle of champagne.

The Act Two finale whizzes through with Jeffrey taking some hair-raising tempi, leaving us breathless at the interval.

The Act Three duet for Susanna and the Count is one of Mozart's loveliest inventions. 'Why do you tease me and lead me on?' he asks her. And slowly but surely she appears to become entrapped in his net. Nothing too overstated, but the underlying sexual tension is there for everyone to feel and hear. With Marie it's never the same thing twice – in fact we deliberately try to alter the emphasis of each point each time. With this freedom to explore new ideas, we'll be lucky not to rate an X Certificate by the time we get to the last performance.

My aria is set at as fast a tempo as I've ever sung. But it works, and the anger and strength of the Count are well demonstrated.

Judging by the reactions of press and public, the evening has been a great success.

Before the next *Figaro* performance, I have space to talk over with my manager, Robert Rattray, plans for the coming years. I've been fortunate throughout my career in having sufficient offers of work to enable me to pick and choose. My problem has always been to allow enough time for study and memorising. It's more important now than ever before. In the coming months I have two operas to learn, *Peter Grimes* and *The Yeoman of the Guard*, both for recordings; a revision of the *Italian Songbook* of Hugo Wolf; a vast Schubert song programme to be recorded with Graham Johnson; a new work dedicated to me written for the Proms by John Casken; the *Sea Symphony* of Vaughan Williams to revise for a recording; as well as the other engagements that involve me in works supposedly always at my fingertips.

There are never enough hours in the day. Once or twice I've found myself landing at Heathrow and scuttling home to pick up a pile of music for a rehearsal with Roger Vignoles en route to the next recital venue. It's a relief to talk to colleagues and find that we're all tarred with the same brush. We take on too much. But I prefer a hectic pace. There will be times a'plenty, I've no doubt, for taking things easy. For the moment, my energy level is high and my workload stimulating. I'd probably find life dull if I worked in a musical Utopia where time for contemplation and reflection was an in-built part of routine.

There are two performances of *Figaro* before Christmas and then nothing until a week afterwards, so there is the luxury of Christmas at home and not even the worry of having to work on Boxing Day. Some of my German colleagues find themselves having to be in the theatre on Christmas Day itself.

After the break it's hardly surprising that the cast are feeling their way back into the piece.

But more on my mind is the fact that rehearsals are now due to begin on the new *Don Giovanni*. Johannes Schaaf seems to create very different impressions in people wherever he goes and depending on what department he's dealing with. But the overriding factor for me is that, underneath his shaggy and sometimes rude exterior, lies a man of great warmth of heart and generosity of spirit. I've no doubt that on several occasions over the next four or five weeks writing these words will seem like the action of a saint.

*

We are called to the first rehearsal of *Giovanni* on the afternoon of 30 December. The previous evening I received a telephone call to say that Carol Vaness has a virus infection and that Hans-Peter Blochwitz, our German Don Ottavio, is also ill and confined to his sick-bed in Paris.

The whole company is called on this first day to the opera rehearsal room in the Opera House. At one end of the room where 'teacher' sits is assembled a model stage with the set in place, while to the side a display board is covered in photographs of the various scenes and lighting changes envisaged for the production, plus an assortment of costume sketches. This is the first opportunity most people have had to see how the new Covent Garden *Giovanni* is to look. It's dark and very sombre. A sky cloth hangs over the set from start to finish, and we watch it pass through a series of atmospheric states. The initial impression is of the whole thing taking place within a vast squash court whose walls move in or out to suit the scene we're playing.

Dozens of people are with us on this first morning. All the cast, except the two invalids; production staff; lighting; design. Many are familiar. What I hadn't expected are the extras. Actors and actresses outnumber singers by three to one. They are to be servants of the nobility, henchmen of Don Giovanni, and so on.

Johannes starts with his talk on his feelings about this great work. It will be his first production of *Giovanni*. He visualises the Don as having more in common with the Marquis de Sade than with Casanova.

Various ideas are put forward. Was Donna Anna raped by the Don in the first place or does there remain some unfinished business? What motivates Elvira? And so on.

During a tea-break, Richard, one of the extras, asks me how the roles he and his colleagues are to play are normally presented. They are to represent '*I Bravi*', the band of brigands and muggers who are swept up in the maelstrom created by the Don, his refuse men and his guardians. He's rather surprised to learn that as far as I know there is no precedent. Johannes has invented them to serve the purposes of his concept. Donna Anna will also have a duenna constantly at her side, and Elvira will be accompanied in her travels by a maidservant. Giovanni, of course, refers to this maid when talking to Leporello at the beginning of Act Two, but few producers have thought through the idea of Giovanni's interest in her, and her possible demise.

Several members of the cast have not met before. The Zerlina (Marta Marquez), a Puerto Rican trained in America, now attached to the opera house in Düsseldorf, is a singer new to me. Masetto is to be sung by the young Welsh bass-baritone Bryn Terfel, who, since a successful appearance in the Cardiff 'Singer of the World' competition, has seen his career rocket forward. This is to be his debut at the Opera House. Robert Lloyd is luxury casting as the Commendatore and the others are also well-known to me – Carol Vaness who, when recovered, will be Anna; Karita Mattila, Elvira; Hans- Peter Blochwitz, Ottavio; and Claudio Desderi, Leporello.

Claudio and I have worked together on several operas, including *Falstaff, Figaro* and *Don Giovanni*. We performed *Giovanni* together for the opening of the La Scala season, the feast of St Ambrogio, in Milan in 1987. We spent many hours in knockabout routines, breaking down all barriers between us. The background work we did then, and the fact that we know one another so well, is a tremendous asset to us.

Everyone has seen productions where two men at the centre of the action are supposed to have close brotherly ties. The fear of treading on one another's machismo prevents them from getting within a yard of one another. The clasping of hands is done at a safe, manly arm's length. The problem becomes even more exaggerated in an epic Greek drama such as *Iphigénie en Tauride*, where the bond between Oreste and Pylade is of heroic propor- tions. In such a situation the need to embrace one another without the infantile sniggering that rises from the pit at such moments is abolutely essential. Were such scenes to be portrayed in a straight play, there would probably be no problem. Add music and a sensitive tenor or a callous maestro with an ill-timed remark, and the relationship takes on connotations that were never intended and often greatly misunderstood.

*

Logically, we wish to begin at the beginning. The understudy Donna Anna is called on to sing immediately.

I make a rough calculation of the number of Don Giovannis I've sung. It's just over a hundred. Yet, with all that experience, when it comes to starting again I feel as though I've never been in this position before. As I rush on to the set ahead of Donna Anna, a voice in me is saying: 'No, this is not right. This won't do – it's not truthful!' A translation of that might read: 'Johannes is watching you, and you can't get away with this false bravado. How would you play this scene were you really in the skin of Don Giovanni?' But of course I won't be able to answer that question for some time. I know how I like to present Don G. But my ideas may be in conflict with what the producer has in mind. Then I have to tell myself harshly: 'Get on with the job and stop worrying. If you're hesitant about committing yourself now, no-one will make any headway at all.'

So we begin with this enormous clean slate, on which we write a short first sentence.

Don Giovanni walks away from Anna's house, having assaulted her, and seeks to escape.

The slate can always be cleaned off later if the statement is wrong. At least we have the first sentence. My experience tells me that Johannes will make us question everything. It's a healthy sign. When he says he wonders what would happen if Giovanni strolls calmly away rather than runs in desperation, he's sown a seed that will germinate over the days that follow. Perhaps we see Don Giovanni at a moment in his life when he no longer runs. The world is shortly to end for him and these are the clues to that ending.

We then work on the Commendatore, father of Donna Anna, he of the old school, who demands satisfaction of the Don. It helps to think of them as two Colossi, dinosaurs of a former age. We discuss the duel and how and where the old man dies. More often than not, this scene is put aside for rehearsal with a fight director (as in Los Angeles). Swords on stage worry me and I'd rather have a qualified instructor deal with us elsewhere at a separate time.

Fencing is a skill I've not trained for, but with proper coaching combined with some sporting ability and such gift for acting as I have I can manage to present a passable imitation of an experienced swordsman. On several occasions I've faced Commendatores and witnessed all sense of reason and control drain from their faces as they saw the opportunity to be glorious one last time. At that moment, Olympic rings dangled before their eyes and they lost themselves in a flurry of blows that would have gained them victory at Agincourt, never mind over the unfortunate Don G, desperate, fighting for his life. Entering over-enthusiastically into the part is not a temptation confined to basses. Tenors singing Faust are capable of misdemeanours and, considering some fiery tenor temperaments, probably become even more dangerous in the circumstances.

On this occasion, the discussion is not solely concerned with the moves and choreography of the conflict. Johannes wants to avoid the ritual that surrounds a formal duel. What emerges after some time is that this Giovanni is a bit of a beast. Superficially, he demonstrates the decent behaviour necessary to be accepted by the society to which he belongs by rank; but this disguises only thinly the nature of a much more sinister individual beneath. It will not be easy for me to tread this thin line which separates the man who is totally repugnant (who manifestly has qualities which are extremely attractive) from the aristocratic charmer with charisma and magnetism (who is manifestly cruel and manipulative). Men of extremes – be they heads of state, captains of industry or figures familiar to us from literature – tend to combine the vile with the alluring.

We start to explore the idea that Giovanni is driven by his curiosity. He is avid for each new sensation as it arises. He can take on the nature of the necromancer, the alchemist, observing and relishing each tiny moment of change as it unfolds before his eyes. It's rather like what one experiences during an accident. Everything seems to go into slow motion and for a moment one is disembodied, observing the action from some external point distanced from oneself.

And so we decide to kill off the Commendatore more brutally

than I would ever have dared, with several savage knife thrusts. He dies, clinging to me in a pose reminiscent of a *Pietà*, and as he sinks to the ground I watch, through the slow triplets of the postlude, as he exhales his last.

Silence. I watch death take over.

The recitative that follows comes out as too concerned. It does not fit in with the interpretation we've been working on. If the Don is the observer and Leporello the recorder, the delivery of the words should be much more matter of fact. I try it. Giovanni is now chillingly unconcerned with what has just happened. His mind is occupied with observing how Donna Anna will deal with the situation when she comes round from her faint and discovers that her father is dead.

I have to remind myself that this is only the first rehearsal and yet it seems to me we're doing some new and interesting things. With a few clues and the germ of an idea for the kind of man Giovanni is, a character will undoubtedly emerge very different from any I've played previously.

It would be easy to call a halt at this moment to any further development along these lines. The course we're following is not one that will endear this Don to the public and he'll finish up with few, if any, admirers. For fifteen years I've presented a figure who has worked for me. It looks as though I'll have to put that aside. Doing the same old thing would be a boring safe option. I want to explore new avenues, to find out more of this man's nature, and to allow myself freedom to follow a risky new line under Johannes' eye.

Some time ago my stepson Rob gave me a novel by the Russian writer Mikhail Bulgakov. *The Master and Margarita* has become something of a cult piece. It deals with the events surrounding the arrival from nowhere of the Devil in Moscow. Bulgakov's imagination and invention of characters is extraordinary, from the cat that walked on hind-legs and talked, to Azarello, the wall-eyed, yellow-fanged acolyte of the Devil Woland, himself depicted in one scene dressed only in black underwear louchely disporting himself upon cushions. Throughout the book the various guises and manifestations of the Devil Woland are a source of constant wonder. This, I believe, is the talent within Don Giovanni. He can be anything he wishes to be at any time. A man first and foremost, but with far-reaching vision that seems to transcend other human boundaries. Over the next few weeks the opportunity will arise to pursue these thoughts.

Carol and Hans-Peter are now recovered and join us for rehearsal. It's never quite the same with an understudy. We depend on one another enormously for input, and, when someone is absent, everyone knows that whatever work we do will be subject to considerable change once the artist who will play the role is brought into the picture.

The greatest difficulty I shall have over the next month will be leaving my mind free to accept new ideas. Despite myself, I can feel the old familiar route opening up ahead of me. Before each step in that direction it will be wise to remind myself to explore any side turnings along the way.

Our schedule runs from a 10.30 start in the morning. We finish for lunch at 1.30, and recommence for a further three hours at 2.30. Each day as I go downstairs for lunch I look back. The sight that always meets my eyes is of Johannes in deep consultation with his long-suffering assistant, Harvey. Harvey has already lit up a longed-for French cigarette. He's not allowed to smoke at other times – most singers are paranoid about smoke, and the paranoia is increasing. Unlike many producers, Johannes has no clear picture of the final product he seeks. So each rehearsal is repetitive, potentially infuriating and usually results in a wonderfully successful end-product. We are, however, beginning to find it difficult to remember what each end-product is.

For example, we spend the whole morning discussing and trying out various positions for the scene between Don Giovanni and Zerlina. It culminates in the duet '*La ci darem la mano*'. Only in the last ten minutes of the rehearsal do we find what we're looking for, and then only enough time remains to run it through once. Because another scene and other singers are called for the afternoon session, we won't have a chance to continue where we left off; and because of the way the schedule is planned, we may not do the scene again for more than a week. By that time the subtleties we have found today in the last among many versions may well have been dulled, if not forgotten altogether.

Within this short scene we also touch on the very interesting problem of dialogue or recitative leading into a set number with orchestra. In this case, it's the duet, but another example is Cherubino's aria *'Non si piu cosa son, cosa faccio'* in Act One of *Figaro*, which is preceded by recitative between Susanna and Cherubino. Because the 'tunes' are so well-known, it can appear that they are the only thing of importance, whereas they are a result of equally important dialogue that has just taken place.

Johannes pores over his own copy of the full score. Some producers have little musical training (or even none) and content themselves with a simplified vocal score. The advantage in being able to read the full score is in having every musical detail mapped out before one's eyes. And since all the answers lie in the music, the score becomes Johannes' vital prop. His search is for the musical links that will help bridge the gap between the recitative and the beginning of the duet proper.

We try out various ideas.

Don Giovanni has said to Zerlina: 'Let's not waste time with this banter over who's the gentleman and who's the peasant. At this moment – I ask you to marry me.'

'You!' she says, stupefied.

And then begins his seductive prelude to the duet, though we are still in the dialogue of recitative with nothing accompanying us but the occasional tinkle from a distant harpsichord.

'Certainly me,' says the Don at his most chivalrous. 'That "small house" is mine,' – casually indicating what we know to be a minor palace – 'There we will be alone' – ever more private in his words to her – 'And there, my jewel, we shall be wed.' After which we can slip smoothly into the first line of the duet in the same mood as the recitative that has gone before with no apparent gear-change.

The recitative sounds simple enough and appears at face value open and honest. But the use of the words can present a wholly different colour to the scene and, I believe, show the true, hidden intentions of the Don, beneath the surface.

For some time now I've sought to produce a particularly suggestive colour on the word '*soli*' when the Don says, '*Soli, saremo*' ('We will be alone'). The 'o' vowel of the word is closed in Italian and closing it as much as possible produces the effect I require. Similarly, although he says '*E la gioello mio ci sposeremo*' ('we will be wed'), the word '*sposeremo*' ('marriage') is not at all the uppermost thought in his mind – as we all know. There is a way of making it sound as though it has become severely tarnished, by leaving the mouth almost completely closed and allowing the words to ooze through the slash that is created.

Should Zerlina be alert enough to pick up either of these two give-away 'colours', the Don, in his capacity for rapid change, reverts immediately to the image of gentleman of honour verging on saintly hero.

A further section of recitative is almost hypnotic. Giovanni dismisses all the arguments presented by Zerlina. 'And another thing,' he says. 'You who possess those roguish eyes ("*occhi bricconcelli*"), those lips so beautiful ("*labbretti si belli*"), these so slender fingers ("*ditucce candide*"). . . .' three items with which to flatter her in identical musical phrases. The effect is that of a hypnotist entering into the well-practised routine of causing a subject to fall under his spell. The repetition of the phrases is totally charming and utterly seductive.

For the duet, he employs subtle confidences whispered in her ear, the words ever more gently pressing. 'I can change your life,' he promises. 'Just give me your hand, you shall be mine.' Under such pressure, she is unable to resist his attractions and the second half of the duet is taken up with their coming together as she surrenders. 'Let's go, let's go, my love,' they sing.

Though they sing of innocent love, by the end of this consummate seduction it is as much as either of them can do to resist running off to begin their love-making.

And so they would, were it not for Elvira's arrival at the moment of their flight. She presents a tirade against Giovanni. Zerlina confesses her confusion. Giovanni invites the advice of the god of love.

Taking Elvira aside, he explains he was out simply to enjoy

himself a little. 'Is it true what she says of you?' interrupts Zerlina. And here Giovanni demonstrates once more the baseness of his nature. 'The poor woman is in love with me,' he explains quickly to Zerlina. And then pointedly and, I believe, with the intention that Elvira should hear: 'And out of pity I *pretended* to love her for I am a man . . . of . . . good heart.' It's the most terrible put-down imaginable.

Elviras's life has been changed for ever by the memory of three days spent in deepest love with Giovanni in Burgos. Now he allows her to overhear that he was pretending love out of pity. It is the action of a despicable person and begins to indicate the depths to which he will sink.

Exploring a hundred ideas is one method of arriving at a valid theatrical and musical truth. It seems to pay off. But it's very time-consuming and can be frustrating for everyone. It is the cause of some tension in fellow artists, but by some miracle we seem to be able to recapture the mood of the scene when required.

For the moment we're working with a mock-up of the set at the main rehearsal room. We move soon on to the stage where we shall see the real thing for the first time in all its looming blackness.

15 *January*. After the morning rehearsal, I have a meeting with the composer John Casken. He's just completed a work for me which will be performed at this year's Proms season in the Albert Hall. After a strenuous morning, I'm happy to see him.

We first met two or three years ago at Durham University, when I was given a Doctorate of Music by the then Chancellor, Dame Margot Fonteyn. It was a day full of incident. In the same ceremony, Professor George Rylands of Kings College, Cambridge, mentor of so many theatrical folk, received his degree of Doctor of Letters, and two scientists got awards for research. I felt dwarfed by lofty academics.

Afterwards, we had tea in the Music School on Palace Green and my mind went back nearly thirty years to when I came to this place in my school uniform to sing and have my voice appraised by Professor Arthur Hutchings. It was in a nostalgic and rather sentimental mood that I first met John and the idea of him writing something for me was born.

Now here he is with a more or less completed full score of a piece very much inspired by his feelings for the North-East of England. We make for the conductors' room at the Royal Opera House, where we can read through the score undisturbed for an hour or so. He's written, for a large orchestra, settings of poems by Jon Silkin, Gael Turnbull and Rodney Pybus; and has chosen the title '*Still Mine*' for the work, which is clever as it suggests two meanings – the closure of the mines and a man's enduring love for his distant wife.

I'm not the kind of singer who can make musical sense of splodges on a piece of blotting paper, as is the nature of some modern music, but I'm able to make a reasonable stab at sight reading what John has written for me. The first impression is very encouraging indeed. Each poem has been sensitively set with due regard for voice and text, and also a deeper feeling for some of the environmental issues that are behind the sentiments. Spurred on by this first read-through, John now has to return to Durham to think about the preparation of a vocal score for me, after which my hard work has to begin.

London is a place of extraordinary contrasts. This evening I have to be at the Stationers' Hall.

Some months ago, and very much out of the blue, I had received a letter from the Worshipful Company of Musicians informing me that I had been chosen as a recipient of the Sir Charles Santley Memorial in recognition of my work. The prize was a cheque for £250 which I was to spend on something of value which could be suitably inscribed. At a loss for some time as to what to buy, I finally settled on a Scottish Quaich (drinking cup), which I'd spotted in George Street during the Edinburgh Festival. Tonight is the occasion on which I am officially to receive my Quaich.

As a member of no societies, secret or otherwise, I find myself amazed by the out-of-hours activities in the City of London which go on in all sorts of places in the name of all kinds of crafts and skills, and which are a source of much charitable work. I am led before a board of worthy gentlemen in their ceremonial robes and subjected to their well-tried ritual of the handing over of the Sir Charles Santley Memorial. Very gratifying, and a new experience in my already uncommon life. Johnny Dankworth is another prize-winner this evening, receiving the first medal they've given for services to jazz. I leave wondering how many other lovely halls are being put to such use in the City this evening, what other ceremonies, what other awards.

The following day, the new Santley Memorial holder resumes work on stage.

Rehearsals now take something of a nose-dive. I miss a day for a performance of *Figaro* and at the same time Karita falls foul of some throat complaint. It seems she must leave immediately and will have to cancel her first two performances.

This is a terrible blow, since Karita presents such a depth of intelligence on the stage, but within hours the Opera House has traced the American, Patricia Schumann, and she will begin rehearsing tomorrow.

Over the years I've suffered one or two unfortunate mishaps in the course of my work. A moving set nearly severed both my feet during rehearsals for Busoni's *Doktor Faust*. On another occasion, rehearsing *Billy Budd*, a canvas shute down which I was meant to slide gave way and I dropped ten feet on to my back and head. (As far as I know I've made a full recovery. . . .)

John Dexter's production of *Billy Budd* at the Metropolitan Opera, New York, was rather terrifying. The set, designed by William Dudley, was a thing of immense presence. In Act Two the music built to an enormous climax as the crew mustered on stage in preparation for the battle. All that time the cross-section of the ship had been rising until, finally, a complete cut-through ship was represented on the stage, every deck filled with the requisite ship's complement. (It was hardly surprising to learn that when the audience left the theatre, they were humming the set and not the tunes. . . .) Similarly impressive was the last scene, in which Billy was hanged from the yardarm. In this production Billy was required to climb from the main deck, hands tied behind his back, up the companionway that took him to the side of the ship where a rope was put around his neck. He then had to walk the length of a cricket pitch along a three-foot-wide board, thirty feet above the stage, until he reached the safety of the wings.

They tried to reassure me that a fail-safe device had been built into the rope around my neck, should I stumble. No one explained how I would survive the thirty-foot drop, should I fall.

I didn't freak out then, and I'm unprepared for an accident this morning. At one point during the rehearsal I have to get up from a chair and simply walk to the front of the level stage. After a couple of steps I stop suddenly, aware that something has gone wrong in my left leg. A pulled muscle? A torn ligament? Whatever it is, it is now painful to move at all. Work grinds to a halt. I am the latest contributor to what is becoming an unlucky show. We console ourselves with the thought that at least we aren't doing the Scottish play. I take a seat in the stalls and wait for the theatre nurse to come and examine the problem, then spend the rest of the morning watching proceedings with my foot wrapped in towels and an ice pack.

Fortunately, I have a wife who is a tennis fanatic and she is in contact with a number of sports physiotherapists. I leave for home with a pocket full of ice-packs.

I can't help thinking how easily such a mishap has occurred. In the process of putting one foot in front of the other I've done some damage to tendons in my leg. I hope that it's not going to become a regular event.

Under the treatment of Inge and Carol, now my two favourite physios, I am walking more or less normally within a week. I then spend a couple of days taking it rather easier than usual, sitting in a chair with my leg rested, while my colleagues busy about their work. The strapping gives tremendous support but both physiotherapists have warned against putting weight on to my leg too early. Parts of costumes are beginning to appear. I intend to wear my high-heeled boots as much as possible in order to feel safe and comfortable.

The pocket that I had planned on using for the purse of money or 'kerchief has not been provided. I'll have to remember that and invent new business.

From my privileged view of rehearsals it's rather easier to make an assessment of how the production looks. It will certainly lean heavily on the cruelty of Giovanni – mental and physical – and also on the torment of the two main ladies in his life – Donna Anna and Donna Elvira. Giovanni will follow a clearly defined path that will take him from his brutal murder of the Commendatore to his descent into hell – a long, slippery, inescapable slope. There will be a nice touch – a cyclical effect – when the image of the *Pièta* is repeated: first the Commendatore dies in Giovanni's arms; then, in the supper scene, he returns to 'nurse' Giovanni in a similar pose, as Giovanni is about to make his own last journey. These two Colossi seem to stand apart in the drama from the other characters, who say their lives will be different now, but, like so many others who intend to change, may well in fact fall back into life as they have always known it.

The entire outfit for Don Giovanni is black, apart from cuffs and a lace collar. The jacket is made in beautiful detail. The sleeves have a series of overlapping sections such as one would find in a suit of armour – or indeed an armadillo.

I'm always hugely impressed at the skills of Wardrobe departments and other specialists in the theatre. In Covent Garden, for example, there is a millinery shop where hats are produced as required. They're always lovely – and, sadly for the hard-working designer, seldom worn. To be a milliner must be one of the most frustrating jobs in opera theatre, as all singers, as far as I know, run a mile rather than wear a hat. The act of singing is much easier if the head is free.

I remember Monteverdi's *Ritorno d'Ulisse* in Salzburg several years ago, when I had to make a quick change from being old Ulysses to being the young warrior. This meant a rush to get into armour, including a helmet. If, for reasons of hurry, the helmet did not go on to my head in the correct position first time, singing the following scene became a nightmare. Suddenly I was able to hear only a portion of what I wanted to hear and all the vibrations and sensations I associate with certain sounds and levels in my voice were impaired. I lost the sensation of singing.

So hats, beautiful though they are, I tend to discard at the drop of a . . . .

3 February. This morning is our Dress Rehearsal. I slept well, partly because Don Giovanni is one of the roles that doesn't cause me to worry unduly over the music and the singing. That may sound blasé, especially when applied to a role that we all consider to be something of an Everest, but its problems lie in the dramatic intensity of the piece and in the immense concentration required to be wholly convincing.

I take a taxi to the theatre. These days are always exciting. They're a mixture of fun and relief. Fun in that we are, after everything, at the end of a rehearsal period, but still in a position to try things out before the real performance day in two days' time. And relief because tomorrow we can relax and after that life becomes relatively normal once more. The excitement begins at the sight of the queues of people waiting outside the theatre. They are the Friends of Covent Garden plus the families and guests of those concerned with the production – cast, orchestra, chorus, technical and Wardrobe. Once past the clamour at the stage door, I make my way to the dressing room to prepare for the next few hours' work.

We are trying out new dressing rooms. Several years ago we moved into a new extension to the Opera House which included offices, rehearsal and dressing rooms. Now it has been found necessary to lease out certain parts to private enterprise for the next twenty-five years in order to create some capital on which the theatre can continue to exist. The idea horrifies me. For the past year an old area of the theatre under Floral Hall has undergone renovation and development for the use of Wardrobe departments and to provide us with dressing room facilities. Shortly after we debunk to this area, the north-west corner of the new Opera House extension is to be sealed off to be converted into cafés and restaurants – lost to the theatre. I think it's shameful that the one international opera house in the country should be reduced to such financial straits. Where will this philistinism stop?

But, for now, I have to get used to my new dressing room. I might appear relaxed backstage, but I create a carefree exterior pose to cloak the anxiety I'm feeling internally. There is no escaping the fact that we're involved in a dress rehearsal this morning. Each tannoy announcement is made with that extra sense of urgency. Everywhere there is a heightened sense of the occasion. Orchestral noises filter through the sound system as the early warming-up processes begin. I apply what little make-up is required of me and Ron Freeman, the wigmaster, calls me into his make-up room to slick my hair into shape for the part and to give my beard a trim.

I've neglected to shave for the past two weeks in order to have my own beard for the production. This makes a great difference to me as a singer. The glue that holds a false beard in place tightens on gauze and skin, making normal facial movement much more difficult. Also I live in fear of the damned thing falling off on stage. On one occasion in New York, the moustache I wore in a production of *Die Fledermaus* started to peel off halfway through Act One. I developed a strange habit of holding my index finger to my top lip in order to keep it in place. This gesture I then had to incorporate into the next two acts in order not to be inconsistent.

No such problem this morning.

This is a great rehearsal. Only the so-called 'Champagne Aria' causes me concern. Schaaf wants me to play against my natural inclination to become more and more expansive as the aria progresses. I understand him to mean that the passion and the mania to organise this great feast, with which the aria deals, become distilled and more and more internally focused. Doing that successfully on stage is extremely difficult. It's an approach that might work well on film; but I'm not at all convinced I can make it succeed here. Afterwards he insists that it's good but I feel totally straitjacketed by the idea and, for the only time in the opera, as though I'm playing against the spirit of the music. It's worrying for me because my feelings are always dictated by my instincts, and I rely heavily on feelings and instincts in my work.

There's a lengthy notes session after the rehearsal. The main problem lies in negotiating the sets. Backstage at Covent Garden is often restricted because of the confines of this old theatre. In this production it's even worse. The two huge walls that constitute the major part of the set move in and out to create rooms or streets as if by magic. In fact, they're operated by teams of men and a hydraulic system. The pipes and cables of the mechanism run into the wings where it is reasonably safe when the walls are close together. When they move towards the wings to create space on stage, the whole offstage area becomes a snake pit as these pipes slew around the floor and coil up against walls and any passing personnel. Principal singers are not excluded and we are forced to spend a large part of our time dodging and weaving our way through this heavy industry of the opera world. It's not the safest place to be at such times, and being in the dark makes it worse.

I now have a day and a half to lose myself in some painting. Little did I know as a child how useful the allotments and pigeon crees of the North-East would become. When I first started to be interested in golf, I joined the club at Seaham Harbour with my father. The view on most golf courses is of traditional English parkland and woods, or of the gorse and marram grass of the links; at Seaham, we had a panorama that included at least half a dozen coal mines, the docks at Sunderland and allotments as far as the eye could see.

Golf in a Lowryesque landscape is what I remember best, and what now occupies me when I'm looking for something to paint.

5 *February*. Cards, flowers and letters await me at the stage door for the *Giovanni* première. I'm managing to put on a reasonably calm show as I move down to the dressing room area.

Julio Trebilcock, our pre-Columbian Wardrobe master, has everything ready for me. The props department are doing their rounds, delivering my pack of cards and the purse for my money. Ron tidies up my beard and slicks down my hair with one of his magic gels. I half expect him at this point to ask the question: 'And something for the weekend, sir?' He's one of the great characters in the Opera House and his 'salon' becomes a sort of commonroom where we all meet. His room is a memorial which he has created to the artists who have passed through his hands – a regular black museum. Forbes Robinson, Jon Vickers, Ingvar Wixell, Martti Talvela. . . . It is interesting to look at them, to recognise friends and colleagues and to indulge in a little nostalgia. He has a separate part of the room for the photographs of those no longer with us.

The tradition of theatrical make-up is rather extraordinary and never more so than in the opera. Particularly interesting are the stylised creations devised for some of the Wagner operas or the weird and wonderful characters created by Richard Strauss.

This evening there will be no such extremes. I've prepared a basic make-up concentrating quite heavily on my eyes, which always need a special emphasis – it's because of the way my face is made. We have fun, Ron and I, on these occasions. Some years ago I sang Malatesta in *Don Pasquale* at Covent Garden for the first time. I had an idea for the sort of character I wanted to present and how he should look. I imagined a man from whom you'd buy snake oil in Dodge City. . . . Ron studied my sketch and created him out of my own hair and various gels and setting agents. It became a most satisfying experience because my ideas had been realised, carried out and made successful by a skilled practitioner.

The first visitor to wish me well is Bernard Haitink. He makes it a rule to call on his artists early and then disappear to make his own preparations. It's a tactic for which I'm grateful, as the flood of people who usually follow on a first night can be very distracting. Stella Chitty, Covent Garden's stage manager supreme, is next. Her calling card is the very lightest of gentle taps on the door – we all know it could only be Stella. She's the most thoughtful and conscientious person and I'm very fond of her. After a few encouraging words she also leaves.

A few moments later Schaaf and Peter Pabst, the designer, arrive. Schaaf starts to give me final notes and reminders, but basically the production has gone from him and he must now trust it in our hands. Jeremy Isaacs follows, and is clearly in happy anticipation of this new Mozart production.

And all the while the tannoy has buzzed away with calls to technicians to deal with problems, stage management to check a table and chair, dressers to go to the stage door where, no doubt, an artist's guests – not mine, I hope – are standing without tickets for the performance while orchestral pipings and scrapings intensify as the hour approaches.

The half-hour has been called – all calls are given five minutes in advance of the actual time. Like the good publican who calls time at 10.55, the opera house calls the half-hour with thirty-five minutes to go.

The five-minute call has gone. I hear applause from out front and a moment later the overture has begun.

Most of my anxiety is in making sure I don't mess up the various bits of business I have with props. It won't do to fumble with my gloved hands the moment I produce the dagger to kill the Commendatore. Shortly after that I have a purse to handle and coins to hand over to various silent characters about the stage. I must produce a handkerchief from my sleeve to dry the tears of the distraught Zerlina. Worst of all, I have to sit during Elvira's Handelian tirade, '*Ah fuggi il traditor*', and play a hand of patience. I am the butt of many a joke within my family for my lack of skill in anything to do with cards.

Everybody is in form from the start. Carol has developed into an artist of such power, with such a wide range of colours and dynamics to her acting and singing, that her Donna Anna is a resounding success. It's marvellous to be on stage with someone you know well and admire enormously, and to enjoy her triumph with her. As Masetto, Bryn Terfel makes as big an impact as we all expected he would, proving yet again that there are no small parts, only small people – and he's certainly not that, in any sense. Marta's Zerlina is terribly vulnerable, a mixture of awe and fear of the dangerous path she follows under the influence of Giovanni. I produce the cards cleanly and manage a decent job of laying them out on the table in front of me.

At curtain call the reception from the house is generous. Thank God. It's a very dark interpretation for me. One critic at least will remark on the fact that no woman he knows would go within a mile of such an unattractive character. I can only say in reply that the world is a strange place, full of many contrasting per-sonalities, with their own likes and dislikes. Several people I meet within the course of the next few weeks, and the many letters I receive, indicate that the nature of man is so many-sided that even so extreme an interpretation – with its coldness, its clinical observation, its cruelty – will hold a fascination for many spectators.

The run of *Giovanni* continues for seven more performances, interspersed with two performances of *Figaro* to add relative lightness to my diet.

A Royal Gala is the occasion of the second performance. It's in honour of Her Majesty the Queen, to celebrate the forty years since she came to the throne, and it is to be televised. It also happens to be twenty years since my debut at the Royal Opera House, so the evening has a further significance for me.

But for the addition of television cameras in the theatre and their technicians' vans outside it, nothing should be different about this performance. But there is no escaping the fact that a heightened sense of occasion is in the air. Bunting and awnings bedeck the front of the theatre and a red carpet marks the spot where 'she' will set foot. Below stairs, we can watch on television monitors the arrival of the Royal Party at the same time as preparing for the performance. Eventually lights dim, applause is heard for Bernard in the pit and the opera is under way.

I've been involved in several such evenings over the past twenty years, from Common Market celebrations to Royal Jubilees, and the Opera House always comes splendidly into its own in honouring whichever event we celebrate.

Several weeks previously, Jeremy Isaacs, General Administrator of the Opera House, had stopped me in the street with a proposal that I should lead everyone at the end of the opera with a round of songs of loyalty. 'Naturally,' I said, 'I'd be honoured and delighted!'

Now, at the end of an exhausting second performance, and feeling almost voiceless as I always am after *Giovanni*, I'm beginning to doubt my sanity in accepting the task. From somewhere a shot of adrenalin arrives and I find myself with enough voice left to deliver a newly learnt *'Here's a health unto Her Majesty'*. It's obvious that no-one else can remember any of the words. I'm grateful to get support from cast and audience for *'For she's a jolly good fellow'*; and the music of the evening is over. Confetti glitters in the lights as it tumbles from the dome of the House and the event is completed when the Royal party comes to the stage to thank the assembled company. It's the end of a glorious evening, captured for ever (as far as we know) on videotape.

There now remain one performance of *Figaro* and the other six *Giovanni* evenings.

Chapter Ten

A SINGER'S DIARY

FTER *Don Giovanni* I leave for La Scala, Milan, and a new production of Gluck's *Iphigénie en Tauride* to be conducted by Riccardo Muti and directed by Giancarlo Cobelli.

In the meantime, I have to plan a preliminary rehearsal with Graham Johnson for the Schubert recording I'm soon to make with him. Graham is involved in the long-term, mammoth enterprise of recording the complete songs of Schubert with many different singers. My contribution will be thirteen songs, all to texts by Schiller. It's a considerable task as none of the songs is known to me and one or two are colossal both in length and in the technical demands they make on the singer. We don't begin recording until the middle of May but it's by no means too early to begin the early groundwork as we're now in mid-February.

My third task is to prepare my approach to learning the new work by John Casken that I'm to record for the BBC in June, followed by the live 'Prom' performance in late July. Reading it through once again fills me with excited anticipation at the study that lies ahead.

The BBC studio recording of the Casken falls at the same time as a new recording of Vaughan Williams' *Sea Symphony*, which is preceded by concerts of the *Sea Symphony* in Birmingham and London. Then I have to record Captain Balstrode in *Peter Grimes* for EMI. Normally I prefer to record only those roles that I have sung on stage, but Balstrode is an exception as I've sung Ned Keene in many performances of *Peter Grimes* and have by now more or less learnt, by osmosis, my way with this other, bigger character in the same opera.

I'm also giving recitals of Wolf's *Italienisches Liederbuch*, and in mid-May have to fit in two performances of *Don Pasquale* with the Bayerische Staatsoper who are making a fleeting appearance in the 'Fränkische Festwoche' in Bayreuth. I am amused to think of being in Bayreuth as a singer but not for the usual reasons. This will be my second appearance in the Wagnerian mecca: the first time I played golf with Graham Clark, who was legitimately involved with Wagner; this time I'm to sing Donizetti in the small rococo Markgräfliches Theater.

Readers interested in my complicated schedule of recordings and performances are referred to page 224.

Instinct tells me to treat this work schedule rather in the way the alcoholic looks at his life – on a day-to-day basis, one step at a time. If the steps are planned well enough, and if there's a certain amount of rest and leisure time built into this plan, I shouldn't suffer too much.

Chapter Eleven

A NEW SEASON BEGINS

MILAN is not my favourite city. It has a climate that can change rapidly. (It brought me down a few years ago with a cold from which I thought I'd never recover.) Secondly, it's the home of a theatre known the world over for its association with all the greatest names that have ever sung opera. That alone would be intimidating were it not for the presence of that group of shady characters known as 'the claque'.

These 'professional' cheerleaders emerge towards the end of the rehearsal period in the manner of so many farmers gone to market to prod with their sticks at the meat that is paraded before them. Searching for the tender, the vulnerable, spot, they seize on an innocent singer – young or old – and unnerve their victim to the point where it seems safest to play along with their game. For they are a protection racket. Other explanations of their worth and existence may be given, but as far as I can see they are there to take money from singers who feel it best to ensure that they've gone some way towards avoiding the cockpit booing and baying that has become such a feature of performances in some great theatres. The Milan claque actually gain access to backstage areas and dressing rooms. Since La Scala have a strict security system, it's difficult not to think that they sanction this.

My first encounter with a claque was at the Teatro Communale in Florence many years ago. In the corridors of the dressing room and backstage area I'd noticed for several days the presence of two benign-looking old men, one of whom was reminiscent of my own paternal grandfather. I felt a warmth of spirit and generosity towards them, as one does to a much older generation, passing each day with a friendly: '*Buon giorno,*' to be met with an even friendlier: '*Oh buon giorno, maestro – come sta?*' A good way to start the day, I thought to myself, doing my bit for the early days of a European Community. Until, that is, the day that they entered my dressing room and the following dialogue took place.

'Our compliments on your singing – it's very beautiful.'

'Thank you,' said I, 'that's kind of you. It's lovely to be in Italy, singing Mozart in Italian.'

'Very good,' said he. 'Do you like applause?'

'I can't deny we enjoy being appreciated,' I replied, modestly English to a fault.

'We lead the applause,' he explained, 'so the singer traditionally pays for us to have dinner or drinks.'

'Sorry?' said I, as if believing something had been lost in translation, though I'd been forewarned and was playing deliberately dumb.

They then produced from their jacket pockets wadges of official tickets which showed, quite clearly, that they were to have access to the private areas of the theatre because they led the claque in Florence.

'And for this clapping, you pay,' he explained, his grandfatherly smile now sickening. The other, I now noticed, had a sinister cast in his left eye.

Playing as naive as I dared, I ventured: 'What a strange custom. When in England I can get people to clap for me for free. Thank you for coming. That was most interesting. *Arrivederci!*'

They didn't bother me again, but I'm aware it's a ploy that, once used, cannot be repeated. I spend some time prior to trips to Italy setting up possible behavioural patterns and trying to imagine how I shall deal with the scowl of the *capo da claque* when he realises that he'll have no campari and soda on me tonight. I pride myself on having faced them off so far, but I know they may at any time turn unpleasant. I am resolved never to surrender to their blackmail.

La Scala is an extraordinary place. It has an acoustic that is most rare. There would appear to be a certain spot on stage, just to the right of centre and ten or twelve feet upstage, where the voice takes on a very pronounced extra resonance. For all the world, you imagine you've stepped into an echo chamber. For this reason, clever singers, and even some tenors, organise things so that they deliver their big tunes from this 'spot', or, as it is known locally, '*la punta di Callas*'. I worked there some years ago with the Italian director Giorgio Strehler. He amused us by explaining that it was all very well for an aria, but what about the problems of, for example, performing the sextet from *Lucia di Lammermoor* – with all six members wanting to be there. The picture beggars the imagination!

For the first few days in Milan we're involved in a combination of musical and stage rehearsals. Often, in my experience, music is dealt with at rather a late stage. This can cause conflict with staging that has already been rehearsed for some weeks. If the sound is not to the Maestro's liking because of the position of singers on stage, the singers will have to move. It has always been the case that the music comes before any other consideration and not for the first time do I hear Maestro Muti explain that, if he can't find the right balance between singers and orchestra, he will simply indicate from the pit that the artist is to abdicate the production and walk forward until given a signal to stay there. It hardly requires me to describe the frustration this can cause directors, who've spent weeks mapping out the geography and psychology of a production only to see it jettisoned at the crooking of a finger. Frustration also rises in the breast of the artist who, naturally, wants to be heard at his best and so acknowledges the signal, only to spend the next few hours trying to work some logic into a move on stage that has no reason except how it sounds. With some forethought, such conflicts of interest can be resolved at an early stage, if there's co-operation between stage and pit.

But the restaurants at least are good in Milan, providing me with my favourite cuisine and havens of sanity away from a theatre that can, at times, become rather temperamental in true southern-European style.

I stroll through the famous Galleria this morning, 7 March, with Carol Vaness, who is the Iphigénie of this production, and we're approached by three tiny waifs, begging, and tugging on our clothes as they do so. While my attention is taken with the one yanking on my left arm, a second child wafts a newspaper under my nose with one hand and with the other casually lifts the wallet from my inside pocket. The incident takes five or six seconds. An old Italian gentleman becomes incensed at the shame brought on his country and attacks the waif to my left quite viciously. My initial feeling is that he's over-reacted but, discovering my wallet gone, a desire for justice, if not blood, overtakes me and I give chase. I manage to catch one of them but the others escape, it seems with my money. Police are quickly on the scene and we're whisked off to the local station to make a report.

In the courtyard of the police station I watch the behaviour of this child who has robbed me. She prowls like a trapped animal, her street sense and cunning highly tuned to the kind of life she leads. She's exhibiting an animal survival instinct. I'm told shortly afterwards she's 'clean' and my wallet has gone. I enquire who they are and where they come from, these street urchins. Nobody seems entirely sure, but they're part of a migrant population of Zingari or gypsies, who might be from Albania or Romania. Since the breakdown of Communism and the easing of borders, Milan, along with other European cities, has become overrun with refugees whose presence has become a matter of some shame to Italian citizens. It's apparent that, over the next few years, Europe will have an enormous problem as the huge differential between affluence and abject poverty incites confrontation. Regrettably, it would not require a great stretch of the imagination to understand the success of Fascism in such a situation, and it's probably no coincidence that during my time in Milan the granddaughter of Mussolini is running a highly publicised campaign as a candidate for election on a familiar right-wing ticket.

Two days later, I see the same gypsy child in the same place in the Galleria, going about her business in the same time-honoured manner, ripping off punters under the eyes of the police.

*

The première of *Iphigénie* has worked quite successfully. Carol has found a new role to suit her commanding voice and presence, and the Swedish tenor Gösta Winbergh is in great form as Pylade. The Dress Rehearsal and the first four performances are being turned into a commercial recording, but with four chances to get it right, as it were, we have some sort of cushion against pressure.

Jeannie arrives and we slip off for a two-day break in Venice. We choose a small hotel, La Fenice, near the opera house. Venice is not crowded, and we wander all day and enjoy the hidden places of this amazing city.

On a previous visit, a day-trip from Florence, I happened to be walking along one of the elegant arcades that border the Piazzo San Marco, when I noticed something odd about the couple approaching me with their dog held firmly on a leash. It was only as they were within a few yards of me that I could see this was no dog but an ocelot on a substantial chain. Whilst feeling terribly for the animal, I couldn't help but think that they might have been delegates of some Eastern potentate presenting their credentials to the Doge of Venice some three or four hundred years earlier. I looked around to check the reaction of others in the square. Hardly anyone had noticed, their attention held more by the elegant shopfronts than this hugely exotic creature, so far from home, in their midst.

Each turning in the city brings new wonders, and I am able to spend a restful time simply enjoying the light and the views. But it's a strange and rather sinister place, too. I quite understand why Daphne du Maurier chose to set her story *Don't Look Now* in Venice, for here are all the elements for murder and mystery under cloak of darkness and mist. It's easy to lose oneself – so many similar alleys, so many bridges crossing tiny canals all seemingly going nowhere, so many walls rising on either side making miniature canyons and creating the unique atmosphere that is Venice.

Back in Milan, I nod knowingly to the *capo da claque* each evening, with an unenthusiastic '*Buona sera*'. It seems to me that we've been sizing one another up for years, like a pair of Sumo wrestlers prior to locking grips.

Originally my schedule showed that I would have my final performance in Milan on 3 April. With a *Don Giovanni* in Munich on 4 April this would have been taxing, but in the end we completed our schedule of *Iphigénie* performances on 1 April. Time enough to change clothes and money before moving on to Munich, in a much more relaxed state than I had envisaged.

When Munich appears in my diary I view it with a sense of relief. I'm happy there. The production of *Giovanni* is old; I know it well, which is fortunate as on this occasion I don't get even one rehearsal. Stafford Dean is my side-kick which pleases me as he's terribly consistent in what he does on stage and is always there when I want him. He was the original Leporello in 1973, so he knows the production as well as anybody.

Sadly, these are the first performances I've done in Munich without Wolfgang Sawallisch. He had been intending to conduct but required hospital treatment and is now convalescing. In his place we have the conductor Ralf Weikert, whom I last worked with a good many years ago in Barcelona on Verdi's *Falstaff*. Our only contact tonight is a chat of a few minutes before the curtain goes up. Amazingly – yet again – things run along quite smoothly on this precarious system. Most of my colleagues agree: we like either no rehearsal or lots of rehearsal. Problems arise when we indulge in a little rehearsal, which seems to serve only to confuse and to create indecision.

The Donna Anna on this occasion deserves a very special mention. The role is being sung by Edita Gruberova – in my opinion the greatest coloratura soprano of our day. Listening to her is like hearing a perfect mechanical reproduction of a voice, with warm human musicality added to it. We've worked together many times, since *Die Zauberflöte* at Glyndebourne in 1973, and her skill has staggered audiences for more than twenty years.

*

10 April. A sad note in the obituary columns of my English newspaper this morning. I read of the death of Ronald Eyre.

We met first at the Buxton Festival of 1980. I liked him immediately, partly because of his open Northernness and partly because he was a lovely person to be around. Good talk poured from him. Sometime later, when we were involved on *Falstaff* in Florence, we helped keep each other sane, while all around were bowing to some Italian musical deity, be it conductor or singer.

At one stage in his career, Ron was engaged by the BBC to present a series of religious programmes, a new venture for him. Seeing me one evening, seated before the mirror in my dressing room in fear and trepidation, he told me of a trick he'd learnt during those programmes. He'd look at that funny comic's face of his, and enter upon a routine with his mirror along the lines of: 'Well, what a funny nose you have. But there's a kind twinkle in your eye.' And: 'What a sad mouth that is – but a moment later there's a nice thought in your head and your mouth has a lovely smile.' And so on. His director always knew, when Ron faced the camera, whether he'd done his exercise or not.

We shall all miss this poetic Bardolph figure.

I'm glad when the next two Munich *Giovanni*s are safely over, as I've now reached the point where I can take a long-awaited holiday.

After the performance on 11 April I return to London where I'm able to catch up on family news with my son Stephen and his fiancée Julia. Jeannie and I are packed and ready to leave the following day.

My diary for the day has a reminder for me to pack, along with my warm-weather clothes, scores of *Don Pasquale*, *Yeomen of the Guard* (for a recording), the *Italienisches Liederbuch*, John Casken's *Still Mine*, *Peter Grimes* and the Schubert/Schiller songs. Is this a holiday or a study leave?

Jeannie's father lives in a small village about a hundred miles south of Durban. Up the coast are the small towns of Margate and Ramsgate and further on is a Southport. But it's a far remove from the Kent and Lancashire coasts, this Indian Ocean shore line of

Natal. After a week, the climate has worked its spell. I've joined the slow pace of life here. It's not only seductive, but essential. I spend my time walking from one beach to another, enjoying the life-giving pounding I receive from the breakers and seeking out a stand of eucalyptus or a banana plantation as subjects for painting. As an alternative, there's the golf course, bordered by some of the most attractive plants imaginable, where Vervet monkeys in their dozens watch the efforts of the golfers. Barbets and fiscal shrikes flit from tree to tree. Scenically, South Africa is one of the most beautiful places on earth. Not so politically, but President de Klerk has, it seems to me, brought about a new and enlightened way of looking to the future of this troubled, lovely country. There have been many years of injustice and discrimination in South Africa (and in many other places in the world, too) but change is happening slowly and I feel cautiously optimistic.

Time passes too quickly. We return to London via Johannesburg, refreshed.

My first task, two days after returning, involves a solid morning of work playing through the Schubert songs with Graham Johnson. Though we've known one another for some years, this will be the first occasion on which we've worked together. It is difficult not to be impressed by Graham. His house in London is filled with the library that supports his rightly renowned encyclopaedic knowledge of the song repertoire. As the man behind the *Songmakers' Almanac*, he seems hardly ever to utter a frivolous or unconsidered thought in rehearsal.

The greatest problem in the recording that we're preparing quickly becomes apparent. Two or three of the songs are so long, and written over such a wide vocal range, that, with a limited amount of time in which to complete the record, it would be tempting to fall into the trap of recording the shorter, 'easier' songs first, leaving us with 'huge bleeding chunks' and too little time in which to do them justice. After three hours we agree to take the long songs in easy stages. Before we meet for a second rehearsal, I will work out a timetable that will make the best use of our time in the studios.

*

Later that day Jeannie and I catch a train from King's Cross to Durham. I love taking this train, for one very particular reason: when my spirits are low or I'm feeling tired, my mood changes at Darlington. I know the train will soon pass through a cutting to emerge shortly afterwards high above Durham City. On the right is one of the most glorious sights in all the world. Durham Cathedral. Each time I see it my heart beats faster and I sense my pride in having been born nearby. I love that place and its surroundings. As a child I loved going to the Cathedral, and now, because I see much less of it, each glimpse is savoured and cherished.

In the days of a thriving coal industry, 'Durham Big Meeting' or 'The Gala' was the highlight of the mining year. All the lodge banners were brought to the city from the many mining communities in the county. There was speech-making from the balcony of the County Hotel – Gaitskell, Wilson, Benn, Callaghan, Foot, the Labour Party stars – much drinking and picnicking on the racecourse and along the banks of the Wear, and a service for the miners held in the Cathedral – which dominated proceedings, proud, massively overpowering and dignified. The miners' hymn, 'Gresford', was played with passion by the assembled prize bands. Each village had its own music. Services were always emotional, even more so in the years when accidents and disasters had befallen these tight-knit, unbeautiful communities.

So on 6 May 1992 I look once again on Durham Cathedral with all those memories racing through my head. But this time we are coming for an academic occasion. Tomorrow will see the installation of a new Chancellor at Durham University. Sir Peter Ustinov is the man chosen for the job, maintaining the theatrical and musical tradition of his predecessor, Dame Margot Fonteyn.

7 May. The sun shines down, and with honorary graduates, professors and local dignitaries we make a procession from the castle to the Cathedral. Sir Peter gives us some expertly chosen words. He describes his early years and the despair with which his father looked upon his lack of academic success and the even

greater despond into which he fell when he announced that he was entering upon a theatrical career. 'So,' says Sir Peter, 'I became aware that without the necessary scholastic qualifications I should never be able to enter such an august establishment as the University of Durham, other than from the top.' And so we witness his entrance in just such circumstances. A memorable day, with new friends made, and a host of thoughts to take home .

9 May. The Schubert is taking shape with Graham but it isn't easy to concentrate: Cup Final Day is special this year as Sunderland are playing Liverpool at Wembley.

The last time Sunderland were in the Final, in 1973, I was involved in a performance of Delius' *Mass of Life* under Vernon Handley in Guildford. Most people there didn't notice that I was being kept informed of progress by a sort of semaphore system from someone in the hall. Then, they won. Today, they played well in the first half and should have been ahead, but rather fell away under the pressure of the Liverpool machine in the second. In 1973, industry improved its output in Sunderland because of the pride felt towards their team. In 1992, with no shipbuilding to speak about and barely any mining, the knock-on effect is unlikely even to turn a head at the already smooth-running Japanese car plant.

But the extraordinary passion of the North-East is not yet stifled. This morning in a rainy London, the only colours to be seen are those of the Sunderland club and its gallant band of supporters, which bedeck many a famous landmark. The southerners from Liverpool are cowering somewhere out of the rain while the Roker roar grows and grows.

The following day I go to see some British pictures coming up for sale in the following week at Sotheby's. What a privilege to stand in front of so many wonderful canvases. Two huge Lowry industrial landscapes hold my attention. His style looks simple and childlike but in fact disguises his artistic achievement. Speaking as a singer, I'd say that Lowry has a unique voice. I love the football match on what seems to be a white pitch. The streets and rows of chimneys are all identifiable and starkly impressive.

There are pictures, too, by Burra – odd watercolours of inflatable warring peoples – by Stanley Spencer, and by David Bomberg – with the most extraordinary clear light. Something must surely rub off on to me as I spend time with these marvellous works. I can only hope so. In my few spare moments I've taken time to produce one or two sketches, a couple of watercolours and an acrylic, with the thought that unless I try I shall never become skilful whereas by trying I might. Having the talent for it is, I acknowledge, a different matter altogether from having the enthusiasm.

11 May. Recording starts on the Schubert. The venue is the Unitarian Chapel on Rosslyn Hill in Hampstead. This has become a favourite 'room' for small recordings of this type. London enjoys a reputation as the centre of a recording industry but the number of suitable studios, halls and rooms is seriously limited. Traffic noise is the biggest problem, below, above or at street level. Here at Rosslyn Chapel it varies. During some of the sessions we have constant interruption from noise and at other times it runs with strange smoothness. This plays on my nerves, and has the curious effect of sapping my energy.

Some years ago I made a record of English song in what we all planned to be the ideal situation – a country church nestled on the Berkshire/Hampshire borders. No sooner had we started than the beat of the vicar's lawnmower poisoned the stillness; an hour later, the local farmer decided it was high time he brought in his cereal crop. In country and town, noise pollution is part of our everyday lives. We wouldn't recognise silence if we heard it.

Our plan to break down the bigger Schubert songs into manageable daily sections is the key to good work. We throw in a shorter, less demanding song every now and then, and this keeps us well up to schedule for the four days we record in the Chapel.

Graham is interesting to work with. He will play a certain phrase in a particular way during rehearsal and then have a sudden attack of artistry during the recording and invent something new. As I'm also prone to the occasional flight of fancy, this makes for a greater awareness and livelier interpretation. Some songs go to several takes, and a final version emerges only after several acceptable but rather sterile attempts. That's not to say that the preliminary work was not done or was not sufficiently thorough, but simply that in cutting through several early efforts one emerges on the other side with something that has a stamp of original creativity about it. It doesn't always work this way, but when it does it's apparent to everyone concerned.

These songs are unfamiliar to all but the best-informed Schubert fanciers, and each one unwraps its surprises like so many Christmas-present offerings only after hours of preparation and practice.

Chapter Twelve

DONIZETTI IN BAYREUTH
AND OTHER PASTIMES

T WO days later I fly to the new Munich airport, collect my hire care and set off along the autobahn. I feel there should be a crescendo of horns as I near Bayreuth, but no-one is celebrating these two performances of *Don Pasquale* in the tradition of Wagner.

I'm conscious of a tremendous contrast. The Schubert songs were rehearsed in every detail; the Donizetti will be so little prepared that there's potential for catastrophe. The cast, Spanish tenor and bass-baritone, American soprano and I, meet for a peremptory morning rehearsal followed by an evening run-through in costume with orchestra. This is slapdash; only occasionally does one artist interact satisfactorily with another in a remembered piece of detail. We manage to survive, but the two performances are not my proudest moments on the lyric stage.

A redeeming feature of the job is provided by the beauty of the Markgräfliches Theater. Its wonderful wooden interior in dark green and gold is a delight to the eye. The landscape of Germany could be England, in these days of European conformity. Everywhere is a sea of vast golden oil-seed rape.

I return to London ready to begin another recording. This time it's Gilbert and Sullivan's *Yeomen of the Guard* in which I'm to sing the jester, Jack Point.

Two days are spent just on the dialogue, under the watchful guidance of Ian Judge, who was tremendously helpful to me when

I made a record of excerpts from great musicals. I had no hestitation in suggesting him to Eve Edwards and Erik Smith at Philips Records as our G. and S. tutor.

Sir Neville Marriner is the conductor, with his orchestra, The Academy of St Martin's. He and I have made several records together, and each experience has been enjoyable and different from the others. He relies heavily on his metronome and, during playbacks, on his acutely trained ears. Thus he makes whatever subtle changes are necessary for the ideal sound balance and texture.

We have five days to complete this recording in the happiest of atmospheres at St John's, Smith Square. Away from our concert and operatic workloads, we singers relish this opportunity to enjoy the somewhat lighter music of G. and S. Sylvia McNair is a charming Elsie Maynard; Kurt Streit, the American tenor, sweet-voiced as Fairfax; Jean Rigby a delicious Phoebe. My long-time friend and Durham-born colleague Anne Collins – opera's Dame Edith Evans – makes a perfect Dame Carruthers and Stafford Dean is ideally bucolic in the role of Sergeant Meryll. Add Bryn Terfel as a powerful Welsh Shadbolt plus the luxury of Robert Lloyd as the Lieutenant of the Tower (as befits his former Naval rank) and it's not difficult to see why we are all having such a very pleasant time. At the end of the recording, we agree what great value can be had from something outside our normal repertoire. It has served as a refreshing tonic for us all.

31 *May*. This is the day, long-awaited, that I devote to golf. The Royal Opera House Golf Society have been invited to spend the day at the Stoke Poges Club, and to play against a team of their members. It's been some twenty-seven years since I played regular competitive golf, and time and lack of application to the game have not been kind. But for once the old axiom of 'it's like riding a bicycle' seems to apply and for some reason known only to the golfing muses I manage to win a match with a score of seventy-six gross. At the end of the day I find myself as euphoric as if I'd made a hugely successful debut in a big new role in a major opera house.

*

The week ahead involves me in rehearsals for the Italian Songbook concerts with Flott and Geoffrey Parsons. From successful golf to subtle Wolf is for me a beautiful transition. These forty-six songs shared between two singers are sheer joy from beginning to end. They deal with almost every emotion imaginable, while the back-and-forth nature of the programming allows each singer to bounce ideas and commentary off the other.

5 *June*. Our first port of call is the opera house in Lisbon. Two English singers and an Australian pianist have brought to Portugal Italian words translated into German and set to music by an Austrian. These intriguing statistics don't inhibit the audience in their enjoyment of the concert.

The next venue is very different – Harewood House, where George and Patricia Harewood have managed to promote a concert series for the past twenty-four years. There's something awesome about singing in the room set aside for music. The familiar Italian paintings are as beautiful as I remember them from my recital in November, and I remind myself to pay another visit to the aviaries.

There are several specimens with which I'm now familiar from my travels in Africa, but my favourites are still the Snowy Owls. On one occasion many years ago I went as far as the Shetland Isles to do a concert in the hope of catching a glimpse of these birds. I don't like to see them caged, but at least this affords me an opportunity to see how beautiful and commanding they are.

The third and final setting for the Wolf Concert is the Symphony Hall in Birmingham. Entering the auditorium is as inspiring now as it was the first time. Over the stage looms a huge lighting rig, raised and lowered to the requirements of that evening's concert. We try out a few songs, taking it in turn to go out into the auditorium and listen to each other. With a capacity of 2,200 – equivalent to Covent Garden – the hall is big for a concert of this sort. But there's no acoustical problem, no vocal adjustment required of us. Every note, every syllable, can be heard. The evening gives me great pleasure, and I'm feeling very contented as I drive back to London, having eventually found the road out of Birmingham.

I have one free day in London to continue work on *Still Mine* and to revise the *Sea Symphony*. Both are registering very strongly with me: John's piece, because, of course, he's chosen the text with me in mind, and the Vaughan-Williams setting of Walt Whitman's words because it deals with the sea and ships and few things stimulate me more than those particular subjects. I was born by the sea and I miss it more and more as time goes by.

12 June. I spend the evening with the Philharmonia Orchestra and Chorus under the American conductor Leonard Slatkin, rehearsing the *Sea Symphony* in Holy Trinity Church, in Southwark. The building was deconsecrated some years ago and renamed the Sir Henry Wood Hall, and it's now one of the regular rehearsal facilities of the London musical scene. The soprano soloist is Benita Valente, an American colleague. Last year we made a record of songs with guitar accompaniment, and it's good to see her on this side of the Atlantic for one of her too rare appearances. The rehearsal goes smoothly, though in the acoustics of this hall it is difficult to judge how the sound will be in Birmingham.

I return to Birmingham on the following day, and we give the *Sea Symphony* to a slightly recession-hit house. Having travelled back to London by car after the concert, we repeat it in the older surroundings of the Royal Festival Hall the following day.

For the past year I've quietly been buying recordings of the Vaughan-Williams symphonies, not realising that I am part of a trend to give more exposure to his work. I hadn't listened to him properly since my student days in the late 1960s. There's some wonderful writing in the *Sea Symphony* that sums up everything that is English music. In the same way that Janacek, for example, uses an orchestra to produce a sound unique to him, so it is for Ralph Vaughan-Williams.

The week of 15 June is busy, and I have to plan each day carefully.
On the morning of the first day, I continue to work on the

Casken, and look through the role of Captain Balstrode in *Peter Grimes*, just to remind myself of its shape.

The afternoon is spent with David Syrus, a pianist and coach at the Opera House, for whom I have the utmost respect. He's in charge of music preparation on the forthcoming *Grimes* recording and it's that which occupies our time this afternoon. It isn't a huge role, but there's sufficient material to build an interesting character, and the final moment of dialogue, when he instructs the broken Peter to take his boat to sea and sink it, is something I've long looked forward to. I feel as if I've shed the skin of Ned Keene and jumped into that of Balstrode, the man who stood alongside him in all those performances over several years.

The following day is taken up with interviews, the first at my home on the subject of Glyndebourne on the eve of the big changes that will take place there, the second with Richard Baker for his series *Comparing Notes*. We jabber on for what seems like hours, comparing many more notes than we shall need for the programme.

On Wednesday I make an early start learning the Casken, now with an underlying piano accompaniment. For this I've engaged, as a coach, Mary Nash whom I've known for many years. We'll work together for two or three three-hour sessions before I go to the studio to record with the orchestra.

From Mary's home I drive to Watford Town Hall, which is the venue for the recording in a week's time of *Peter Grimes*. Today we're having a preliminary play-through with the orchestra under Bernard Haitink. For *Grimes*, as for *The Yeomen of the Guard*, a strong British cast has been assembled. Anthony Rolfe-Johnson is Peter; Flott, Ellen Orford; Stuart Kale, Bob Boles; Stafford Dean, lawyer Swallow; the New Zealander Patricia Payne, Auntie; and Sarah Walker, Mrs Sedley. Simon Keenlyside sings the part of Ned Keene, which has on so many occasions been my role, and I enjoy listening to his interpretation. We don't compare too many musical notes, spending time instead discussing ornithology since this is a shared interest.

I've sung so much Benjamin Britten, from college days on, that it never ceases to surprise me when people say they have problems listening to his compositions. I am steeped in his music. Indeed, *Billy Budd* became so much a part of me it is as familiar as any of the more easily assimilated nineteenth- and eighteenth-century music that I sing. Once again it's wonderful to be in the middle of 'sea' music. *Grimes* I find even more poignant than Vaughan-Williams' *Sea Symphony*, since it's set on the east coast, about two hundred miles from landscape which I know so well.

We're all greatly excited at the prospect of beginning the recording next week.

The first part of Thursday is set aside for Mary Nash and more work on Casken. I then spend the afternoon at home to get into my head what I've learnt in the morning.

Friday morning is for resting, as the afternoon and evening will be spent in intensive labour at the Abbey Road Studios recording the *Sea Symphony*. The Philharmonia have already recorded the other eight symphonies under Leonard Slatkin and this will complete the set. Surprisingly little time is needed, or so it seems to me, to complete such a major task. The first session lasts from 2.30 p.m. to 5.30 p.m. We begin again at 6.30 p.m. for a further three hours, and by Saturday have finished making the recording.

Ursula Vaughan-Williams, the composer's widow, has been in attendance throughout the sessions. She makes a short speech of thanks, saying she has no doubt R.V.W. would have approved and been delighted with the results. It's one of the nicest and most touching endings to a recording project I can remember.

I can now rest for most of Sunday until 8 p.m. when I have a short piano rehearsal and meeting with Matthias Bamert, the Swiss conductor of *Still Mine*. John Casken will be there.

Matthias Bamert and I haven't met before, but have an instant rapport. He beats the bars exactly as indicated, which is not always the case. John is happy with the outcome and the two hours set aside have been reduced to an hour and a quarter. I can now have an early night. Tomorrow Bamert will conduct the studio recording.

22 *June*. The BBC Maida Vale studio is a curious place, with which

I've had a long association. I first sang here in choruses as a student, and in many varied projects since then. It's some time since I've been here. It has been redecorated and air-conditioning is now in operation in Studio One. The effect on me is less than ideal. I feel as if a cold compress has been laid across my chest and breathing becomes more trouble than it should be.

We begin the recording. The BBC's long-serving producer Stephen Plaistow is in the box, and shortly after 2.30 p.m. we hear for the first time the sounds of *Still Mine*.

The cues I've previously heard only from the piano are now coming at me from all directions of the orchestra. I've had a full score to work from, of course, and I know that certain lines will be coming from the violas or cellos or, at one point, from a distant cor anglais, so it's not altogether a surprise and I learn to cope. The tasks of solving the riddles, as it were, turn out to be enormously enjoyable and, from the first movement, also successful. We have a couple of retakes to allow for the 'cold compress' effect on me to clear and for my voice to be clean, one or two orchestral retakes, and the recording is completed within the time allotted for the first session. This means that everyone has an unexpected work-free evening, which I shall use in a steam bath, breathing deeply.

On top of the problems that singers experience with air-conditioning – as if these aren't enough – there's a strange, sterile, almost a-musical ambience in certain studios. We need studios for our work, but there are some that seem light years away from the actual business of live music, which is what we do best and what they should do their best to capture.

It would be a real pleasure to rest now and I feel I've earned it after the exertions of the past few days, but the following afternoon, 23 June, is my first rehearsal of *Figaro* at the Opera House, in preparation for the company's visit to Japan in early July. There's not much time to put together the three da Ponte operas (*The Marriage of Figaro*, *Don Giovanni* and *Così fan tutte*) but the fact that the two in which I'm involved, *Figaro* and *Giovanni*, were performed very recently will be a tremendous advantage to me now.

*

24 June. Today we begin recording *Peter Grimes*. It's a trek out to Watford Town Hall but necessary for the same old reasons of lack of space and too much noise in London. (Anyone who retains any illusions about the glamorous life of the singer must be having second thoughts. . . .)

Last week's preliminary run-through has served as a useful exercise for the recording engineers of EMI to get the kind of placement and balance they require for their microphones. As a result, a lot of time has been saved and today we are able to make our way through the early part of the opera without too many stops and starts. Thursday and Friday are spent on the recording and by Sunday afternoon the whole thing has been completed.

The fact that we've finished ahead of our scheduled time allows me to race round the M25 orbital road to get to a game of golf with my son, Stephen, in Surrey. It's a rather intimidating experience these days as he's on the verge of signing his papers as a professional and suddenly every shot has become rather more important than it was two weeks ago. Though he's played golf since he was upright enough at the age of two to hold the sawn-down golf club I thrust into his hands, he's now learning how to swing the thing properly for the first time. His boss, John Hoskison, is a fine player, winner of many titles, and is in the process of taking Stephen through all the steps of the game properly. Since I've had no formal lessons, I'm hoping he might pass on that information some day. Who knows, I may yet make the British Amateur Championship! Now if I could also get a picture into the Royal Academy Summer Exhibition, my pastimes would really prove themselves to have been worthwhile. . . .

The following three days we alternate rehearsals of *Don Giovanni* and *Figaro*.

The prospect of three weeks in Japan with the company is very exciting. It's thirteen years since I first made the trip in 1979 but this time there'll be no time for paying homage to the shrines of Kyoto and the bath-houses of Tokyo. With nine performances –

five of *Figaro* and four of *Don Giovanni* – I'll be concentrating on
negotiating the journey from hotel to theatre and back again.

Chapter Thirteen

MOZART IN JAPAN

4 July. Independence Day in the United States and their election fever is building. Here in London it's the day the main body of the Covent Garden company leaves for Tokyo. Something strange generally happens to me whenever a trip to Heathrow is imminent, especially when it's for a long flight. I can't analyse it but it's something akin to childish excitement: I wonder what the airline has in store, what goodies there will be in the little toilet bag, what they'll serve as food, what film will be shown. I'm hardly ever disappointed, even when the toilet bag holds only a plastic comb and a toothbrush with annoying detachable bristles. When we're a company of 240 travelling together there's an even greater sense of fun and – inevitably – an end-of-term spirit.

Over the next three weeks, chorus, principals, orchestra and stage crew alike have an opportunity to meet, discuss, eat and work with one another in a way not possible on home territory. The various elements that make up an opera company will be thrust together. This is my fourth trip abroad with this Company and it will, I'm sure, like all the others, produce a tremendous sense of pride, team spirit and confidence in the work we do. I hope that this will carry over and be of benefit to the forthcoming seasons when we've returned to home shores.

We leave Heathrow at 15.30 and arrive at Tokyo's Narita Airport the following afternoon at 13.50, a flight of just over fourteen hours, plus an eight-hour time difference. The following day is understandably scheduled as a free one. Rehearsals in the Bunka Kaikan theatre begin a day later on 7 July. Our first performance is of *Don Giovanni* on 9 July. Before that I have a piano run-through, followed by an orchestral dress rehearsal of *Giovanni* on the 7th, and a rehearsal for *Figaro* on the 8th. Our greatest concern is that enough time has been allowed to acclimatise ourselves to the humidity and, even more so, to the effects of jet-lag. From this point, the schedule seems a mammoth task.

Both rehearsal days are very strenuous and I find it necessary to rest as often as possible, regardless of the correct time for bedtime or naps. There's little enough time as it is before we open. The journey across Tokyo from hotel to theatre is best done by subway train. Door-to-door takes about forty minutes. On one occasion when I was here with the Bayerische Staatsoper I elected to go by the car provided and found myself in a total panic as a result of the heavy traffic which caused me to arrive at the theatre ten minutes after the start of a dress rehearsal. Never again, I vowed. By lunchtime on performance day I'm still feeling very tired and wish I could stay in bed. I manage to sleep a short while after lunch but with a six o'clock start it's difficult to decide how best to plan the day.

I needn't have worried so much. Everyone in the cast is feeling this extreme form of jet-lag, but fortunately it does little to prevent the performance from being an outstanding success. The Japanese audience, restrained in their appreciation during the performance, are rapturous with their cheering and clapping at the curtain calls. We all agree that the production has matured since its unveiling earlier in the year. It is now one of the most exciting performances of *Giovanni* I can remember.

Two days later we perform *Figaro*. Again a success, but *Figaro* never generates quite the electricity one experiences from *Giovanni*. It is silly to try to compare these two operas by their effect on audience and artist. They are so different from one another that the 'gut feeling' reaction is bound to be completely different.

A party is given for us by the two organisations most closely concerned with the visit. The first is Rio Tinto Zinc (RTZ), who are very happy to have this association with the Opera House, the second the Japan Performing Arts Association (NBS). It turns out to be a particularly auspicious occasion, as Mr Higuchi, the man behind Asahi breweries, our other sponsor, announces that the success of our two performances has so fuelled his enthusiasm that he has offered a substantial contribution to the Royal Opera development fund. In the course of conversation I learn he owns a large slice of Buckinghamshire – in the form of a golf course.

We continue our work. I'm two down with seven to go – three more *Giovanni*s and four more *Figaro*s.

Jeannie arrived on the evening of the *Giovanni* première, sadly too late to witness the excitement. Three days later we receive news that her father is seriously ill in hospital in South Africa. Understandably, she goes immediately to join him, though this entails flying back to London with a connection to Johannesburg later that same day. She'll be travelling for thirty-two hours. I don't envy her and it worries me a lot that she has to do it. But we both of us know that it has to be done. When my own mother and father were still alive I found myself in just such a situation on several occasions.

Two days later there's an opportunity to meet up with friends from the chorus at a ten-pin bowling alley across from the hotel. Though I find the game mindless in the extreme, this one-off session is an ideal way of relaxing on a rare free day. Bob Lloyd also joins the party and the Japanese attendants almost lose their inscrutability for once as they search for a pair of size fourteen bowling shoes for him. In the computerised system that operates, our names come up on a television screen telling us when to bowl and how to score. Bob's name has been most appropriately mis-spelt and from now until his last days I shall think of him as Bob *Loud*.

Two more performances follow, one *Figaro*, one *Giovanni*. For some reason – tiredness, perhaps – my concentration lapses in Act One of *Figaro* and a line of recit that comes out every night like a two-times table explodes on my tongue into the biggest stream of gibberish I've ever uttered on a stage. I thank God we're not at La

Scala. Marie McLaughlin struggles almost successfully to keep a straight face. Her look of shock is something I shall treasure. *Giovanni* the following night causes no like problems, thank goodness, but it is with some relief that I welcome the completion of our performances.

My impression is that we'll be leaving Tokyo with a *Don Giovanni* to remember. Bernard has taken fire and produced all the excitement of which he's capable and which I remember so well from Glyndebourne in 1977 and 1982.

18 July. I leave for Osaka by bullet train. This is my favourite form of travel. For three hours modern Japan passes by the windows of this quiet luxury train. From Tokyo to Osaka there's more or less continuous urban development in a succession of living areas and light and heavy industries, small businesses, and the giant green cages that have almost replaced the chrysanthemum as the emblem of Japan. These are the multi-tiered golf driving ranges that have sprung up in their hundreds all over the land. For the majority of the folk who desperately smash balls into these cages hour after hour it's probably the nearest they will ever come actually to playing a round of golf. The impact of the game in this part of the world is difficult to describe to anyone who has not witnessed it. Suffice it to say that dedication to golf is now as intense and passionate as the enthusiasm once devoted to Bonsai, Kabuki or Noh. Indeed such traditional cultures appear to have been supplanted by this preferred Occidental pursuit.

Osaka is yet another vast development of the modern Japan. Rather more sedate than Tokyo: there actually seems to be space to move around the streets here. Our 'opera house' here is the Festival Hall. Access to this is gained via the kitchens and back stairways of the adjoining Grand Hotel. As stage doors go, this is not altogether unusual. My favourite stage door entrance is that of the Teatro Liceo in Barcelona. Somewhere hidden away on the Ramblas, the promenading avenue in front of the theatre, is a newspaper and magazine kiosk. Side-stepping one's way through this small business, one arrives at a little door giving on to a flight of stairs which takes one, a few moments later, into the dressing

room area of the theatre. It's rather what I imagine it must have
been like to have gained access to the inner sanctums of MI5 before
it went public.

In Osaka I have a free day before two consecutive performances:
on 20 July there's our last *Giovanni* followed by our third *Figaro*.
Bernard will leave the tour after the *Giovanni* in order to be present
at Glyndebourne's Gala Evening. Jeffrey Tate will then take over
the conducting of the remaining three *Figaro*s as well as continuing
his own *Così fan tutte*.

This planning is very difficult for me. Unused to consecutive
evenings, opera singers take fright at such times. To follow *Don
Giovanni* with *Figaro* is particularly hard, since as Giovanni I rant ✓
and rave and spend so much of myself in the course of an evening.
On this occasion I try to discipline myself into giving slightly less
and into not overdoing the histrionics of the last scene. The
following evening I apply the same principles to *Figaro*. By
reminding myself simply to *sing* at all times, I learn a useful lesson.
I cannot deny a sense not only of relief but of accomplishment at
the end of two evenings.

With two free days I'm virtually on holiday. . . . I can allow myself
a couple of excellent Japanese beers.

The tour is dwindling. Already, those in the *Don Giovanni* cast
not involved with other performances as either principles or
understudies have left for London. There's a feeling of '*Heimweh*' in
the Company now. Those with enough energy to withstand
Osaka's heat and humidity have made their pilgrimages to the ✓
temples of Kyoto and Nara. I've been outside twice – on both
occasions to pay my respects to the theatre. Otherwise I've
contented myself with the air-conditioned atmosphere of our
hotel. I make my return to Tokyo on a hot day of brilliant sunshine.

My ticket is pre-booked, first class. For about £20 I am to travel in
car number 8, a 'Green Car', to Tokyo main station. There are three
green cars – non-smoking areas. Cars 1 to 5 have seats available for
those not having made a reservation.

The platform is marked with car numbers. The train arrives and as if by magic conforms to the signs exactly. I sit on the raised upper deck. Below me is a self-service cafeteria and beyond that private rooms in which the busy Japanese executive can sit in stylish comfort, in touch with his interests by telephone and fax while in transit. It's an impressive set-up. A request is made in English and Japanese, over the train's announcement system, that passengers refrain from using portable telephones as this can upset other passengers. The first-class monk in front of me, who is dressed in robes of a shade of such delicacy it defies description, leaves his seat and makes for the solitude of the corridor, where he is allowed to use his portable telephone without breaking the rules of the cabin attendant. How many monks, I wonder, carry personal telephones about their habits? And what can be so urgent in a monk's life that he needs this modern appendage?

Announcements keep us informed of the train's progress. A dot-matrix indicator board such as one sees these days in estate agents' windows gives further information in English and Japanese. It's now welcoming aboard the passengers who have joined us at Nagoya. Across the other platforms I can see half a dozen varieties of train. (Modern Japan must be a spotters' paradise.) Mostly privately owned, they're dazzlingly new-looking – perhaps just clean and glistening in the afternoon sun. Air vents of the type found on aeroplanes cool the passengers, many of whom also produce their own fans and waft them in long-learnt tradition before their faces. We've just been informed that the conductors' rooms are in cars 7 and 10. I have visions of Solti, Giulini, Kleiber, Muti, Davis and Haitink sitting there practising their baton-wielding in conductors' caps. (Well – perhaps not Kleiber as he makes a rule of nonconformity.)

Every inch of ground we pass now seems to be put to use as we near Tokyo. Even the driving ranges, never large enough, have reduced in size. The last one I glimpsed can have been no longer than the length of two cricket pitches.

There's a bewildering array of greenery wherever space permits. Ornamental conifers like overgrown Bonsai stand alongside rice-paddy fields. Many other vegetables are being reared on small plots of land reminiscent of allotments at home. Try as I might, I've not been able to spot any prize leeks as yet. Electric pylons seem to be the staple crop of many of the other fields, sprouting among the houses in the mountains by the water's edge, humming to keep Japan going forward at its breathless pace.

Hot towels are now being handed out so that we can arrive in the capital looking our best. Meanwhile, on Network SouthEast, fallen leaves have brought the service to a standstill and the last bacon butty was sold before the train left the terminus. All courage to Richard Branson, I say!

Through the haze, which I shall try to think of as heat-inspired rather than man-made, I catch my first glimpse of Mount Fuji since my arrival here three weeks ago. Straight up at both sides and flat along the tip, it seems designed to harmonise with its environment. Fuji means 'wisteria'.

In London the racemes of a beautiful wisteria plant spread from my neighbour's garden happily into mine, while she shares my honeysuckle.

I've seen little of either this year. . . .

Gardening is not the ideal hobby for a travelling minstrel. You either put in your plants and miss their flowering or vice versa. You're never there to see the year through. But that's in the nature of your work.

Next week I shall once more see the Austrian summer meadows of Salzburg. . . .

One day I'll see my garden through: I'll finish the projects I started ten years ago and more.

In two days' time someone will hand me an air ticket and I'll be off. . . .

For the moment I'll think of the world as one big back garden and take my pleasure from that.

A CODA

The form of this book is a journal. My aim was to capture a representative slice of the life of a singer during one year. This life has, of course, continued.

Jeannie has showed a good recovery. It would seem she suffered the effects of a delayed concussion. She has now resumed her place travelling with me around the world. However, a shiver runs along her spine at the sight of turbulent water, and she's not entirely happy to step into a powerful shower.

Following its return from Japan, the Covent Garden company settled back into life at the Opera House. I returned there for a revival of *Don Giovanni*. I've also been involved in a production of *Don Carlos* in San Francisco.

I have learned to appreciate Paris – the elegant lady of European capital cities – through unprejudiced eyes. This was while taking part in *Queen of Spades* at the new Bastille theatre of the Paris Opera. Tchaikovsky's underrated masterpiece, in a production by Konchalovsky, proved to be magnificently Gothic, and the work in the theatre ran smoothly.

And now I continue to prepare for the future with a new production of *Die Meistersinger von Nürnberg* at Covent Garden, in which I shall be singing the role of Sextus Beckmesser for the first time; *Madama Butterfly* and *Death in Venice* at the Metropolitan, New York; and *La Traviata* in Munich. With many orchestral concerts and recitals added to my programme of operatic roles, and the challenge of studying and learning parts new to me, another year proceeds apace. Envelopes from travel agents remind me of my obligations as they drop on to my front-door mat.

ENGAGEMENTS

From my diary: February to July 1992

Feb.	5	*Don Giovanni* première	London
	8	*Marriage of Figaro*	London
	10	*Don Giovanni*	London
	12	*Marriage of Figaro*	London
	14	*Don Giovanni*	London
	16	British Youth Opera – Gala Concert	London
	18	*Don Giovanni*	London
	20	Record video promotion for ROH development	London
	22	*Don Giovanni*	London
	25	*Don Giovanni*	London
	26	Preliminary rehearsal with Graham Johnson	London
	27	*Don Giovanni*	London
	29	} 2-day preliminary rehearsal for	
Mar.	1	} *Iphigénie*	Milan
	3	*Don Giovanni*	London
	4	} Fly to Milan to rehearse *Iphigénie* Rehearsals	Milan
	17	}	
	18	*Iphigénie en Tauride* première	Milan
	19	} HOLIDAY – 2 days	Venice
	21	}	
	22	*Iphigénie en Tauride* (Simultaneous recording for Sony)	Milan
	24	*Iphigénie en Tauride*	Milan
	26	*Iphigénie en Tauride*	Milan
	28	To the theatre: *The Madness of George III*	London
Apr.	1	*Iphigénie en Tauride*	Milan
	2	Fly to London	London

	3	Fly to Munich (no rehearsal for *Don G*)	Munich
	4	*Don Giovanni*	Munich
	7	*Don Giovanni*	Munich
	11	*Don Giovanni*	Munich
	13	HOLIDAY – 2½ weeks, with books	Africa
May	6	Rehearse Schubert Songs with Graham Johnson	London
		Evening	Durham
	7	Installation of Sir Peter Ustinov as Chancellor	Durham
	8	Rehearse Schubert/Graham	London
	9	Rehearse Schubert/Graham + Cup Final Sunderland/Liverpool	Wembley
	10	Sotheby's British pictures – Lowry/ Bomberg/Spencer	London
	11 12 13 14	Recording Schubert Songs/Rosslyn Hill Chapel with Graham Johnson	London
	17	Fly to Bayreuth (car from Munich)	Bayreuth
	18	Reh. a.m. *Don P.*, eve. orch. *Don P.*	Bayreuth
	19	*Don Pasquale*, Bayerische Staatsoper	Bayreuth
	20	*Don Pasquale*, Bayerische Staatsoper	Bayreuth
	21	Fly Bayreuth/Frankfurt/London	
	22	Golf with Stephen	London
	23	Rehearse dialogue and music *Yeomen of the Guard*	London
	24	Rehearse *Yeomen*	London
	25	A.m. study *Still Mine*	
		Eve. record *Yeomen* dialogue	London
	29	A.m. meet Stephen's boss	London
		P.m. record *Yeomen*	London
	30	Record *Yeomen*; dinner afterwards	London
	31	ROH golf	Stoke Poges
Jun.	1	FREE DAY	London
	2	A.m. Mary Nash – Casken	London
		Rehearse *Italian Songbook* with Geoffrey Parsons	London

	3	Rehearse *Italian Songbook* with Flott/ Geoffrey	London
	4	Fly Lisbon – San Carlo Theatre	Lisbon
	5	Recital with Flott/Geoffrey Parsons	Lisbon
	6	Fly to London – p.m. RA Summer Exhibition	London
	7	Drive to Harewood House	Yorkshire
	8	Recital – *Italian Songbook*, Harewood House	Yorkshire
	9	Drive to Birmingham	Birmingham
	10	Recital – *Italian Songbook*. Symphony Hall	Birmingham
	11	Study *Sea Symphony*/Casken at home	London
	12	Eve. rehearsal *Sea Symphony* (Slatkin)	London
	13	*Sea Symphony*, Symphony Hall	Birmingham
	14	*Sea Symphony*, Royal Festival Hall	London
	15	Study Casken/*Peter Grimes*	London
	17	A.m. study Casken	London
		P.m. run-thru' orch. *Peter Grimes*	Watford
	18	A.m. study Casken	London
	19	Eve. record *Sea Symphony*, BMG Abbey Road	London
	20	Eve. complete *Sea Symphony*	London
	21	8–10 a.m. rehearse with Matthias Bamert *Still Mine*, BBC	London
	22	P.m. record Casken *Still Mine*, MVI	London
	23	Rehearse *Figaro* for Japan, ROH	London
	24	P.m. recording begins *Peter Grimes*	Watford
	25	A.m. record *Peter Grimes*	Watford
	26	A.m. record *Peter Grimes*	Watford
	27	A.m. record *Peter Grimes*	Watford
		P.m. Wimbledon	Wimbledon
	28	A.m./p.m. record *Peter Grimes*	Watford
	29	A.m. rehearse *Don Giovanni*	London
		P.m. rehearse *Figaro*, ROH	London
	30	A.m. rehearse *Don Giovanni*	London
		P.m. rehearse *Figaro*	London
Jul.	1	Cancelled – sore throat	London
	2	Cancelled – sore throat	London

3	FREE DAY	London
4	ROH company fly to Japan	
8	Rehearsals	Tokyo
9	*Don Giovanni* première	Tokyo
11	*Figaro* première	Tokyo
14	*Don Giovanni* (2)	Tokyo
16	*Figaro* (2)	Tokyo
17	*Don Giovanni* (3)	Tokyo
20	*Don Giovanni* (4)	Osaka
21	*Figaro* (3)	Osaka
24	*Figaro* (4)	Tokyo
26	*Figaro* (5)	Tokyo

INDEX

229

VENUES

Index

Index